BRAZIL
THE CHALLENGES OF THE 1990s

BRAZIL
THE CHALLENGES OF THE 1990s

Edited by

Maria D'Alva G. Kinzo

The Institute of Latin American Studies
University of London
and
British Academic Press
London · New York

Published in 1993 by
The Institute of Latin American Studies,
University of London
and
British Academic Press
45 Bloomsbury Square
London WC1A 2HY

175 Fifth Avenue
New York
NY 10010

British Academic Press is an imprint of I. B. Tauris & Co Ltd

In the United States of America
and Canada distributed by
St Martin's Press
175 Fifth Avenue
New York
NY 10010

A CIP record for this book is available from the British Library

A CIP record for this book is available from the Library of Congress

ISBN 1–85043–613–4

Typeset by Photoprint, Torquay, Devon
Printed and bound in Great Britain by
WBC Ltd, Bridgend, Mid-Glamorgan

CONTENTS

CONTRIBUTORS

Maria D'Alva Gil KINZO is professor of political science at the University of São Paulo (USP) and researcher at the Instituto de Estudos Econômicos, Sociais e Políticos de São Paulo (IDESP). She was a research fellow at the Institute of Latin American Studies, University of London (1991–2). She is the author of *Representacão Política e Sistema Eleitoral no Brasil* (1980) and *Legal Opposition Politics under Authoritarian Rule in Brazil – the Case of the MDB, 1966–79* (1988). Her articles on political parties, elections and democratization in Brazil have appeared in various edited volumes and journals.

José Márcio CAMARGO is professor of economics at the Catholic University of Rio de Janeiro (PUC–RJ). He has published, with C. A. Ramos, *A Revolução Indesejada* (1988) and edited, with F. Giambiagi, *Distribuição de Renda no Brasil* (1991). He is author of several articles on economic stabilization, unemployment and income policy in various specialized journals.

Gustavo H. B. FRANCO is professor of economics at the Catholic University of Rio de Janeiro (PUC–RJ). He also works as a consultant for international agencies such as UNCTAD, OECD and ECLAC. He is the author of *High and Hyperinflations: cross-country patterns and the design of stabilization* (1991) and has published articles on current Brazilian and Latin American inflation, trade and foreign investment policies and the monetary history of Brazil in various journals.

Maria Helena GUIMARAES de CASTRO is assistant professor of political science at the University of Campinas (UNICAMP) and researcher at the Núcleo de Estudos de Políticas Públicas (NEPP–

NICAMP). She has published articles on social policy in Brazilian journals and is co-author with Vilmar Faria of 'Social Policy and Democratic Consolidation in Brazil' in *The Political Economy of Brazil: Public policies in an era of transition*, edited by Lawrence S. Graham and Robert H. Wilson (1990).

Bolivar LAMOUNIER is professor of political science at the Catholic University of São Paulo (PUC–SP) and researcher at the Instituto de Estudos Econômicos, Sociais e Políticos de São Paulo (IDESP). He has published *Partidos e Utopia: O Brasil no Limiar dos anos 90* (1989), *Depois da Transição – Democracia e Eleições no Governo Collor* (1991) and, with R. Meneguello, *Partidos Políticos e Consolidação Democrática no Brasil* (1986). He has edited *De Geisel a Collor: O Balanço de Transição* (1990), *A Opção Parlamentarista* (1991) and *Ouvindo o Brasil – Uma Análise da Opinião Pública Brasileira Hoje* (1992). He has also published articles on democratization and institution-building in numerous edited volumes and international journals.

Carlos Alberto LONGO is professor of economics at the University of São Paulo. He is also member of the editorial board of the newspaper *Folha de São Paulo* and has worked as a consultant for the World Bank and IMF. His books include *Em Defesa de um Imposto de Renda Abrangente* (1984), *Caminhos para uma Reforma Tributária* (1986) and *Estado Brasileiro: Diagnósticos e Alternativas* (1990). He has published numerous articles on taxation, trade and monetary policies, stabilization and external debt in journals such as *Revista Brasileira de Economia*, *Revista de Economia Política*, *National Tax Journal*, *Public Finance Quarterly* and *Journal of Development Economics.*

José Alvaro MOISES is professor of political science at the University of São Paulo (USP) and researcher at the Centro de Estudos de Cultura Contemporânea (CEDEC). He was visiting fellow at St. Antony's College, Oxford (1991–2). His books include *Lições de Liberdade e Opressão – O novo sindicalismo e a política* (1982), *Contradições Urbanas e Movimentos Sociais* (1977), *Cenas de Política Explícita* (1986), and *Cidadania e Participação – Ensaio sobre o Referendo, o Plebiscito e a Iniciativa Popular na Nova Constituição Brasileira* (1990). He has also co-edited with J. A. Guilhon Albuquerque, *Dilemas da Consolidação da Democracia* (1989) and published various articles on democratization and political culture in Brazil.

Alkimar MOURA is professor of economics at the Fundação Getúlio Vargas–São Paulo (FGV–SP). He was director of Brazil's Central Bank during Economic Minister Bresser Pereira's term in office (1987–1988). He has published 'Rumo à Entropia: a Política Econômica de Geisel a Collor' in *De Geisel a Collor*, edited by B. Lamounier (1990), and is co-author with Lamounier of 'Economic Policy and Political Opening in Brazil' in J. Hartlyn & S. Morley, *Latin American Political Economy: financial crisis and political change* (1986) and 'A recuperação econômica e o inicio da Nova República: problemas y perspectivas' in *Estudos Econômicos* (1985). He is also the author of various articles on trade and currency exchange policies in Brazil.

Ricardo PAES de BARROS is professor of economics at the Catholic University of Rio de Janeiro (PUC-RJ) and researcher at the Instituto de Pesquisa Econômica Aplicada (IPEA). He has edited, with G. Sedlacek, *Mercado de Trabalho e Distribuição de Renda: uma Coletânea* (1989) and published various articles on the labour market, wages, income distribution and poverty in Brazil in journals such as *Revista de Econometria*, *Journal of Development Economics* and *Sociological Inquiry*.

Maria Herminia TAVARES de ALMEIDA is professor of political science at the University of São Paulo (USP) and researcher at the Instituto de Estudos Econômicos, Sociais e Políticos de São Paulo (IDESP). She has co-edited, with Bernardo Sorj, *Sociedade e Política no Brasil pós–64* (1983). Her articles include, 'Novo Sindicalismo' and Politics in Brazil' in *State and Society in Brazil: Continuity and Change*, edited by J. Wirth *et al* (1987), 'Difícil Caminho: Sindicatos e Política na Construção da Democracia' in *A Democracia no Brasil – Dilemas e Perspectivas*, edited by F.W. Reis and G. O'Donnell (1987) and 'El reformismo democrático en tiempos de crisis' in *Capitalismo, Democracia y Reformas*, edited by N. Lechner (1991).

INTRODUCTION

Maria D'Alva G. Kinzo

Few countries in Latin America have undergone as much economic and social change in the last 40 years as Brazil: an annual average rate of economic growth of 7 per cent between 1950 and 1980; four decades of state-led import-substitution industrialization; rapid urbanization which in less than 30 years transformed a predominantly rural country into one in which two-thirds of the population live in cities; a significant enlargement of the middle classes whose mass society values and consumer expectations came to match those of the developed world.

Yet, in spite of all these changes, Brazil stagnated in terms of income inequalities and levels of poverty: one-third of its population (about 50 million people) is today living beneath the poverty line, another one-third is just a little above it, facts that make Brazil one of the countries with the most unequal income distribution in the world. Moreover, Brazil entered the 1990s immersed in the most serious and prolonged economic crisis in its history, a crisis that had already lasted for more than a decade causing the 1980s to become known as the 'lost decade'. The successive efforts, from the early 1980s onwards, to shake off the downward economic trend have only resulted in higher unemployment, lower wages and a further deterioration in living standards.

At the same time the 1980s witnessed a transition from military to civilian rule and 1990 saw the country enthusiastically embrace the option for democracy, symbolized by the inauguration of Fernando Collor de Mello as the first democratically elected president in almost 30 years. Brazil's military regime lasted 21 years (1964–85) and, as is well known, the process of democratic transition was quite singular: a gradual and controlled liberalization that took more than ten years to re-establish civilian rule and another five to put a directly elected president into office; a negotiated transition that involved co-operation between the opposition and former collaborators of the military regime; a process which survived the sudden death of its leader – President-elect Tancredo Neves – and the ascension to office of Vice-president-elect José Sarney, a former loyalist to the military.

In spite of all the setbacks, a competitive and pluralist political system has been established. A National Constituent Assembly worked for 19 months to produce a new constitution, which was promulgated in October 1988. Although frequently criticized for its imperfections and inconsistencies, the charter was the result of a democratic process which involved the mobilization of all organized sectors in society. The interplay of pressures during the working of the Constituent Assembly, with the most diversified interest groups vying to influence the decision-making process, was certainly a rare event in Brazilian political history. Inevitably, however, the debate and decisions on fundamental and controversial issues made it difficult to achieve a coherent, well-structured and consensual charter. In the end, so many points were lacking consensus that a door was left open for a revision of the constitution five years after its promulgation. Thus, in September 1993 a plebiscite will be held to decide on the system of government (parliamentarism or presidentialism) as well as on the form of government (either constitutional republic or monarchy). One month later Congress will take on the powers of a Constituent Assembly with the task of reforming the entire constitution.

The still uncompleted institutional process and the uncertainties concerning economic and social questions are interrelated elements that make the portrayal of Brazil in the 1990s both complex and problematic. These are the issues with which this book is concerned.

Rather than offering an overall analysis of Brazil's economy, polity and society, the volume concentrates on some of the pressing problems which we believe to be essential keys to the understanding of the questions of social and economic development and democratic consolidation.

The three essays that make up Part I analyse the economic question, dealing with Brazil's current crisis, the policies that have been devised to tackle it and possible alternatives. Alkimar Moura examines the various economic programmes implemented since civilian rule was re-established in 1985, thus providing an evaluation of the various stabilization shocks administered during the Sarney administration (1985–90) and during the first two years of the Collor government (1990–92). Gustavo Franco concentrates on the inflationary process, specifically analysing the factors causing the hyperinflation which developed during the first civilian government. Carlos Alberto Longo provides a critical analysis of the Collor administration's policies as regards both the question of inflation and the other issues involved in structural adjustment: privatization, administrative reform, deregulation and trade liberalization.

Part II offers a discussion of the social question. Why has so much poverty persisted in Brazil in spite of the country's rapid economic growth? José Márcio Camargo and Ricardo Paes de Barros analyse the origins of poverty, underscoring the problems related to the low qualification of the labour force and the under-utilization of available human resources. Maria Helena Guimarães de Castro concentrates on the social policy question which was brought into debate during democratic transition. She examines the formation of the new agenda of social reforms in the early 1980s, the advances achieved in this sphere with the 1988 Constitution and the present problems of social policy formulation and implementation in the face of the economic crisis and of the dominant ideology of neo-liberalism. Focusing on the labour movement, Maria Herminia Tavares de Almeida analyses trade union reaction to economic stabilization and, in particular, their strategies in response to the policies implemented during the Sarney administration. The unions' struggle for wage indexation and their confrontational approach *vis à vis* the government are thoroughly analysed.

Part III is concerned with the political question, more specifically with assessing the role played by both the institutional framework and political culture during the consolidation of democracy in Brazil. The two first essays in this section discuss the institutional constraints which lie at the root of the problem of governability, and pose obstacles to democratic stability in Brazil. Bolivar Lamounier deals with problems related to the electoral system, party organization and the structure of government, arguing that Brazil's institutional model has stimulated political fragmentation and worked against government stability. My own essay concentrates on the problematic state of the party system, questioning the parties' role in creating conditions for governability and the consolidation of democracy. Focusing on political culture, José Alvaro Moisés discusses the significance of democratic values for the stabilization of democracy. Based on opinion polls, his analysis provides evidence that changes in the direction of a democratic view of politics are taking place in Brazilian mass political culture. (As I am reading the proofs of this book (December 1992) Brazil is facing dramatic changes as a consequence of the impeachment of President Collor de Mello, the outcome of which will be determined in the coming weeks.)

The papers brought together here were first presented and discussed at the University of London's Institute of Latin American Studies within the programme of activities I organized as the co-ordinator of the Centre for Contemporary Brazilian Studies in 1991–92. Apart from the regular Brazil seminar held every week, a special conference 'Brazil: The Challenges of the 1990s', was held between 31 October and 1 November 1991. The Brazilian Embassy in London, the British Council and the Foreign and Commonwealth Office provided part of the funding for the conference. The travel costs of participants were paid by CAPES – Coordenação de Aperfeiçoamento de Pessoal de Nível Superior and the Nuffield Foundation. The Institute of Latin American Studies covered the remaining costs, in part from the grants awarded to the Centre for Contemporary Brazilian Studies by British Petroleum, Lloyds Bank and the Brazilian Ministry of Foreign Affairs (Itamaraty).

This volume would not have been possible without the support of Professor Leslie Bethell, Director of the Institute of Latin American Studies. Being a research fellow and coordinator of the Brazilian programme at the Institute of Latin American Studies was a stimulating experience due largely to the dynamism of Professor Bethell who was always willing to support the activities I developed at the Institute. The help of several other individuals was crucial to the completion of this project. Anthony Bell (administrative secretary of the Institute) helped solve the numerous problems associated with the organization of an international conference. Hazel Aitken, Alison Loader and Maria Cristina Silva also helped organize the conference. Moyra Ashford was responsible for revising the English translations of the essays in this volume. None of the institutions and individuals supporting this project is responsible for the views that are expressed here. The opinions are those of the individual authors.

London, 2 June 1992

1· STABILIZATION POLICY AS A GAME OF MUTUAL DISTRUST:

The Brazilian Experience in post-1985 Civilian Governments

Alkimar R. Moura

Introduction

The objective of this article is to describe the main elements of Brazil's various economic stabilization experiences since the re-establishment of civilian rule in March 1985. It encompasses the five-year period of the Sarney administration and the first two years of the Collor government. During this period, short-term economic policies were conducted through a series of successive stabilization shocks aimed at curbing an inflationary process within an international environment permeated by the foreign debt crisis. The twin problems of internal stabilization and external adjustment have imposed monumental challenges to the successive federal administrations since the first oil shock in 1973. Previous works have already dealt with the economic responses of the military governments to those difficulties.[1]

The study is entirely descriptive. It does not present any original analytical view on Brazil's poor macroeconomic performance nor does it display any new piece of empirical evidence on the subject. The essay is organized in three sections: the first deals with the Sarney administration; the second covers the first two years of the Collor government. Finally, the third section explores the dilemma faced by the present administration with respect to the stabilization game.

The Sarney Administration and the New Republic: Paradise Found and Lost

When the Sarney administration made its debut, one would have thought that Brazilian technocrats had already exhausted the stock of economic policy mistakes that every administration is entitled to exhibit. Even if only as a matter of probability calculus, given the experience of the Figueiredo period (1979–85), the new administration should have made fewer policy errors. However the economic chronicle of the New Republic shows a succession of plans aimed at stabilizing the economy which were a complete failure in terms of stabilization, not to mention their poor record as far as growth and income redistribution are concerned. Worst of all, they affected credibility in the sense that economic decisions increasingly tended to be viewed as a war game among economic agents, in which mutual distrust reigned between the main partners – the government, the private firms and the workers.

Sarney inherited a cabinet patiently built by Tancredo Neves to reflect the divergent political forces supporting the transition to civilian government. These contradictions soon emerged in the conflicting views held by the economic authorities about the nature of the Brazilian inflationary process. On the one hand, there were those who advocated domestic fiscal and monetary austerity as the prerequisite for the resumption of growth. On the other, there were those who favoured renegotiation of the foreign debt in order to reduce the burden of its service on the government budget and generate funds to finance much needed social expenditures. Of course, government actions in this period reflected this ambiguity. A rather restrictive monetary policy was implemented based on the massive sale of government bonds at record real interest rates.[2] On the fiscal side, however, control of administered prices and tariffs on public utilities increased the public sector borrowing requirements.

In August 1985, Sarney made the first change in his economic team by replacing those defending conventional macroeconomic stabilization methods. From then on fiscal and monetary policies became more important. Interest rates were reduced while public expenditures were increased. At the year end, real money supply had grown by 20.6 per cent (compared to a −6.8 per cent reduction in 1984) and the operational deficit/GDP ratio increased by 62 per cent (from 2.7 per cent to 4.4 per cent, respectively in 1984 and 1985), in spite of the vigorous GDP growth in the latter year (led by capacity utilization and higher levels of consumption expenditures). Not surprisingly, the inflation rate also hit a record level of 235.1 per cent in 1985.

The Cruzado Plan

Naturally, the high and rising inflation rate was eroding the government's socio-political and parliamentary support. In February 1986, Sarney reacted with a surprise attack – the Cruzado Plan – the first of the several heterodox stabilization plans which, despite their cataclysmic effects on the Brazilian economy, did very little to generate a minimum of stability and growth. The Cruzado Plan contained all the ingredients of the heterodox-inertial therapy for curing Latin American inflation, that is, a price and exchange rate freeze; monetary reform with the introduction of a new currency; abolition of all types of indexation for periods of under one year; *tablitas* in order to discount future inflation built into existing contracts, financial operations and business sales practices; a wage policy aimed at restoring the average real wage of the previous 12 months.

In order to accommodate the expected increase in the demand for money due to the abrupt fall in price level, the Central Bank adopted a highly expansive monetary policy in the months following announcement of the plan. Signs of potential disequilibrium soon appeared in the goods, factories and asset markets. The excessive money supply led to higher prices of all types of real assets (urban real estate, rural land, stocks of raw material and finished goods), to a stock market boom and to a rising premium on the parallel rate over the official exchange rate.[3] Furthermore, the simultaneous combination of a price and exchange rate freeze with a wage bonus plus low interest rates led to an explosion of aggregate demand, a movement which came on top of an underlying growth trend of consumer spending. Finally, the strong demand bubble leaked to the external sector, reducing exports and increasing imports.

The initial success of the Cruzado Plan allowed the government to buy legitimacy and popularity in advance. Much needed measures to reduce the public deficit were postponed until after the November 1986 elections, exactly as General Figueiredo had done four years earlier. This old piece of electoral expediency paid handsome dividends to the most important political party forming the governmental coalition. Sooner rather than later, the bill was presented to the nation in the form of abrupt increases in utility prices and indirect tax hikes. This cumbersome tax increase became known as the Cruzado II Plan. The drastic inflationary acceleration in January 1987 marked the disintegration of the Cruzado Plan. The fall-out also reached the external sector with a trade deficit in December 1986, the first after six consecutive surpluses. With no foreign reserves to service its foreign debt, the country was then forced to declare an unilateral moratorium on medium- and long-term interest payments to commercial creditor banks.

In spite of its stridency, the February 1987 moratorium did not evoke harsh retaliatory measures from the banking community nor did it reverse the declining trend of popular support for the government. Many factors can account for the dramatic worsening of the economic situation in the first few months of 1987, such as the rising inflation rate; the fall in economic activity, in employment and in real wages; and the emergence of a financial crisis affecting particularly the highly indebted sectors (farmers, small- and medium-sized firms and municipalities). Given the potential for instability embodied in a faltering economy, Sarney's dominant tactic prevailed again: a change in the economic team in April 1987. A new surprise attack on inflation was carried out two months later.

The Bresser Plan

Far less ambitious in its objectives than its predecessor, the Bresser Plan had two aims: firstly, to stop the inflationary acceleration and the subsequent tendency towards disorganization in productive activities; secondly, to eliminate the prospects of a foreign exchange crisis. At the plan's inception, there was a 9.5 per cent exchange rate devaluation and an upward adjustment in government administered prices, including utilities. Prices and wages were frozen for a maximum three-month period, after which prices would become increasingly flexible while wages would be allowed to increase in accordance with the average increases in the consumer price index over the previous three months. Indexation in the financial markets was preserved. Monetary and exchange rate policies were conducted so as to maintain nominal interest rates and exchange rates in line with the current inflation rate.

The plan was successful in improving the external accounts and the financial situation of the state-owned firms. It also made considerable

Table 1.1 Monetary and Fiscal Policy Indicators

Years	(1) Real Money Supply (%)	(2) Real Interest. Rate (%)	(3) M1/GDP (%)	(4) PSBR/GDP (%)
1985	20.65	12.70	4.9	4.4
1986	146.54	1.70	11.2	3.6
1987	−55.91	−11.20	4.8	5.7
1988	−41.07	1.87	2.9	4.8
1989	−21.06	44.21	1.7	12.4 (6.9)
1990	54.50	−4.17	3.3	−1.2
1991	−26.20	13.10	2.3	2.2*

* preliminary
Column 1: Annual changes in the money supply deflated by changes in the general price index (IGP-DI);
Column 2: Monthly average interest rate (at annual rates) on short-term Treasury/Central Bank bills, deflated by changes in the general price index (IGP-DI);
Column 3: Money supply (at year end);
Column 4: Public Sector Borrowing Requirements/GDP ratio: operational concept. The Consumer Price Index (IPC-IBGE) was used to arrive at the operational PSBR. For 1989, the figure in parenthesis refers to nominal PSBR deflated by next-period change in consumer price index, according to Central Bank methodology.
Source: Central Bank Brazil, *Economic Program*, several issues

progress in institutional reforms designed to separate Treasury and Central Bank operations. The wage policy, however, met with enormous obstacles in the larger state bureaucracies. Higher wage concessions in the public sector were soon extended to the better-organized workers in the private sector. Moreover, a tax reform proposal submitted by the finance minister failed to receive support from either the executive or the legislative branches of the government. The minister resigned and a new economic cabinet took office in January 1988.

The 'Rice and Beans' Interregnum

After two successive and unsuccessful stabs at the heterodox experiment, the Sarney administration decided to use conventional fiscal, monetary and exchange rate policies to stabilize, not prices but the rate of inflation. The new authorities were also committed to re-establishing Brazil's connections with the international financial community. The 1987 moratorium was suspended in January 1988 and in June, Brazil and the bank advisory committee reached an agreement to reschedule the US$ 63 billion debt, over a 20-year

Table 1.2 External Sector Indicators

Years	(1) Real Effective Exchange Rate	Trade Balance	Internat. Reserves
	1985=100	US$ Million	US$ Million
1985	100.0	12,486	7,690
1986	105.0	8,305	4,585
1987	109.2	11,172	4,433
1988	98.5	19,184	5,359
1989	81.4	16,120	7,268
1990	68.9	10,990	8,751
1991	83.8	10,622	8,552

Column 1: Average of monthly indexes of real effective exchange rate – for total exports. The currency basket is weighted by the share of the exports to 10 industrialized countries in the aggregate Brazilian exports for the period 1988/1989.
Source: Central Bank, IPEA – *Boletim Conjuntural*, January 1992

period, corresponding to principal maturities of Brazilian medium-term foreign indebtedness owed to commercial banks and due in the years 1987 to 1993. An IMF stand-by loan and an agreement with the Paris Club, in June and July 1988 respectively, completed the effort to save the country's reputation as a worthwhile borrower. Moreover, the enormous trade surplus in 1988 (US$ 19.1 billion or 6.8 per cent of GDP) led to accumulation of foreign reserves which helped to stabilize the external accounts.

On the domestic front, however, the story was completely different. The objective of trying to stabilize the inflationary process at a very high and unstable rate proved to be a self-defeating exercise. As the previous Brazilian experience had made abundantly clear, the very effort of producing a trade surplus fuelled the inflationary motors. Another piece of bad news came from the agricultural sector: growth in real output was ten times less than in 1987, which may explain the wild fluctuations in prices of farm products observed in 1988. As a whole, the 'rice and beans' policy yielded an explosive combination of zero GDP real growth and a 684.6 per cent inflation rate for 1988. Again, the Sarney administration reacted to the worsening of the economic situation in accordance with its internal logic: by delivering a new heterodox plan. Announced in January 1989, the Summer Plan had already been anticipated by the majority of the relevant economic agents.

The Summer Plan

In fact, the Summer Plan was a re-enactment of the Cruzado Plan, now accompanied by official pledges of monetary and fiscal austerity. From the heterodox prescriptions, it copied such devices as monetary reform (the 'new cruzado' replacing the former cruzado as the national currency); deindexation of financial assets and contracts; use of *tablitas*; price and exchange rate freeze after a 17 per cent devaluation against the US dollar; centralization of all types of foreign exchange operations with the Central Bank; a wage policy based on a rule designed to restore average real wage level in the previous 12-month period. The plan's orthodox component consisted of a monetary policy centred on setting an extremely high real *ex-post* interest rate. Fiscal policy, which in the words of President Sarney, would be the strictest in Brazilian history, reduced itself to official pledges of not allowing the government to spend more than its revenues.

The actual functioning of the plan revealed its many inconsistencies. The so-called administrative reform, aimed at reducing the number of government agencies and expenditure on personnel in the public sector, was stalled by the disputes between the executive and the legislative on the responsibility for spending cuts. Lacking the fiscal adjustment, the high interest rate policy reduced itself to a mechanism of income transfer from the public to the private sector, besides having a negative effect on the fiscal deficit. Finally, the persistence of high domestic interest rate in a fixed exchange rate regime led to enormous inflows of foreign 'hot' money, which, in turn, caused a sharp increase in the monetary base. Given the artificial conditions prevailing in both money and exchange markets, such inflow of foreign resources soon left the country, as domestic interest rates were expected to fall and the exchange rate was certain to depreciate.

For all practical purposes, with the disruption of the Summer Plan in June 1989, the Sarney administration came to an end, though it still had a nine-month mandate to complete. The June inflation rate more than doubled in relation to its May figure. Daily devaluations of the exchange rate were back again as well as the daily coefficients for indexing financial assets and contracts in the economy. From then on, until March 1990, the policy-makers had just two objectives: firstly, to make sure that the November presidential election would be held and secondly, to avoid hyperinflation. Two initiatives justify this assump-

Table 1.3 Inflation Rate

Monthly Changes in the General Price Index (IGP-DI)							
Month	1985	1986	1987	1988	1989	1990	1991
Jan	12.6	17.8	12.0	19.1	36.6	71.9	19.9
Feb	10.2	22.4	14.1	17.6	11.8	71.7	21.1
Mar	12.7	−0.9	15.0	18.2	4.2	81.3	7.2
Apr	7.2	−0.6	20.1	20.3	5.2	11.3	8.7
May	7.8	0.3	27.6	19.5	12.8	9.1	6.5
Jun	7.8	0.5	25.9	20.8	26.8	9.0	9.8
Jul	8.9	0.6	9.3	21.5	37.9	12.9	12.8
Aug	14.0	1.3	4.5	22.9	36.5	12.9	15.5
Sept	9.1	1.1	8.0	25.8	38.9	11.7	16.2
Oct	9.0	1.4	11.2	27.6	39.7	14.1	25.8
Nov	15.0	2.5	14.5	28.0	44.3	17.4	25.7
Dec	13.2	7.6	15.9	28.9	49.4	16.4	22.1

Source: Central Bank Brazil, *Economic Program*, various issues

tion. The first was the decision to stop the interest payments to foreign commercial creditor banks in order to protect the country's foreign reserves. Thus, in a less strident manner, Brazil resumed the 1987 moratorium on her external obligations. The second initiative refers to an official effort to organize co-operation between businessmen, workers and government with the idea of establishing consensual increases in prices, wages and public utility rates. This so-called social pact tried to avoid a price explosion followed by social unrest and disorganization of productive activities.

The pact did nothing to prevent the exponential increases in the rate of inflation observed in the second half of 1989. The year's inflation hit 1,782 per cent on a 12-month basis, the highest ever in Brazilian history. But this is not surprising, considering the fact that the government's financial behaviour reinforced the worst expectations. Both the absolute and relative size of the public deficit in 1989 was monumental: the public sector borrowing requirements (operational concept) reached 12.4 per cent of GDP (or 6.9 per cent of GDP using the following month's price increase to deflate the current month's deficit, according to the Brazilian Central Bank's presentation of the 1989 figures for PSBR). Almost 70 per cent of that result was explained by the budget deficit of the Federal Government. Moreover, an increasing fraction of the public debt was being monetized by the Central Bank as investors became reluctant to hold government securities maturing after March 1990. These factors account for a 1,288 per cent rate of money expansion in 1989. Inflation continued to rise in early 1990. In February 1990, the last month of Sarney's administration, the daily inflation rate reached almost 2.0 per cent, meaning that the general price level would double every 35 days.

The Collor Administration: A Modernizing Messiah?

After the many unsuccessful surprise attacks unleashed upon the Brazilian economy by the Sarney administration, it is hardly any surprise that a new attack was launched by the first directly elected government in almost 30 years. Yet, the so-called Collor Plan (March, 1990) did provoke a striking effect on the economy initially, both by its sheer boldness and the amateurish and authoritarian manner of its implementation.

The plan consisted of the five following measures:

(a) a monetary reform, with the return of the 'cruzeiro' as the new domestic currency and a freezing of almost 70 per cent of all monetary and financial assets in the hands of the private sector. These assets were compulsorily transformed into deposits at the Central Bank, to be returned to their owners in 12 monthly instalments, from September 1991 on. Yields on the frozen deposits were fixed at 6 per cent per annum, plus monetary correction based on a modified consumer price index;
(b) an administrative reform, abolishing some governmental agencies and state-owned firms, including a reduction in the number of ministries. There was also a bombastic announcement of a sharp cut in personnel expenditures in the federal government;
(c) a once-and-for-all capital levy was imposed upon private financial wealth (including holdings of financial assets, gold and shares). Furthermore, all types of bearer transactions in organized financial markets were prohibited, including the successful bearer mutual fund;
(d) a 'fluctuating' exchange rate replaced the pegged exchange rate mechanism, which had been in operation almost continuously since 1968. Afterwards, it was known that the Central Bank was substituting its exchange rate target for a target based on the desired level of foreign reserves;
(e) an 'incomes policy' centred on a temporary price freeze coupled

with a pre-fixing of wages, rents, and other types of contractual payments.

For the medium and long term, there were pledges for the privatization of state-owned enterprises, deregulation of economic activities and trade liberalization (consisting of a programme of tariff reduction and elimination of some non-tariff barriers).

The plan's impact in the first few weeks was devastating, leading to a virtual paralysis in production, distribution and sales throughout the economy. Moreover, being extremely interventionist, the Collor Plan required competent and flexible operational management, qualities in short supply in the small group of academic economists responsible for its implementation.

In the months preceding March 1990, large industrial firms had accumulated enormous stocks of raw materials, intermediate and final goods, as a hedge against the expected price freeze and as a flight against financial investment in government bonds. Their initial reaction to the sudden drop in demand was to promote a sharp decline in production, adjusting it to their decreased level of working capital. The *cruzeiro* became a scarce commodity by virtue of the tremendous liquidity constraint imposed upon the economy. To generate the domestic currency, holders of final products cut their prices, exporters sold foreign exchange, and workers in the private sector agreed to temporary wage reductions. As a result of this stock adjustment, in the months after March 1990 there was a drastic reduction in both industrial output and the inflation rate, accompanied by an overvaluation of the foreign exchange rate.

A permanent decline in the inflationary level, however, would require more than a liquidity squeeze, since the latter had also contributed to a contraction in supply, due to disorganization in industrial activities. As early as April and May, the plan suffered its first and unexpected setback, with the enormous real liquidity expansion which somehow prevented a further decrease in the aggregate level of expenditures. Many factors account for the sudden increase in the monetary base in those two months: (a) an expansion due to channels which had been contemplated in the original plan or had otherwise been created legally afterwards, thanks to sectoral pressures; (b) an 'endogenous' creation of new money, through the emergence of a private market trading in formal or informal liabilities denominated in the old currency, and (c) a flow of budget expenditures by the states and municipalities. Local and state treasuries received an unexpected windfall gain represented by an increase in tax revenue, since taxpayers could pay their taxes using their frozen deposits. In fact, due to this mechanism, states and municipalities shared with the Central Bank the monopoly of issuing the highly demanded cruzeiro. As 1990 was an electoral year, this once-and-for-all tax bonus was easily transformed into a permanent increase in state expenditures. Of course, such short-term expediency contributed to worsening the fiscal crisis of the states in years to come.

A rather restrictive monetary policy was implemented during the period from June to September 1990, based on very tight monetary control and an extremely high and volatile real interest rate. This experiment had to be abandoned as soon as it was perceived that it could trigger a wave of bankruptcies in the private sector. Moreover, the high interest rate policy was harming state and municipal finances. Worst of all, the inflation rate did not show any significant decline and the exchange rate was clearly overvalued.

By the end of 1990, devaluation of the exchange rate was accelerated, backfiring on a rising inflationary trend. As the inflation rate reached almost 20 per cent per month in December, together with the dramatic fall in economic activity and the growing difficulties that the Central Bank was experiencing in rolling over the domestic debt, it became clear that the government was ready with another surprise attack, repeating the tactical manoeuvres of the Sarney administration. At the end of January 1991, the Collor Plan II was announced in the midst of a wave of disenchantment and pessimism.

The Collor Plan II: The non-cooperative game again

The traditional items of heterodox therapy were back on stage: a price freeze following a large increase in tariffs and administered prices (including energy); discretionary rules for nominal changes in wages and rents; for the financial system, a prohibition on the issue of repurchase agreements in short-term operations involving public and private securities (the so-called market for overnight funds). The plan also paid lip service to orthodoxy by promising a 10 per cent cut in current expenditures by the government-owned enterprises. Certainly, the most controversial decision was to replace the backward-looking indexation scheme (based on past price indexes) with a supposedly forward-looking mechanism: the 'reference' interest rate.

Table 1.4 Real Annual Growth Rate of GDP. Per cent.

Years	GDP	Agriculture	Industry	Services
1985	7.9	10.0	8.3	6.5
1986	7.6	−8.6	11.8	8.2
1987	3.6	15.0	1.1	3.3
1988	−0.1	0.8	−2.6	2.3
1989	3.3	2.8	2.9	3.9
1990	−4.2	−3.7	−7.9	−0.7
1991	1.2	2.1	0.0	2.6

Source: Central Bank Brazil, *Economic Program*

Based on a sample of interest rates paid by banks to small investors in certificates of deposits, this became the prevailing rule for indexing financial operations. Moreover, due to a highly penalizing tax on short-term funds, these had to be compulsorily invested in open-ended mutual funds, whose portfolio composition was defined in such a way as to provide cheap finance for the public debt and for private long-term investment projects.

The initial results of the Collor Plan II were in line with the previous version of the same experiment: a temporary drop in the inflation rate and in the nominal interest rate and a modest gain for nominal wages. Both factors led to a recovery in sales and production, particularly for those sectors more responsive to changes in the interest rate, or where the price freeze could be enforced more forcefully. In fact, after reaching a very low level in February 1991, industrial production (adjusted for seasonal factors and for number of working days) registered a 17.4 per cent gain in the following three months. In the same period, the consumer goods industry grew by 9.4 per cent (15.5 per cent for durable goods) while intermediate products and capital goods production increased by 22.2 per cent and 11.5 per cent respectively. According to data presented in Table 1.5, industrial GDP grew 13.65 per cent in real terms between the first and second quarters of 1991.

However, the evident change in the direction of economic activity was not enough to reduce the growing dissatisfaction with the distance between economic promises and results. On the domestic front, the administration became more isolated, with mounting criticism of the low quality and increasing centralization of its economic decisions. On the international front, foreign commercial

Table 1.5 Quarterly Real GDP Index (1980=100)
(with seasonal adjustment)

Period	GDP	Agriculture	Industry	Services
1985 (I)	103.52	117.37	95.93	108.31
1985 (II)	103.68	121.29	94.06	109.76
1985 (III)	107.95	122.29	100.34	112.63
1985 (IV)	111.23	120.16	105.41	115.41
1986 (I)	111.20	112.18	106.03	116.97
1986 (II)	112.97	111.02	108.18	119.15
1986 (III)	116.00	107.50	113.01	121.98
1986 (IV)	118.93	116.47	114.99	124.25
1987 (I)	120.43	116.22	118.05	124.46
1987 (II)	120.03	128.77	113.76	124.79
1987 (III)	116.55	133.75	106.02	123.81
1987 (IV)	119.06	128.44	110.52	126.28
1988 (I)	120.79	131.51	112.58	127.23
1988 (II)	119.70	128.13	110.25	128.27
1988 (III)	118.68	127.44	108.47	128.05
1988 (IV)	116.74	128.19	104.87	127.25
1989 (I)	117.82	133.94	104.69	128.43
1989 (II)	123.49	132.93	113.47	132.43
1989 (III)	124.25	128.55	115.20	133.58
1989 (IV)	124.39	130.89	114.22	134.37
1990 (I)	121.35	122.46	110.77	133.40
1990 (II)	112.18	127.45	94.36	128.52
1990 (III)	119.54	129.44	106.54	131.84
1990 (IV)	116.98	129.92	101.18	131.64
1991 (I)	112.57	126.99	93.89	130.18
1991 (II)	120.94	129.01	106.71	135.22
1991 (III)	122.08	133.11	107.62	135.74
1991 (IV)	119.50	131.94	103.38	134.68

Source: IBGE

banks, multilateral institutions and government officials from the creditor countries all resented the new Brazilian approach towards the renegotiation of the foreign debt. According to this approach, service of the foreign debt should be conditioned by public finance and not by the balance of payments situation. Therefore, any payment to foreign creditors would be conditional on the existence of a government budget surplus.

Contrary to the previous pattern of response to internal and external tensions, the Collor government reacted with a sweeping change in its economic cabinet in May 1991. The then Brazilian ambassador to the United States was recalled to be the economic minister. This event marks the beginning of a Collor Phase III programme.

The Collor Phase III: Back to the fundamentals?

A combination of moderate inflation and economic recovery afforded the new economic team a four-month period of grace, which lasted from May until August 1991. During the second quarter of 1991, the average monthly inflation rate reached 9.7 per cent and real GDP growth rate jumped to 7.4 per cent relative to the previous quarter. (On a four-quarter cumulative basis, however, the growth rate was still negative at −2.4 per cent). This apparent tranquillity led the authorities to bring forward by a month, to 15 August 1991, the devolution of the first instalment of the frozen deposits at the Central Bank.

At the end of August, it became increasingly clear that the inflation rate was again on an upward course. Given the fact that monetary and exchange rate policies were pegging nominal interest rates and the exchange rate to a lagged 'reference interest rate', such a policy rule was leading to an untenable combination of a negative real interest rate with an overvalued exchange rate. The government's reaction consisted of a series of interest rate increases and a 15 per cent currency devaluation on 30 September 1991. At the same time, the Central Bank announced that it would stop its daily interventions in the domestic gold market, a mechanism which had been used since March 1990 to control the premium of the parallel ('black') over the official exchange rate. These changes seemed to appease domestic financial and exchange markets at the cost of aborting the fragile recovery in the industrial sector, due to the very high level of real interest rates prevailing in the last quarter of 1991.

As the Collor administration reaches the end of its second year in office, its economic policies seem to fall into two groups. The first is directed at short-term stabilization problems, using monetary policy to keep domestic interest rates high; fiscal policy to maintain public tariffs 'in tandem' with current inflation rate, and exchange policy to establish a realistic exchange rate. Moreover, in late January 1992, Brazil signed a stand-by agreement with the International Monetary Fund in support of the stabilization programme. This paved the way for a renegotiation of the government-to-government foreign debt with the Paris Club which was completed one month later. A private debt settlement with the commercial banks was expected to follow.

The second part of the government's effort seems to have been directed at creating an economic environment conducive to growth and stability in the medium and long term. As most of Latin America is learning the hard way, a change in policy concerning the financing of the public deficit is crucial to the latter objective. The administration is trying to get congressional approval for a fiscal reform which would change some constitutional provisions related to the distribution of revenue and expenditures between the three levels of government: federal, state and municipal.

Together with the effort to improve the public finances, there have been attempts to promote structural changes in the economy through privatization of state enterprises, reduction of tariff and non-tariff barriers to trade, deregulation, incentives for direct foreign investment in the Brazilian stock markets, and other decisions aimed at creating a more open and competitive economy.

Financial and capital markets abroad have apparently reacted favourably to the new policies of the Collor administration. In the second half of 1991, Brazil experienced the first large voluntary inflow of foreign currency since the 1982 debt crisis. According to Salomon Brothers, capital flow to Brazil reached US$ 11,626 million in 1991, second only to Mexico's US$ 16,072 million. This is 2,761 per cent more than the US$ 406.3 million inflow in 1990.[4] Money came into the country either as direct investment in the stock market or as portfolio investment (Brazilian firms issuing securities abroad). Part of this inflow is said to be a repatriation of domestic capital which had left the country in order to reduce its exposure to Brazilian risk during the successive economic shocks and the mega-inflation period at the end of the Sarney government. Irrespective of its origin, the money inflow has caused a stock-market boom, has promoted an increase in the monetary base, in foreign reserves and in the internal debt and has also led to a negative premium on the parallel exchange rate.

On the domestic scene, support for the stabilization programme is problematic due to the coexistence of a very high inflation rate and deepening recession, which is more pronounced in the urban-industrial sectors of the economy. Lacking any stable parliamentary or political basis, the government has been forced into negotiation with

Table 1.6 Indicators of Employment, Wages and Income Distribution

Years	Average Rate of Unemployment	Monthly Real Wage Rate	Gini Index
1986	3.56	109.0	0.589
1987	3.75	100.1	0.595
1988	3.85	102.5	0.617
1989	3.34	99.3	0.639
1990	4.31	86.0	n.a.
1991	4.72*	78.3**	n.a.

* January to October
** January to November
Column 1: Average monthly rate of unemployment as percentage of economically active population, with seasonal adjustment;
Column 2: Index number for the average monthly real wage rate in the manufacturing sector in the São Paulo State, 1986=100
Column 3: Gini index for income concentration for the economically active population, excluding the rural population in the North Region
Source: IBGE, IPEA

Congress on every issue relevant to its new orthodox posture, some of which require constitutional amendments (fiscal reform, wage policy, social security financing, new patent law, breaking-up of state monopolies in important industries and services, and so on). Of course, 'quid-pro-quo' arrangements have been part of the negotiation process, such as the virtual 'federalization' of the US$ 57 billion of state and municipal public debt. (The highly indebted states have promised to give support in Congress to the government-sponsored package of fiscal reform, in exchange for a 20-year plan to reschedule the state debts with the Federal Treasury and federal financial agencies and also for rolling over the outstanding state government internal debt.)

GDP growth in 1991, though positive, was still 1.2 per cent, below the rate of population growth. This result was particularly affected by the poor performance of the industrial sector which, in turn, had its effect on employment and wages. Data in Table 1.6 indicate an increase in the unemployment rate in 1990 and 1991 for the country as a whole. The same table shows a dramatic fall in the real wage rate in the manufacturing sector in the state of São Paulo: between 1986 and 1991, the index of average monthly real wage rate fell by 28.1 per cent.

Other macroeconomic statistics provide a desolate picture of the deteriorating social conditions. The combination of high inflation rate and economic stagnation has caused a worsening of income inequality in a country which has not been a model for a civilized pattern of income distribution. The Gini index for income inequality increased between 1986 and 1989. (See Table 1.6) For more recent years, an income distribution survey for the Greater São Paulo Metropolitan Area showed increasing inequality between 1989 and 1991: the poorer 30 per cent of the economically active population saw their income share drop from 3.2 per cent to 2.8 per cent.[5]

Final Remarks on the Stabilization Game

This article has reviewed the main lines of the short-term economic policies in Brazil in the post–1985 experience of civilian government. Judging by their results, it is only fair to conclude that the quality of the economic decisions was no better than those prevailing in the military-authoritarian regime. Judging by their methods, economic policy-making can best be described as a type of non-cooperative, non-zero sum game among many agents, in which the dominant strategy of the main actors consists of a series of surprise attacks designed to stabilize the economy. Not one of the six successive interventions (considering the Cruzado II as another attempt of the same type of experiment) produced the intended results.

It is interesting to note that, according to some modern theoretical macroeconomic hypothesis, an inflationary economy is the logical outcome of a non-cooperative, non-constant sum game between the government and its central bank on one hand and the public on the other. Given the assumed short-term surprise effect on output and employment, the government has a discretionary incentive to inflate once the public's inflationary expectations have been set. The public, however, learn by experience and with an appropriate deterrence mechanism they can determine a sustained rate of inflation, lower than the government's discretionary rate.

It may be that the same logic explains the failure of the surprise-based heterodox plans to stabilize the economy. A surprise attack represents the maximum use of the policy-makers' discretionary power in allocating resources, income and wealth in the economy. Therefore, a first surprise attack may have real economic impact, giving the government time to attack the fundamental inflationary causes, mainly fiscal adjustment. This is one of the theoretical justifications for a heterodox strategy in countries with chronic high inflation.[6] However, each failed attack damages the attacker's reputation and credibility, thus lowering the efficiency of the next attack, which requires that each attack be more interventionist than the previous one. Once such a pattern is perceived by the public, each new shock is fully anticipated and it may not have any real economic effects whatsoever, a result which may be similar to the well-known impact of a fully anticipated monetary shock. Even when the government seems to be firmly engaged in a no-shock strategy, like the Collor administration in the initial months of 1992, it takes time to convince economic agents of its commitment, given the recent experience. In other words, the conventional macroeconomic stabilization policies may end up being longer and harder than they would have been otherwise.

A simple example can illustrate the type of dilemma that policymakers face in choosing the appropriate stabilization path. Suppose there are two methods: on one hand, the conventional macroeconomic combination of monetary and fiscal policies in whatever mix is appropriate to the situation; and on the other hand, the surprise attack, with its plethora of price, wage and exchange rate freeze followed by interventions in contracts and in other rules of the game. The public understands the government's behaviour and forms its expectations according to its previous experience. The payoff table can be represented as follows:

	GOVERNMENT CHOICES	
PUBLIC EXPECTATIONS:	Shocks	Macro policies
Shocks	A	B
Macro policies	C	D

If the government chooses a surprise attack, but the public also expects the same (A), the economic effect would be nil. The expected value of an expected surprise attack is zero. In fact, a sequence of shocks may have worse consequences since it may lead to higher inflationary instability. Studying the lessons of the heterodox stabilization programmes, Kiguel and Liviatan arrive at the conclusion that the failure of a heterodox programme is more likely to destabilize inflation than the failure of an orthodox programme.[7]

Alternatively, if the government chooses the conventional mix of monetary and fiscal policies as a stabilization weapon, and the public expects this (D), the economy may eventually move towards price stability. If the government chooses shocks, while the public expects conventional macro policies (C), there is a surprise effect which can be favourable provided that the shock is followed by an orthodox component. Finally, if the government is committed to conventional stabilization policy, but this commitment is not fully credible because of past experience, so that the public expects a shock to occur (B), the conventional policies will take longer to deliver favourable results. Output and employment losses will be larger and inflation will persist longer than in the typical adjustment process towards price stability. This delay will, in turn, lead some agents to expect a shock for different reasons, that is to say, out of fear that the government can not afford to sustain a combination of recession-cum-inflation for a long period. It is easy to see that this is not a process which converges to an equilibrium position. In March 1992, the Collor administration is completing its second year in office. After two unsuccessful surprise attacks, it has publicly announced a commitment to a no-shock strategy. This commitment is being enforced by a short-term monetary policy centred on maintaining a high real interest rate; for the medium and the long run, fiscal and structural reforms have high priorities on the governmental agenda. So far, results have been meagre: negative real per capita income growth and high inflation rates. It remains to be seen whether Collor can reverse these outcomes without another surprise attack.

To conclude, it seems ironic that it has been the fate of the new democratic governments in Brazil and elsewhere in Latin America to resort to shocks as a mechanical formula for intervention. Other social scientists may be able to explain this exotic preference for non-democratic methods of economic management, precisely when the slow construction of democratic institutions calls for participation, so that the sacrifices of adjustment can be shared equally rather than being arbitrarily imposed.

(São Paulo, 10 March 1992)

2· BRAZILIAN HYPERINFLATION:

The Political Economy of the Fiscal Crisis

*Gustavo H. B. Franco**

Introduction

This article, which is divided into two sections, offers a discussion of some important regularities, as well as some crucial contrasts, in cases of hyperinflation in the twentieth century and, against this broad background, isolates some peculiarities of the Brazilian case. Its emphasis is deliberately analytical and critical, reducing descriptions to a minimum for the reader not acquainted with the Brazilian experience. The key issue under discussion is the process by which, for almost exclusively domestic reasons, Brazilian hyperinflation developed during the period of the New Republic (1985–9). The paper argues strongly that the political economy of the budgetary process was a crucial element in producing an unsustainable fiscal situation at the end of the Sarney presidency in 1989.

Brazilian Hyperinflation in Perspective

During the few months preceding the inauguration of the newly elected Collor government, it was commonly argued that Brazil was *not* experiencing a hyperinflation: either because economic disorganization had not reached the levels presumed to have been reached in the 1920s, or because Brazil barely touched the 50 per cent monthly inflation rate threshold, the 'definition' established in Philip Cagan's classic 1956 paper.[1] Yet, no qualitative meaning could possibly be associated with this unquestionably arbitrary definition. For Latin American countries with a long experience of chronic inflation, the slow approach to the 50 per cent threshold of 'hyperinflation' was somewhat uneventful: living with 50 per cent monthly rates seemed no different than with 20 per cent or 30 per cent. The very same 'technologies' (price/cost indexation, search costs, and the flight towards inflation-sheltered assets) that were used to survive under slowly accelerating inflation of 30 per cent could be used, perhaps only in a slightly faster mode, at 50 per cent. Moreover, Latin American hyperinflations seemed to reveal the very same slowly accelerating auto-regressive pattern, the 'inertial' character as it is known locally, that had been observed during the two previous decades. Cagan himself perceived these regularities, to judge from his 'hyperinflation' entry in the recent edition of the Palgrave Dictionary, where he admits that 'there is no well defined threshold'.[2]

It is common, on the other hand, to take hyperinflations as episodes in which the national money disappears as inflation rates display explosive behaviour. Yet the latter are exceptions, and very singular ones, rather than the rule. Indeed, in contrast to the usual journalistic views on the subject, the European hyperinflations of the 1920s followed the same pattern as recent Latin American hyperinflations, namely slowly accelerating, but markedly auto-regressive inflations, with incidental shocks – freezing and de-freezing of prices and exchange rates, for instance – and more or less volatility depending on the specifics of each case.[3]

Each one of the twelve cases of hyperinflation reported in Table 2.1 is associated with an overwhelming economic problem, the nature of which, however, is quite varied. The peace treaties after the first world war imposed very heavy territorial losses on Austria and Hungary, which caused the Austrian Parliament to pass a declaration that the country was not viable under the new frontiers. The reunification of Poland after one century of a tripartite division among hostile powers also represented a major challenge that had to be met simultaneously with a war with the Soviet Union which, in its turn, was undertaking an ambitious social transformation. In one way or another, these challenges resulted in fiscal and balance of payments imbalances that appear as proximate causes of hyperinflation. It is useful, in this connection, to consider the evidence in Table 2.2 on current account deficits, real wages, debt service and on budget deficits for European and Latin American hyperinflationary countries. An important point with respect to these numbers is that one should be careful in considering realized values for current account deficits, as well as budget deficits, as indicators of *ex-ante* imbalances, as these

Table 2.1 Hyperinflations in the Twentieth Century (according to Cagan's definition)

Country	Started+	Ended	Duration @	Average*	Worst month*
1920s					
Austria	Oct. 1921	Aug. 1922	11	47	134
Germany	Aug. 1922	Nov. 1923	16	322	32,400
Hungary	Mar. 1923	Feb. 1924	10	46	98
Poland	Jan. 1923	Jan. 1924	11	81	275
Soviet Union	Dec. 1921	Jan. 1924	26	57	213
1940s					
Hungary	Aug. 1945	Jul. 1946	12	19.800	4.2×10^{15}
Greece	Nov. 1943	Nov. 1944	11	365	8,500,000
China #	Sep. 1945	May 1949	44	78	2,565
1980s					
Bolivia	Apr. 1984	Sep. 1985	18	46	183
Peru	Jan. 1989	Sep. 1990	21	51	412
Argentina	May 1989	Jan. 1991	32	67	196
Brazil	Nov. 1989	Mar. 1990	5	62	84

(+) The month in which 50% was reached. (@) In months. (*) Monthly rates.
(#) Wholesale prices for Shanghai.

Sources: Cagan (1956) 'The Monetary Dynamics of Hyperinflation' in M. Friedman (ed.) *Studies in the Quantity Theory of Money* Chicago: University of Chicago Press, p. 26; S. N. Chou (1963) *The Chinese Inflation 1937–1949* New York: Columbia University Press, p. 306; J. A. Morales (1988), 'La Inflación y la Estabilización en Bolivia', in M. Bruno et al. (eds), op. cit.; M. Damill & R. Frenkel (1990) 'Hyperinflación y Estabilización. La Experiencia argentina reciente', Buenos Aires: CEDES, mimeo; and Conjuntura Econômica, Fundação Getúlio Vargas, Rio de Janeiro, various issues.

values incorporate all endogenous influences that worked to 'resolve' *ex-ante* imbalances in the context of the hyperinflation process. In an attempt to avoid this difficulty we report, for European countries, current account deficits for the years immediately after the stabilization, when one important force generating external imbalances – namely very ambitious wage aspirations[4] – was still very much in operation. Inflation was indeed a mechanism through which real wages were kept at low levels and external balance maintained. When these economies were stabilized, real wages experienced very sharp increases and external imbalances reappeared. Note, however, that all these economies experienced sharp increases in unemployment in the years following stabilization, which worked to reduce external imbalances for 1924–6. Another important caveat is that the figures for Germany's current account deficit – only 2.6 per cent for 1924–6 – are a gross underestimation of what occurred in 1922–3 when the full reparation obligation was still in force and represented 76.4 per cent of exports, nearly a quarter of GDP! In 1924–6 this obligation was scaled down to an average of 9.1 per cent of the value of exports. The figures for Polish and Hungarian current account deficits seem rather unimpressive, but an interesting detail with respect to the Polish figures should be noted. The annexation, in 1922, of the German province of Upper Silesia, a coal-exporting district, resulted in doubling Polish exports and in a virtual solution to its balance of payments problems. In Hungary, a relevant consideration was that a right-wing authoritarian government was very active in moderating wage recomposition and effecting external adjustment through the redefinition of wage aspirations. External and fiscal imbalances were definitely important, though to a varying degree, to the development of hyperinflation in these countries.

As far as Latin American countries are concerned, Table 2.2 reports figures for current account deficits in 1981–2, that is, when financing for external imbalances was easy to obtain on the international financial markets. These deficits should provide an indication of the size of the adjustment effort to be undertaken after the Mexican crisis and the drying up of external financing. Note that, except for Argentina, current account deficits were comparable to the (presumed) European ones, and that Brazil, Argentina and Peru endured sharp improvements in their current accounts in the first half of the 1980s, while in Bolivia the picture is quite the opposite. The adjustment effort, in the latter case, was undertaken after 1985 with the implementation of the stabilization programme that terminated hyperinflation. To judge from these numbers, Brazil and Peru experienced hyperinflation after 1985 when their current accounts were already balanced, while Argentina and Bolivia would face it under a considerable external strain.

Budget deficit figures for the two groups of countries seem to indicate that fiscal imbalances were somewhat greater in the Latin American than the European cases. Note also that while European countries experienced a remarkable improvement with the stabilization – which was mostly associated with the Oliveira-Tanzi effect[5] –

Table 2.2 Hyperinflation Countries: Current Account, Wages, Debt Service and Budget Deficits

Country	Current account as % of GDP		Real wages		Debt service as % of exports		Budget deficit as % of GDP (+)	
European countries			(1913=100)					
	1924–26	1927–28	1920–21	1924	1922	1924–26	1923	1925
Germany	−2.6	−4.9	61	102	76.4#	9.1	5.89	−0.6
Austria	−8.4	−6.1	52	94	...	9.5	4.93@	0.1
Hungary	−2.8	−7.7	46	74	...	5.3	5.10	−0.7
Poland	−0.5	−4.8	72	105	...	4.9	5.82	−2.0
Latin American countries								
	1981–2	1984–5	1981–2*	1984–5*	1981–2	1984–5	1981–2	1984–5
Brazil	−6.6	0.0	106	108	42.1	26.6	7.0	3.4
Bolivia	−4.0	−19.5	93	84	28.2	33.7	5.9	12.4
Argentina	−20.0	−7.2	85	117	24.5	35.5	8.5	5.4
Peru	−7.6	−0.5	99	79	36.7	11.6	8.9	5.3

(+) Operational concept. (#) Due values established in the London ultimatum: 26% of exports plus 2 billion gold marks. Details in Keynes (1922). (*) 1980=100. (@) 1922.

Sources: European countries: balance of payments figures from League of Nations (1927/1928/1930) *Memorandum on International Trade and Balance of Payments 1912–1926, 1913–1927, 1926–1928* vol.I & II, *Review of World Trade and Balances of Payments*, Geneva, vol.I 1927, pp. 58–9, 141–51; vol.I, 1928, pp. 180–90; 1926–1928, vol.2, 1930, pp. 91–3; Bank of Poland (1930) *Combined Reprints of the Quarterly Report of the Financial Advisor to the Polish Government*, 4th quarter of 1927 to 3rd quarter of 1930 inclusive Warsaw, pp. 95–6; and R. Nötel (1984) 'Money, Banking and Industry in Interwar Austria and Hungary', *Journal of European Economic History* 13(2) special issue fall, pp. 156–82. Fiscal figures from Franco (1990) 'Fiscal reforms and stabilization: four hyperinflation cases examined', *The Economic Journal*, 100(399) March. GDP figures from B. R. Mitchell (1978) *European Historical Statistics 1750–1970* New York: Columbia University Press, Abridged Edition, pp. 409–12, A. Eckestein (1956) *National Income and Capital Formation in Hungary, 1900–1950* Cambridge: International Association for Research in Income and Wealth, p. 14; and S. Andic & J. Veverka (1964) 'The Growth of Government Expenditure in Germany Since the Unification' *Finanzarchiv* 23, pp. 241–2). Latin American countries: The World Bank, *World Development Report*, various issues; Banco Central do Brasil, *Brasil Programa Econômico*, various issues; Cepal, Comisión Económica para América Latina y el Caribe, *Balance Preliminar de la Economía Lationamericana*, various issues. J. A. Morales (1986a) 'Creación de Dinero y Demanda por Dinero durante la Alta Inflación Boliviana de 1982–85', Documento de Trabajo no 7. Instituto de Investigaciones Socio-Económicas, Universidad Católica Boliviana; and (1986b) 'Estabilización y Nueva Política Económica en Bolivia', Documento de Trabajo no 9, Instituto de Investigaciones Socio-Económicas, Universidad Católica Boliviana; V. Tanzi (1989) 'Fiscal policy and economic restructuring in Latin America' Mimeo; and M. Tuillo (1989), 'Deficit Fiscal, Inflación, Crecimiento y Política de Gasto Público en el Perú, 1968–88', Universidad Católica *Documento de Trabajo* no 86, June.

Latin American countries showed only a small reduction in deficits by the mid-1980s. In fact, through the second half of the 1980s, fiscal accounts in Argentina, Brazil and Peru did not exhibit any significant improvement, this being, according to most observers, the most important cause of the successive frustrated stabilization attempts in these countries. No doubt fiscal imbalances play a very significant role in these countries' hyperinflations, but external imbalances should not be minimized. If anything, we may suggest that both fiscal and external imbalances are present in all cases, which does not authorize an unqualified adoption of any single explanation for each of the episodes in Table 2.2.

One should not fail to note, however, that the overwhelming fiscal and/or balance of payments imbalances mentioned above must not be seen as the sole origins of hyperinflation. Other countries, both in the 1920s and in the 1980s, faced comparable dislocations but not hyperinflations. What seems to be a crucial ingredient in hyperinflation is the government's loss of decision-making capacity in economic policy issues, usually by virtue of political deadlock impeding any meaningful action for a prolonged period of time. This is quite consistent with the common association of the 1920s hyperinflation cases with wars, revolutions and civil disorder which are taken by many authors to be 'critical elements'[6] in hyperinflation. What is interesting to stress is that for Latin American countries, except Nicaragua, policy paralysis may take place without civil disorder or economic catastrophes comparable to what was seen in some countries in the 1920s and 1940s. The debt crisis, as suggested above, is a relevant element, but why did so many other Latin American countries experiencing the same shocks bounce back from the crisis without hyperinflation? The recent history of Argentina, Peru and Brazil does reveal, to a varying degree, the practice of irresponsible populism as well as responsible and ineffective attempts to fight irresponsible fiscal trends. No decisive move towards the correction of fiscal imbalances has been seen for quite a while, and domestic political constraints are certainly to blame. It is somewhat striking that political deadlocks can be such that the whole society has to face the painful consequences of hyperinflation. No general theory can be made of such collective irresponsibility. In what follows we try to align the key aspects of the Brazilian edition of this extraordinary phenomenon.

The Fiscal Crisis: From Open to Repressed Hyperinflation

Late in 1984, when the first civilian government in two decades was about to take office, the economy was experiencing the early phase of a vigorous recovery. As growth resumed without damaging the external accounts, many observers felt that the adjustment to the 1982 crisis had been left behind, thanks to previous efforts of structural adjustment and also the joint impact of the recession and expenditure switching measures. The budget deficit was under reasonable control (between zero and 1.5 per cent of GDP[7]) and inflation, despite a rising trend, was still moderate. There may have been overly optimist expectations of the country's prospects but no observer of the Brazilian scene could possibly have forecast that, five years later, at the end of the Sarney administration, the fiscal situation would become unsustainable (with the budget deficit – operational concept – approaching 10 per cent of GDP) and Brazil would experience the seventh worst hyperinflation in history.[8]

The roots of the fiscal crisis leading to hyperinflation may be assessed with the help of Table 2.3 below, showing a broad summary of the Brazilian government current account since 1970. It is interesting to note that there are two very clear rounds of deterioration, taking 1970 as a benchmark year: the first taking place in the second half of the 1970s, by means of which an overall deficit (operational concept) reached 4.5 per cent of GDP in 1980, when the public sector's savings reached 2.2 per cent of GDP, after remaining around 6 per cent of GDP in the early 1970s, and the second between 1985 and 1989, after which savings reached –5.8 per cent of GDP, and the overall public deficit reached 8.9 per cent. In a widely publicized document, the government acknowledged that, taking into consideration all the measures taken and concessions granted at the end of the Sarney administration, the operational deficit for 1990 was expected to reach 9.15 per cent of GDP. It is also interesting to note that the deficit financing capacity was considerably eroded by the growing difficulties involved in placing government bonds with the public. In 1989 this could be associated with the possibility of the left-wing candidate's victory in the presidential election. Afterwards, this was motivated by the blocking of financial assets and the associated capital levy contained in the March 1990 Collor Plan I. With growing financing difficulties the inflationary repercussions of a given level of fiscal disequilibrium are much stronger.

Table 2.3 Government Current Account, Operational Concept (% of GDP)

	1970	1975	1980	1985	1989
Current revenues	27.1	25.8	23.6	22.3	21.2
Current expenditures	21.0	21.1	21.4	22.1	27.0
debt servicing	0.7	0.6	1.1	3.8	3.3
wages	8.3	7.5	6.2	6.8	9.7
social security	8.2	7.0	7.6	7.1	7.5
other	3.8	6.0	6.5	4.4	6.5
Government savings	6.1	4.7	2.2	0.2	−5.8

Source: Ministério da Economia, National Accounts.

The first round of fiscal deterioration took place during the 1970s through the end of the military cycle in 1985 and may rightly be associated with the domestic fiscal counterpart of the transfer problem created by the debt crisis. Broadly speaking, this is the international component of the Brazilian crisis, i.e. a problem to be found in all indebted countries. The truly puzzling aspect of the Brazilian crisis is the further deterioration occurring after 1985, comprising increased public spending and reduced deficit financing capability, leading fiscal accounts to a chaotic situation at the end of 1989. No doubt this evolution was due to domestic factors; its coincidence with the return to democracy after two decades of authoritarian rule is a disturbing one. It actually suggests that political economy factors may have been important in generating the phenomenon.

Democracy is certainly a factor in Brazilian inflation, just as it was in Weimar Germany. In the latter, the extraordinary increase in union affiliation and activity immediately after the 1918 revolution provoked a very strong drive towards recovering the level of real wages before the war, which was about twice the prevailing level. This was certainly an inflationary influence, and one that made the adjustment effort necessary to meet the reparation obligation even more difficult. In the Brazilian case it is also true that union activity was considerably increased in the second half of the 1980s, and also that this increased 'resistance' on the part of workers to wage cuts required by external adjustment was clearly felt. Yet, the order of magnitude of this 'distributive conflict' effect on inflation was much less important in Brazil. Wage cuts have never been of the same order of magnitude and neither was the external obligation, as already seen in Table 2.2. The mechanism by which democracy facilitated inflation was a different one, running mostly through the fiscal accounts. It is very clear to most observers that by the time of the transition to democracy fiscal and monetary institutions in Brazil were totally inappropriate to the democratic environment. It is usually observed, for instance, that the lack of Central Bank independence as regards government financing was at that time, and still is, a serious institutional weakness of the Brazilian economy, and one that creates a very serious pro-inflationary bias. The solution to this problem is far from simple, since it relates to the delicate issue of the relation between state banks, Caixas Econômicas, Banco do Brasil and the Central Bank, as well as inflation accounting and the treatment of seigniorage revenues. The issues are being discussed within the framework of the law regulating article 192 of the 1988 Constitution regulating the workings of the monetary authorities and the financial system. There is, still, a long way to go.

Serious problems can also be found with respect to fiscal institutions, particularly those related to the budgetary process and the control of government spending. The pro-inflationary bias results from the fact that such institutions were designed to be subject to *ad hoc* control under authoritarian rule. Under democracy, there was no institutional mechanism to regulate an open competition for public resources and regulation or to match demands to available resources. This 'irresponsibility bias' was facilitated by two circumstances: the first was the absolute lack of transparency involving the fiscal accounts. In the mid-1980s the federal budget included only a minor part of public revenues and spending. Other parts were budgeted on the 'monetary budget', the credit operation budget and state enterprises and some development banks were, by and large, outside the budgetary sphere.[9] Avoiding the scrutiny of Congress was an explicit concern of the military. Slowly, during the late 1980s, considerable advances have been made in clarifying public accounts and picturing more appropriately the consolidated financial result of the public sector. But much further improvement is needed as the lack of transparency is still large and so is the scope for creative accounting. The second key aspect of the control of public operations through the budget was that inflation seriously distorted the budgetary process. Because the budget was not indexed, the nominal growth of revenues usually overtook budgeted values within a few months depending, evidently, on the level of inflation. In these conditions, all revenues became 'excess revenues' and thus subject to discretionary allocation on the part of Congress. Likewise, the nominal growth of spending rapidly overtook budgeted values and created a chronic need for extra-budgetary allowances which were also granted discretionarily by Congress. The original lines of the budget were usually entirely lost in this process and, in a context in which Congress no longer accepted guidelines imposed by the executive, the tendency was for the creation of entirely new expenditure in each extra-budgetary round. Besides, perverse incentives were created for individual spending units who felt that the faster they exhausted their budgeted resources the better they positioned themselves in the next round of extra-budgetary bids.

The combination of lack of transparency with lack of indexation in an open political regime was detrimental to fiscal discipline, and the unorganized and unbound competition for public resources bore no relation whatsoever to macroeconomic targets such as budget balance and price stability. The only force capable of enforcing global consistency in demands was the executive, and during the years of the military regime this was quite effective. With the civilian government, however, the executive's role was actually reversed. Given the circumstances surrounding José Sarney's inauguration as president, the lack of political support, both in Congress and from society at large, resulted in destroying any commitment on the part of the executive for fiscal discipline. Quite to the contrary, Sarney displayed a marked clientelistic behaviour that acted as an incentive for special interest groups.

Later on, other problems would be felt. Lack of enforcement of budgetary guidelines and excessive autonomy on the part of spending units were clear and very strong trends during the years of the New Republic which were considerably reinforced by the 1988 Constitution. The latter not only increased the share of states and counties in global public revenues without transferring spending obligations, thus enhancing spending capacity on the part of local government, but also, in view of the number of issues that remained unregulated, established a huge 'grey area', particularly in matters connected to the execution of the budget and the constitution of public debt. The budgetary independence of the states turned out to be a quite disturbing development: their control of the state development banks offered them the opportunity of financial accommodation to cover excess spending and to transform state debts into bids at the Central Bank rediscount window.

Interestingly, the tendency for irresponsible bids from individual spending units is natural in any democracy. Yet, in Brazil there is no market to bring these demands to levels consistent with budgetary balance and price stability. With the end of authoritarian rule, there is a need for institutional guidelines and procedures to establish fiscal discipline. Otherwise, the trend towards multiplying demands for spending and regulation becomes explosive. Indeed, a striking aspect of the fiscal deterioration in 1985–9 is that it is uniform, i. e. there is no clear 'villain' to blame. Interestingly, the burden of debts, domestic and foreign, was reduced (the former because of imperfect indexation, the latter because of non-payment[10]) thus contradicting nationalist claims that the fiscal problem had a 'financial character'.[11] The increase in government dis-savings from 0.4 per cent to 5.8 per cent of GDP is entirely due to the inability of fiscal and monetary institutions to regulate political demands on the budget and the money issue.

Once these problems had produced an unsustainable fiscal situation at the end of the Sarney administration, Brazil faced the concrete threat of hyperinflation. After the failure of the third and last of the 'heterodox shocks' of the administration – the Summer Plan in 1989 – an interesting innovation was introduced as regards government finances. It was openly recognized by the authorities that authorized and mandatory spending was far beyond available revenues including those from seigniorage, i. e. from the inflation tax. At this point, finance minister Mailson da Nóbrega introduced the practice of making expenditure only to the limit of available resources, that is, tax money and seigniorage. This meant a more or less balanced budget 'on a cash basis', despite the existence of a large 'potential deficit', or on an 'accrual basis', thanks to the fact that lots of budgeted expenditures were rationed, left undone, or delayed. The legal loophole allowing these practices was that the budget was only an authorizing document and that, for this reason, the executive was not obliged to undertake all expenditure budgeted. That meant basically that the executive could ration public spending, which was made on an entirely *ad hoc* basis. This is called *contingenciamento*. It is important to note that the potential for corruption and political favouring involved in practices free of any accountability is huge. The recent wave of corruption cases and scandals in public administration is certainly related to this state of affairs.

The clearest implication of the practice of maintaining fiscal balance 'on a cash basis' is that hyperinflation becomes repressed. Apparently, the public still believes that the fiscal problem is not resolved despite actual budget balance, because it perceives that the absence of deficit is due to non-payment. Any bankrupt business can display a cash surplus if not able to pay its bills. A technical denomination for this situation, according to the IMF, is 'fiscal repression'[12] and the basic problem is that it cannot be sustained for a long period of time. It includes delaying payments on current spending, including wages and replacement of materials, which results in dramatic shortages, for example, in hospitals. It includes the postponement of essential investments in infrastructure that will have to be made eventually. Strictly speaking, 'fiscal repression' is like imposing a 'forced' loan on spending units, public employees and contractors. It is public debt like any other and it does involve costs that may be seen in future recomposition of public wages and prices of public contractors. Not to mention the fact that the procedure ruins the very workings of the public sector because it makes relations between government and society increasingly difficult. Prices did not stabilize because it was perceived that the apparent budgetary balance achieved by fiscal repression could not be sustained. Quite to the contrary, the prevailing feeling is that the government is in a permanent state of default with respect to society. Indeed, it assumed obligations far beyond its capacity to meet them, and can only meet part of its promises. Money is certainly one of these promises. It no longer carries the claim of convertibility into gold or silver, but is still bound to honour the promise from the issuing authority that cash can be exchanged for goods and services at a more or less stable value over time. If the government has not been able to keep any of its promises how could it possibly keep this one?

This paradox of an apparent fiscal balance, thanks to 'fiscal repression', and the general perception that there is a large underlying fiscal disequilibrium is one of the distinguishing features of recent Brazilian inflation, which may aptly be described as one of a 'repressed hyperinflation'. To overcome this situation a fiscal reform is needed which tackles several aspects of the budgetary process and abandons many 'authorized' expenditures, making these subject to the approval of Congress in an atmosphere of transparency. The political engineering of this process, however, is very difficult and there are, at present, no signs that the executive is taking steps to undertake it.

3· THE STATE AND THE LIBERALIZATION OF THE BRAZILIAN ECONOMY

Carlos Alberto Longo

Historical Background

The last time a stabilization plan succeeded in Brazil was during the administration of Marshal Humberto de Alencar Castello Branco (1964–7). The government's economic action programme (PAEG) managed to hold inflation down to 70 per cent in 1964, although it had been set to reach 140 per cent in the year by March, when the military took power. In 1965 the annual rate came down still further to about 35 per cent, and from then on it continued to drop until it reached 14 per cent in 1972. Like all comprehensive anti-inflation plans, the PAEG was based on a three-pronged strategy that combined fiscal, monetary and incomes policy targets.[1]

On that occasion the federal government remodelled its budget so as to reduce the fiscal deficit to Cr$ 753 million in 1964, whereas this deficit had originally been expected to rise to Cr$ 2 billion. The actual deficit in the period was Cr$ 748 million. At the same time the government undertook to restrict monetary expansion in 1964 to Cr$ 2 billion, which would mean a 70 per cent increase in this aggregate compared with the preceding year. The actual rate of growth in the money supply was 85 per cent. This was not a radical stabilization programme designed to balance the budget at all costs, but was explicit enough not to give rise to any doubts as to the government's intentions or the direction in which fiscal and monetary policies were moving. As a result, the recession was not profound. Income per head and industrial output, both of which had been stagnant since 1963, began rising sharply from 1967 on. The crisis reached its height in 1965, when industrial output dropped almost 5 per cent.[2]

The programme acknowledged the need for a gradualistic incomes policy. Hitherto, real wages had swung sharply between peaks and troughs due to high inflation and the long intervals between wage adjustments (two years). Instead of calculating wage adjustments so as to restore purchasing power to its previous peak, the new policy instituted a formula whereby the average real wage during the 12-month period in which the newly adjusted nominal rate was to remain in force would be equal to the average real wage in the preceding 24 months.

Alongside the price stabilization programme, the government paved the way for far-reaching changes in the structure of the tax and financial systems. Among many advances and innovations it is worth highlighting the replacement of IVC (Imposto sobre Vendas e Consignações) with ICM (Imposto sobre a Circulação de Mercadorias), the bank reform (Law 4595 of December 1964), the creation of the Housing Finance System (SFH) and of the indexation system known as monetary correction (Law 4380 of August 1964), and regulation of the capital market (Law 4728 of July 1965). The argument is often heard that these reforms were made easier to implement by the absence of political constraints under military rule. The truth is however that harsh criticism was openly directed against the federal executive, both in Congress and by influential state governors (São Paulo, Minas Gerais and Guanabara). Moreover, plans for institutional reform had been made public, and draft legislation covering these questions had been sent to Congress well in advance.

After the Castello Branco government (1964–7), no subsequent administration made a frontal assault on inflation. Hence, over the ensuing 20-year period inflation rates rose steadily as a result of surges in demand or supply. Limited attempts to implement contractionist policies failed because of almost total indexation of prices and incomes, making inflationary expectations highly inelastic: fiscal or monetary contraction had limited impact on inflation but led to recession, which was politically injudicious.

The administration that took office in 1967 decided it would be inadvisable to continue with policies designed to reduce demand. It set itself the goal of promoting economic growth and full employment, despite the fact that inflation was still high at 25 per cent per annum. To some extent, this 'developmentalist' position taken by President Costa e Silva (1967–9), and sustained by President Garrastazú Médici (1969–74), was motivated by the opportunity for an upswing in the economy created by the austerity measures and institutional reforms implemented under the previous administration.

The First Development Plan (1st PND) adopted in 1969 consolidated and extended the import-substitution model introduced by President Juscelino Kubitschek (1955–60) but this time placed the emphasis on exports. Instead of the liberalizing framework of the PAEG, it put its trust in central planning and state intervention in the economy. Indexation through the monetary correction mechanism was extended to all markets, prices were submitted to government control (through CONEP, and later CIP), the PAEG's rules for wage adjustment were maintained, credit controls were introduced, and interest rates capped. The economic programme introduced in 1969 achieved all its aims – high levels of production and employment, a foreign trade surplus, and inflation stabilized at about 20 per cent per annum.

The price paid for this performance (the 'Brazilian miracle') was that relative prices were straitjacketed by monetary correction and excessive state intervention in the economy. Wide-ranging, generous tax and credit subsidies favoured agriculture, exports and industry. Ownership became concentrated in the banking industry, the Central Bank lost its independence, and the official banks became directly subordinated to the Finance Ministry. State-owned enterprises occupied the gaps not yet filled by private enterprise.

During the Geisel administration (1974–9) economic policy frequently changed tack under the pressure of circumstances, especially the inertial inflation inherited from the previous administration and aggravated by the first oil shock. In view of the ineffectiveness of conventional economic policy instruments, the government chose to accommodate the external shock by increasing inflation. The vicious circle created by indexation of prices, wages and exchange rates, with structural balance-of-payments deficits, was alleviated by the abundance of cheap external credit and by compression of prices and rates charged by State Owned Enterprises (SOEs).

The main goal of the Second Development Plan (2nd PND) was to proceed with the import-substitution development model, especially in heavy industry, fine chemicals, and pulp and paper, and to launch an ambitious programme of investment in energy and infrastructure commanded by the state but funded with foreign loans. Implementation of this policy was backed by the same instruments as those employed by the previous government, such as control of prices, wages, foreign exchange and credit. Major distortions in relative prices began to emerge. Domestic demand was buoyed by subsidies to public-service charges and credit, designed to boost consumption and production. Financing of the balance-of-payments deficit depended crucially on re-lending of foreign loans underwritten by the Treasury.

The second oil shock (1979) and the refusal of governments in developed countries to accommodate to their rising domestic inflation brought Brazil face to face with a severe dilemma in the early 1980s. The challenge was to restrict aggregate demand, realign relative prices and temporarily accept low rates of economic growth and high unemployment. The fatal mistake made by the Figueiredo administration (1979–85) was to press on with the now outdated development programme initiated in the previous decade. The argument used was that Brazil was different, that through public investment, subsidies to import-substituting industries (Proálcool, coal, and petroleum prospecting) and preferential treatment for exports of natural resources (agricultural products such as soya bean and orange juice, and primary goods such as ores) it would be possible to go on growing despite the new external constraints and internal distortions inherited from previous governments.

Brazil began the 1980s, in fact, without any planning framework at all. In the absence of explicit performance targets, and with increasingly weak instruments of government action, the executive made even more extensive and intensive use of the administrative controls available. It centralized control of public expenditure and merged into a single consolidated agency – SEST (Secretaria Especial de Controle das Empresas Estatais) – all operations relating to the financing of SOEs and official banks. It created more systems for monitoring and controlling prices and wages (CIP, SEAP, SUNAB, SISE). It stepped up the frequency with which the rules of the game were unexpectedly and suddenly changed, for example by setting the monetary correction and exchange rates in advance (i.e. not indexing them to actual inflation), by announcing massive one-off devaluations of the cruzeiro, and by changing the mechanism for wage adjustment. The result of this opportunistic, ill-managed policy was steadily rising inflation and a prolonged recession (1980–83).

In the mid-1980s another historic opportunity to point economic policy in a new direction presented itself. Once again, however, the government preferred facile measures that guaranteed its popularity, summed up in the motto of the Sarney administration, 'Tudo pelo social'. Under President José Sarney (1985–90), the government recognized that combating inflation must be an end in itself. Yet its stabilization plans also contained major flaws, both in conceptual terms (Cruzado Plan) and in implementation (Bresser Plan, Summer Plan). The nation had not yet become accustomed to the tug-of-war between contending forces that is typical of democracy. The federal administration's shortsightedness and incompetence were compounded by the inexperience of Congress, and even of the law courts, which failed to present constructive suggestions for solutions to the succession of crises linked to the attempts at economic stabilization.

With the economy teetering on the brink of hyperinflation, President Fernando Collor took office announcing bold measures to contain the price spiral, implement institutional reform and improve social welfare. It is no secret, however, that these objectives cannot be attained overnight but are the result of a long process with its own intrinsically necessary chronology. The first step must be to wipe the slate clean of past errors; next, the rate of growth can be stepped up; and finally it will be possible to distribute the benefits of higher growth. Thus, while economic policy-makers during the 'economic miracle' were able to capitalize on the effects of the austerity measures and reforms implemented by the Castello Branco administration, in the 1980s, despite the manifestly populist intentions of governments, they lacked the wherewithal for fulfilling their promises.

The State as 'Enterpreneur'[3]

A pragmatic approach to the analysis of the functions of the state consists of weighing up the costs and benefits of its presence in the economy. The quality of the public sector depends on the effectiveness of its component parts – central, state and municipal governments, official banks and state-owned enterprises. However, obscure fiscal and financial relationships not only distort the application of funds by the state but actually make it impossible to identify how such funds are used.[4]

State-owned enterprises (SOEs) are often used as instruments of stabilization policy, with the Treasury as controlling shareholder and the official banks as the main source of financing. Interbudgetary transfers can take the form of loans, capital increases or subsidies. The way the transfer is classified for accounting purposes does not necessarily correspond to the economic nature of the operation. Capital transfers (loans and investment) are frequently transformed into current transfers (subsidies) during the fiscal year. Thus when SOEs are turned into an instrument of macroeconomic policy, the budgetary process fails to provide clear-cut information as to the nature and effective availability of the funds to which it refers. As a result, the elaboration and evaluation of the Treasury budget becomes a process of aggregation, which combines central guidelines regarding the scarcity of funds on the one hand with requirements for financing SOEs on the other.[5]

A major criticism of the development model adopted by Brazil is that state participation in the economy is excessive. Clientism, corporatism and the absence of stimuli for private investment are among the basic causes of the state's insolvency. There are not even enough funds available to cover the simplest, most everyday items of public spending, and wages have been incessantly depressed by the decline in investment.

The mismatch between public revenue and expenditure is largely determined by long-standing commitments inherited from previous administrations. The consolidated budget procedure recently adopted by the federal executive failed to eliminate several sources of long-term disequilibrium. The executive's draft budget currently being debated by Congress is no more than a desperate attempt to contain the fiscal deficit by means of arbitrary hikes in taxes and tariffs. The exhaustion of the traditional sources for financing the public deficit explains the failure of so many stabilization plans.

Structural disequilibrium derives from the excessive indebtedness of the public sector, meaning all three spheres of government, together with the respective state-owned enterprises and financial institutions. No clear definition exists as to who is legally accountable for these liabilities, and it is therefore virtually impossible to formulate a set of alternative solutions. Systematic transfer of funds (in current and capital budgets) from one part of the public sector to cover default or government guarantee of a debt in another is not compatible with proper budgetary and administrative practice.

There is an urgent need for attributions in the public sector to be clearly discriminated so as to prevent the present situation of interlocking arrears and cross-defaults between agencies from jeopardizing operational efficiency and increasing the fiscal deficit. The concern here is of both a microeconomic and an aggregate nature. It is difficult to envisage any possibility of administrative rationality in production and selling of goods and services when prices are controlled by the Finance Ministry and levels of indebtedness by the Central Bank. In this case, the cash flow of SOEs is defined in terms of what is usually called the 'national interest'. As a result, priorities are not set with a view to protecting the 'interests of the consumer' (quality and price) or those of the shareholder (profit).

Attempts at Stabilization[6]

First Collor Plan

The essence of the Collor Plan was contained in three presidential decrees (known as provisional measures). Issued in March 1990, these comprised a set of fiscal, monetary and incomes policies. The additional parts of the plan (civil service and administrative reforms, cutbacks in subsidies, action to eradicate tax evasion, sales of government property, privatization of SOEs) can be considered complementary in character: they may eventually come to represent the New Brazil (Collor's election slogan) but in isolation they are of little significance to the success or failure of the stabilization programme.

Price and wage hikes were forbidden. To help balance the budget, public-service charges and prices of key SOE goods were raised, as was the Financial Operations Tax (levied on money market transactions, among others). The sharp drop in inflation also contributed. The initial effectiveness of the plan was guaranteed by an immediate reduction of liquidity. Only about a quarter of all financial assets remained at the disposal of the public. Inflationary expectations were abruptly reversed.

The weak points of the plan were excessive centralization, violation of property rights and a high degree of risk. The government could have avoided these drawbacks without impairing the effectiveness of the plan if it had instead opted for modernizing the instruments of economic policy and empowering other decision-making bodies. For example, the Central Bank was still not independent, Congress was not informed of the executive's budget projections, and the judiciary was obliged to perform veritable feats of legal acrobatics for the benefit of a plan which contemplated neither second thoughts nor second opinions.

Rather than reprogramming the budget it had inherited from the Sarney administration and seeking an agreement with Brazil's creditors, Collor's team chose to resort to drastic measures designed to balance revenue and expenditure as quickly as possible. New taxes were created, along with surcharges and compulsory loans, in addition to the seizure of liquid assets: these measures were both inadvisable and of doubtful legality. Moreover, their social cost can be evaluated in retrospect, in that the sacrifices imposed were in vain because inflation is again running at a high level.

It is difficult to appraise the real fiscal situation of the federal sector, since budgets are either out of date or non-existent. Furthermore, the excessive financial interpenetration of the various public entities confuses priorities and discourages the sound application of funds. The only consistent source of information is the federal treasury's cash flow statement, but since this does not discriminate clearly between the rights and obligations of different jurisdictions it cannot be taken as an indicator of permanent balance in the budget.

The return of high inflation after three months is attributable in the sphere of costs to the government's decision to adjust public sector and other prices for inflation occurring in the period. But on the demand side, pressure had also built up owing to the exacerbation of inflationary expectations, despite the drop in the level of economic activity. People were beginning to realize, from the observation of a number of macroeconomic indicators, that the government was losing control of its stabilization programme three months after the Collor Plan was announced.

By August 1990, the crass errors committed in implementing the measures in the first two or three months had led to a 10 per cent rise in prices. Difficulties in communicating with the business community, the law courts and Congress, and delays in negotiations on foreign debt rescheduling were examples of the government's growing inability to conduct the stabilization programme effectively. Indeed, it is not enough to reduce inflation by decree, ensure that the Treasury has a balanced cash flow, allow interest rates to rise to unprecedented heights, and at the same time lift import restrictions. This is a familiar approach, which proved a failure in Pinochet's Chile and in Argentina under finance minister Martínez de Hoz.

The risk of opening up the economy too fast and providing excessive incentives to investors in the financial market, typically accompanied by overvaluation of the local currency, is that decapitalization and obsolescence will ensue for domestic industry, with only limited gains on the inflation front and severe social costs in terms of job losses and wasted production.

Second Collor Plan

Impatient with developments in the economy, in January 1991 the executive launched another incomplete and overhasty economic package. Regrettably, it did nothing to compensate for the succession of errors committed during the implementation of the first Collor Plan. The second plan again consisted almost entirely of measures entailing a high degree of risk and a high social cost – a sharp hike in public-sector prices, another freeze on wages and prices, and a set of complicated changes in the rules for financial markets. This second attempt to stabilize the currency was claimed to be an 'extension' or 'deepening' of the first. The irony is that the government's claim was not altogether unfounded, for Plan II achieved little more than a repetition of the initial failure to stamp out inflation for good and all.

In every respect the style, form and substance of the initiatives associated with the second Collor Plan were similar to those of the previous package. With regard to style, the executive again behaved in an overweening and arbitrary manner. It abruptly changed the rules of the game without any prior consultations aimed to seek the comprehension, let alone the support, of organized social groups and representative institutions (the legislative and judiciary). As to form, the new package consisted of another batch of provisional measures, presidential decrees and Central Bank resolutions, very similar to the approach adopted the first time around.

No financial equilibrium can be expected to result from chaotic, arbitrary initiatives such as postponements of payment, seizure of funds, or raising of taxes and duties. Definitive reprogramming of expenditure would have entailed the questioning of rights and obligations, job security, social security benefits, sharing out of tax revenues among the three tiers of government, and the relations between the federal executive, SOEs and monetary authorities.

The measures introduced by the federal executive ignored, and in many cases actually infringed, accepted principles of administrative decentralization and tax prerogatives. They failed to undertake a comprehensive review of the management, instruments and aims of the federal administration. They failed to pay due respect to the institutions of republican government – in short, to share power.

Thus the Collor administration failed to improve on the fiscal and monetary policies followed by its predecessors.

Change of Style

The Collor administration's disastrous conduct of the economy in its first year of office was matched by the lack of confidence deposited in the executive (verging on deadlock, if not direct confrontation) by the other two branches of government, and by both labour and industry. These misgivings were a reaction to the prevalence until May 1991 of wilful, incoherent economic policy-making and target setting.

Genuine structural reforms of the public sector were not pursued. The executive focused its attention on combating inflation and utilized short-term techniques to this end. It did not concern itself, for example, with undertaking a tax reform, consolidating the budgetary process or overhauling the financial system. Instead, it swiftly and expeditiously seized assets, froze prices, altered indicators and arrested tax evaders.

The legacy of these two stabilization plans is mediocre. There is a need to rethink the meaning and utility of pyrotechnical innovations in the financial market such as the 'Fundão' (money fund, i.e. overnight balances must now be kept in standardized funds) and TR (taxa referencial, i.e. indexed bonds were substituted for the official 'reference' rate of interest). A market solution must be found for the excessively regulated financial sector. Today, disintermediation in corporate and financial investments is becoming as prevalent as it was in the very early 1960s.

When the federal administration suddenly shifted to what it called a 'soft' style in May 1991, it was reacting to the widespread perception that the country was becoming ungovernable. Congress was, in any case, reluctant to ratify any more of the executive's provisional measures; the Supreme Court had put a stop to the outgoing economic team's insistence on dubious legal manoeuvring by granting more and more restraining orders to annul the effect of the two plans. Thus, the balance of power between the three branches of government had apparently been restored.

As price and exchange controls are lifted, the economy is slowly turning to a free market. This time, there is fortunately no risk of hyperinflation as there was after the price freezes imposed by stabilization plans in the past. Prices are being raised not for speculative reasons but to adjust them to repressed costs. For the time being (early 1992), demand remains suppressed because wages are low and liquidity is tight. Inflation is still rising, albeit more slowly.

The problem is how to administer the wage-price spiral in the absence of reliable inflation indices (due to a law which prohibits indexation in the short run). The search must now begin for a means of avoiding universal informal indexation. Thus the solution for the Collor administration will have to reside in yet another stabilization plan. It is likely that, before the end of the year, the executive will change its management of aggregate demand, this time on the basis of a general review of public finances.

Inflation remains high and shows no signs of a downturn of any significance in the coming months. The fact that the curve has flattened out does not prevent speculation about future acceleration. The pessimistic scenario is based on the fact that little has been done to solve the structural disequilibrium in public sector finances.

The managerial flaws of the Collor administration to date have led to a lack of confidence in its programme. There is no major disagreement with the general direction of economic policy – trade liberalization, monetary austerity, privatization of state-owned enterprises etc. But the results achieved so far have been minimal and costly. Besides having failed to make progress with its so-called major reforms, the government frequently finds itself bogged down in Congress and the judiciary over initiatives of an essentially short-term nature, such as emergency economic measures, extension of maturities for state and municipal debts to the federal sphere, or increases in social security contributions.

It is possible to identify several inconsistencies. First, there is the question of timing. Lifting of price controls, opening up the economy and privatizations must all be properly co-ordinated, temporally speaking, with the actual (as opposed to announced) start of institutional reform. The combination of economic liberalization with a crisis of governability leads to industrial decline and an unlimited waste of income and employment.

In this regard it is worth noting that the social cost of mismanaged policies impinges differently on the different participants. Multilateral financing agencies, for example, never place their capital at risk and can resort to 'letters of intent' as a powerful instrument for guaranteeing the liberal agenda, without worrying about the level of activity. Government maladministration also leaves speculators untouched because the mobility of their investments enables them to make large profits without running major risks.

Thematic inconsistencies can also be observed. The government argues that structural issues are covered by the bill it has sent to Congress proposing several amendments to the constitution (the *Emendão*). However, the bill contains no mention of any measures to guarantee a permanent balance in the national accounts. There are no proposals for fiscal or budgetary reform to provide solid backing for the constitutional amendments under discussion. There is no reference to such urgent problems as the need to restructure the rules under which tax revenues are appropriated by the three tiers of government, to reorganize the links between the National Treasury and the monetary authorities, and to reform the social security system.

There is also an instrumental inconsistency. The government does not make harmonious use of its economic policy instruments. The executive concentrates so hard on managing cash flow and controlling real interest rates that it fails to notice that favourable expectations are formed in the light of structural changes. The effectiveness of economic policy has been jeopardized by delays in reprogramming the fiscal budget and in suggesting the replacement or even abolition of outdated tax and monetary policy instruments (Finsocial, PIS/PASEP, IOF tax on financial operations, TR, Fundão).

Nevertheless, it must be said that significant managerial improvements have recently occurred. After Marcilio Marques Moreira replaced Zelia Cardoso de Melo as finance minister in May 1991, the government at last began practising the liberalism it had been preaching for so long. It may be legitimate to ask, none the less, whether it is enough to state intentions clearly and show determination in following the logic of a market economy in a situation where the general level of prices must be stabilized at a politically viable cost.

The ten months since Moreira took office can be divided into two phases. The first lasted until September 1991 and was characterized by a gradual elimination of price controls and reduction in real interest rates. Although most economic actors accepted at face value his promise that there would be no more surprise packages, the financial market none the less signalled its lack of confidence in the local currency. With the first indications that the economic team was slow to get moving and inflation was again out of control, the black market dollar jumped from Cr$ 800 to Cr$ 1,400 overnight. The drain on international reserves was stopped by the firm determination shown by the monetary authorities, who refused to intervene in the foreign exchange market and manipulate the exchange rate. Exporters' liquidations of exchange contracts returned to normal and the black market dollar premium evaporated.

The outstanding feature of the second phase was confusion over the budget. Owing to lack of foresight and the absence of convincing achievements in the structural sphere, the government found itself at loggerheads with Congress over ratification of the federal budget and an emergency tax reform bill. Without the approval of the two measures there could be no agreement with the IMF. With the 1991 parliamentary calendar about to close, the executive 'magnanimously' held out to the opposition the irresistible carrot of a multiyear extension of the maturity of state and municipal debts in exchange for enactment of the two measures.

In January 1992 it was the judiciary's turn to collide with the executive. After a number of lower courts had ruled that social security benefits and pensions be fully adjusted for inflation, the president convened an extraordinary session of Congress to pass a bill that raised the rate of employee taxes and contributions. The bill was at once thrown out and the federal court of audit (Tribunal de Contas) was consulted as to whether the extra funds could be found without any new taxes. After a fierce statistical divergence about the real degree of structural imbalance in the social security system, it finally became evident that no governmental body can accurately say what state that system is in.

At this point a comparison with the Argentinian approach to stabilization may be useful. The Menem administration is now conducting its third attempt at stabilization. The first was the Bunge y Born plan, starting when Menem took office and lasting until December 1989. It was interventionist and short term in nature, contrasting with the government's announcement of liberal intentions, particularly for the financial market (dollar deposits and a free exchange market). Interest rates were capped and no deep-seated changes in public finances were proposed. The contradictory, meandering style of management soon led to a foreign exchange crisis.

From January 1990 to April 1991, the Erman Plan was in force (in versions I, II and III). The executive branch of the federal government ran the economy in line with market principles: it rescheduled the domestic and foreign public debts, sent bills to Congress proposing a new tax structure, consolidated changes in the financial market, cut import duties and stepped up the pace of privatization. This eliminated the risk of hyperinflation but was not enough to kill the expectation that inflation would remain high for some time. Inflation indeed continued at a high rate, uncertainty persisted, and the recession proceeded. Anxiety about an imminent loss of speculative capital and the political instability caused by the steady drop in the level of activity led to the resignation of the finance minister.

The Cavallo Plan, introduced in April 1991, pursued the same economic policy in overall terms but with one important new feature – a fixed rule for conversion of the Argentinian currency into US dollars. Monthly inflation, as measured by indices for exportable goods, has been close to zero since then and nominal interest rates paid by banks have stabilized at around 12 per cent per annum. The main factor enabling Cavallo to topple inflation almost at once (from 5 to 25 per cent per month), in addition to his personal prestige, was the competence shown by his team. Expectations adjusted in an unprecedentedly short period – possibly a few weeks – to focus on the nominal goals set by the government.

Up until the agreement with the IMF (February 1992), the Brazilian approach to stabilization was similar to the Erman phase in Argentina. It centred on all-out liberalism without any admixture of realism regarding managerial issues, i.e. the need for the government to state explicitly the nominal variables to which it was committed and to take an active role in implementing long-term structural reforms. There was only a shaky political constituency in support of using recession as the main weapon, and even this support soon dwindled, as shown in the dollar crisis of September 1991 and the failure to pass higher taxes for social security in January 1992.

The February cabinet reshuffle, based on an explicit political alliance, signalled a strategy designed to neutralize reactions against the gradualistic approach to stabilization. However, no matter how far the government succeeds in obtaining political support and making up for past management errors, it is unlikely to be able to consolidate the downward inflationary trend without putting forward a clear and consistent plan of structural reform.

The Liberalization of the Economy

Privatization[7]

The Brazilian privatization experience began timidly with the National Debureaucratization Programme (July 1979), whose main goals were to strengthen market forces, put a stop to the indiscriminate creation of state enterprises and promote the conditions for transferring controls of SOEs to private enterprise. In 1981 (Decree 86215) and again in 1985 (Decree 91991), rules were set up for issuing SOEs stocks to the public, selling control to private-sector investors, and even shutting some of them down. An Interministerial Privatization Council was created. Some of these rules were changed in 1986 (Decree 93606), when the Council's decision-making powers were enhanced and the BNDES (National Development Bank) was made the agency in charge of executing the programme.

In 1988 (Decree 95886), the liberalization process was intensely reinforced, partly because the federal public sector was already on the verge of insolvency. The Interministerial Privatization Council was abolished and a Federal Denationalization Council put in its place, with representatives of the stock market, BNDES, labour and industry. The restrictions imposed under previous rulings with regard to participation of foreign capital in privatization were lifted.

Finally, Law 8031 (December 1990) created the Programa Nacional de Desestatização, still in force. A Privatization Steering Committee was set up with 11 members, four representing the public sector and seven from the private sector. The BNDES remained in charge of implementation. Foreign investors were now allowed to acquire up to 40 per cent of voting shares and 100 per cent of non-voting shares. Between 1979 and March 1990, when Collor took office, the privatization programme was confined to the devolution to private enterprise of companies that had been nationalized because of financial difficulties. This involved the transfer to private ownership of 38 companies, which were sold both directly and by tender or auction, bringing in some US$ 824 million.

From now on, the plan is to sell SOEs that have always been federally-owned. The monopolies enshrined in the constitution (oil, gas and ore extraction, and shipping lines) will be respected. The programme as it now stands has three main objectives: reduction of the public sector debt, reinforcement of market laws, and further democratization of companies. As of April 1991, privatization projects had been approved for 25 SOEs in the steel, petrochemical and fertilizer industries and their sale was expected to raise US$ 12 billion. Payment can be made in the form of chirographic credits, public debt bonds, transfer of title to Cruzados Novos (old currency) held by the Central Bank, and other similar means.

The supply of credit (domestic and foreign) for acquisition of these companies is potentially high, given the excessive indebtedness of the public sector. Funds deposited with the Central Bank (MYDFA), which are largely overdue external public debt, totalling US$ 35 billion including both principal and interest, entitle the holder to participate in the privatization process with a 25 per cent discount on face value – it is worth noting that on the secondary market these credits are traded with a discount of 65 per cent. The availability of funds for debt-equity swaps was reinforced by seizure of financial market investments during the 1st Collor Plan: the Central Bank holds a total of about US$ 17.5 billion equivalent in Cruzados Novos deposits (August 1991). Other public sector debts which can be used for privatization include debentures issued by Siderbrás (the steel holding company), land reform bonds, and quotaholdings in the National Development Fund (FND). Interest groups have succeeded in delaying privatization through Court decisions that questioned the windfall gains attributed to holders of currently depreciated assets.

The sum total of these credits is sufficient for acquisition of all federally-owned SOEs, estimated to be worth an aggregate US$ 60 billion. The government should not have too much trouble with demand for shares in the most efficient companies, at least during this first stage. The Brazilian privatization experience began with the line of least resistance – first of all, devolution of nationalized companies to private ownership, and now the sale of the most profitable SOEs. The situation will be quite different when the time comes to privatize utilities and commercial SOEs with chronic deficits.

Deregulation

The 'patrimonial' state in Brazil – in which the interests of the bureaucracy interlock with those of the private sector – has deep historical roots. Portuguese laws played a more effective role in political organization than in trade and the private economy. The *Ordenações* (codification of existing laws) enacted by Manuel I and Felipe II of Portugal were fundamentally concerned with allocating public office, including military rank, as well as the property and privileges of the Church. Only after the architecture of administration had been erected did they move on to specify civil, criminal and procedural law. Knowledge of the rights inherent in sovereignty was not sought by studying the ancient customs of the Portuguese kingdom but was borrowed from Roman law. The *Ordenações* were essentially a case of state intervention in the economy, business, shipping, domestic commercial transactions, pricing, export embargoes etc.[8]

Strictly speaking, neither civil nor commercial law existed, only administrative law. Thus the discipline imposed on individuals was not economically inspired but political in content. It did not serve the individual or commerce, rational and calculable in business terms, but the patrimonial state. The logic of laws and decisions was very distant from the impersonality and equality of values, for it was subordinated to the arbitrary rule of the Prince. England, the home of classical capitalism, did not need to consolidate its laws in order to enable its economy to expand to plenitude; it dispensed with codes and with Roman law, for it was driven by the force of its economy, grounded in private property, the context in which industrialization flourished. Thus, through centuries of ancestral assimilation, Brazil became the heir to a long history which dates back to the revolution of John of Aviz and the court of Manuel I.[9]

To cut costs and enhance the efficiency of the federal public administration, Collor announced, within days of taking office, a radical change in ministerial structure. He reduced the number of ministries from 30 to a mere 12, created secretariats, closed public bodies, eliminated posts in the top ranks of the administration, fired or laid off public employees and sold government buildings, flats and vehicles. An initial evaluation indicates that the results were insignificant both financially and in terms of administrative reorganization – not least in view of the difficulty of reforming institutions while macroeconomic instability continues to prevail. A great many of the measures announced were not implemented, and as many again will have to be revised or even abandoned.

In addition to the usual economic, political and legal obstacles, the reforms foundered because of insufficient preparation. No solution was found to the dilemma of how to increase the productivity of the civil service or improve low salaries. The constitution guarantees job security for civil servants, so that it is indeed difficult for the government to cut the size of its work force. The haste with which ministries were merged and autonomous authorities closed meant that the same functions are now performed by 'super-ministries' or 'super-secretariats' reporting directly to the presidency, and this has not led to significant savings or gains in effectiveness.

Liberalization[10]

In June 1990, the executive announced its industrial and trade policy (Portuguese acronym: PICE), reproducing with a few differences the provisions of Decree Law 2433 (May 1988) enacted by its predecessor, the Sarney administration. Its objective was 'to enhance the efficiency of production and trade of goods and services by modernizing and restructuring industry'. Its principal feature was the full integration of industrial and trade policy. According to the PICE, growth in imports will play a key role in fighting inflation because it will stimulate investment and sharpen competitiveness. Among the strengths of the PICE are the recognition that the effectiveness of industrial policy depends on the overall macroeconomic environment.

The problems faced by countries that try to liberalize their economies midway through a failed stabilization programme are well-known. When a stabilization programme is implemented simultaneously with measures to liberalize trade, this tends to put excessive pressure on the import-substitution sector. The changes made to industrial and trade policy since 1988 were designed to alter the development model that prevailed in the 1980s – a closed, uncompetitive, inefficient model that helped undermine the economic and technological dynamism of the decade.

A number of import restrictions were lifted, notably the tax on financial operations (IOF), duties for renovation of the merchant navy and port improvements, the obligation for companies to submit import schedules in advance, controls on import licences, the similarity test and compulsory financing of imports. In 1990 the following measures made trade policy more open: (a) replacement of the crawling-peg devaluation system with a market-oriented system of floating exchange rates; (b) elimination of all special import schemes except drawback, the Manaus Free Zone and international agreements; (c) a phased-in reduction of all tariffs by 1994, designed to achieve an average tariff of 14.2 per cent, with a small standard deviation (about 7.9 per cent). On average, nominal tariff protection will have dropped from 32.2 per cent in 1990 to 14.2 per cent in 1991. For sectors where Brazil has a competitive advantage, and for products without a locally-produced equivalent, a zero rate has been set; for sectors that will be afforded temporary protection, the rate will be 20 per cent.

The dynamism of the export sector derives above all from the behaviour of the exchange rate throughout the liberalization process. In general it is advisable for liberalization to be preceded by a real devaluation so that adjustment by the import-substitution sector and the export sector can attenuate the impact of fiercer foreign competition. In addition, macroeconomic stabilization should be guaranteed before the liberalization process is fully implemented.

The flexible exchange policy introduced in the second half of 1990 was accompanied by the provision of more credit to exporters. The lead time for negotiating foreign exchange contracts in advance of an export operation was increased, exporters were allowed to securitize bills of exchange and, faced with the high domestic rates of interest, exporters easily obtained external lines of credit to finance their activities.

However, a definitive recovery of exports is far from guaranteed. While the accumulated trade surplus in 1988 was US$ 19.1 billion, it dropped to US$ 16.1 billion in 1989, and to a mere US$ 11 billion in 1990. In fact, exports have stayed static at around US$ 33 billion per annum for the last three years, while imports have risen from US$ 14.6 billion to US$ 20.3 billion per annum. This weak performance was made possible only by suspension of foreign debt service. From now on it will be necessary to pay off the arrears and at the same time resume current services.

Trade policy has consolidated approximation with neighbours through the creation of regional blocs in the hope that strategic partnerships can spread to other countries in the continent. The latest agreement relating to regional integration is the Southern Common Market (Mercosul), signed in 1986 by Brazil and Argentina, and later joined by Uruguay and Paraguay (Treaty of Asunción, 1990). Meanwhile, concessions are being made to other trading partners in the framework of the GATT round with a view to eliminating disputes with developed nations. Examples are the effort to introduce stricter laws on intellectual property rights, and the commitment not to resort to Article 18b of the GATT, which permits the use of import restriction measures.

'Integration' can be seen as a step on the road to a common market, whereby independent states relinquish sovereignty in exchange for political participation in a multilateral forum. The issue therefore has broader implications than the immediate costs and benefits of trade liberalization and customs union. In addition to the evident advantages to consumers in the short run, now that domestic market protection has begun to be stripped away there will be qualitative gains from the regional harmonization of economic policies. The main benefit will be a boost to the dynamics of growth, and this more than compensates for the potential disadvantages of a regional agreement.

This kind of broad perspective inspired the Treaty of Rome (1957) as Western Europe pulled itself together after the second world war. The process began with a free trade zone, progressing to a customs union, and finally to the common market. By contrast, in Latin America the Treaty of Montevideo (1960), which set up LAFTA (the Latin American Free Trade Association) – later renamed LAIA (Latin American Integration Association, 1981) – has never been much more than an expression of diplomatic intentions. Over the last three decades, the views that have prevailed are quite different from those that represented the accession of CEPAL's ideas to ruling circles – while the cold war lasted, they were the views of the military governments and of the economists in public administration. Once the winds of democracy and liberalism had swept through the hemisphere, the countries of Latin America decided to move closer to other nations by setting up regional blocs with the aim of building strategic partnerships. The ambitious goal of Mercosul is to create a common market by 1995, as well as a regional parliament.

Brazil's complacency about the Mercosul effort contrasts strikingly with the enthusiasm of its partners. It is easy to explain why Uruguay and Paraguay are so keen on the initiative: intra-regional trade accounts for nearly 50 per cent of their total trade, compared with a much lower 15 per cent in the case of Argentina, and a mere 5 per cent in that of Brazil. Moreover, both countries are small, so that the ups and downs of domestic policies in their two big neighbours have swift and intense internal repercussions. Argentina puts a great deal of trust in Mercosul because it has already forged ahead with its own liberalization and stabilization process. The political strength of traditional sectors, especially the farmers and the financial community, helped the government reduce average import tariffs to less than 10 per cent (in Brazil they are still above 40 per cent) and conduct a stringent fiscal, monetary and foreign exchange adjustment.

Brazil is less committed to Mercosul: as well as having its own specific weight (in terms of a consumer market and industrial base) and a closed economy (imports account for less than 5 per cent of GDP) with high levels of protection for industry, the government has not succeeded in controlling the chaotic macroeconomic situation. It is a strategic error for Brazil to turn its back on the countries of the Southern Cone simply because 80 per cent of its trading partners lie north of the Equator. It is an error, first of all because the developed nations have already begun integrating economically, and in some cases politically. Any concessions from these blocs can only come now as a result of pressure by regional blocs. Thus, it is easier for Latin America to stop the recent decline in its share of international trade (from 8.5 per cent to 3.5 per cent) by resorting to the advantages of economic integration. Indeed, the multilateral diplomacy of GATT negotiation has proved incapable of dealing with the key issues affecting the region, especially Brazil, such as farm subsidies in the industrial countries.

The main advantage of integration, however, is that it forces countries to harmonize stabilization policies in order to enter the common market. Brazil is lagging behind in this regard, and it runs the risk of missing yet another opportunity to diminish macroeconomic uncertainty. In contrast to the other Mercosul countries, Brazil's government has not yet produced a reliable plan of action. Harmonization of fiscal, monetary and foreign exchange policies requires uniform, stable rules of the game. Thus, before it concentrates on setting an agenda for the establishment of free movements of people, services and merchandise, a common external tariff, standardized capital markets and homogeneous public services, the government must bring inflation down to tolerable levels. Not only is Brazil at the back of the queue but it offers no short-term prospect of normality whatsoever.

What Remains to be Done

The federal government has not yet implemented a permanent fiscal adjustment. The measures taken in 1990 and 1991 to achieve a balanced budget were based on an increase in taxes and duties, making the tax system more regressive, inefficient and complex than it already was. They also excessively capped outlays for running costs and investment through cuts, restrictions and levies of doubtful legality and no legitimacy at all.

The way the federal constitution determines how tax revenues are to be shared out is not compatible with the effort to modernize the structure of the budget. The burden of the obligations inherited from previous administrations, and the economic and social heterogeneousness of regions and classes, make it impossible to transfer most of the expenditures currently attached to the federal government to states and municipalities. Since the constitution stripped the federal government of most of its traditional sources of revenue the executive will have to continue resorting to new cumulative taxes not shared with subnational governments in order to guarantee a precariously balanced cash flow.

Very little has been done to pass legislation to minimize the above distortions or to provide ordinary laws for the sections of the constitution on public finance and the financial system. The current budgetary process involves groping in the dark for ways of adapting provisions in the new constitution to the laws and traditions in force before 1988. But the contradictions resulting from this process, aside from the normative vacuum, are very great. Provisions such as the 12 per cent cap on real interest rates, abolition of the National Monetary Council, the procedure for enacting budgetary laws, the ban on fiscal advances by the Central Bank and parliamentary intervention in the administration of public debt are only some of the most conspicuous examples of items that require urgent review and implementation.

The Issue of Governability

Would it be true to predict that a political or social crisis will be the outcome of the growing insolvency of the federal government, and hence its increasing inability to provide services and guarantee republican institutions? Such an outcome is unlikely. The economic stagnation of the 1980s caused only gradual impoverishment; the slow, steady decline in the standard of living in Brazil is not perceptible in a single generation. The impoverishment of the middle class, above all, has not had an intense impact on the majority. Moreover, freedom of expression and free speech are now complete, so that tension is more easily channelled. There is no censorship, nor are there radical groups (in thought or action) with any popular appeal.

However, if the government is to recover the nation's confidence, the legal and institutional framework must be modernized. Ambitious stabilization plans have been implemented but they have flouted a great many legal norms in the name of the 'collective interest'. The resurgence of inflation after so many doses of shock therapy obliges us to question the efficacy of these measures. It is therefore necessary to examine not only the legality but the legitimacy of economic packages.

Inflation, when high and chronic, is an illegal source of funds for the federal administration. Its illegality derives from the fact that there are no provisions in law for 'inflation tax'. Moreover, this tax runs counter to the customary principles of taxation: equal rights to persons in equal positions, and neutral allocation of resources. On the other hand, stabilization packages based on shock treatment weaken the institutions of government by entailing vast and frequent changes to the rules in force. Provisional measures, decrees and directives are not only often mutually conflicting, but seem to be designed to correct administrative errors or serve the interests of the federal executive rather than to modernize institutions. When a state of anomie (lawlessness) becomes generalized, it raises the issue of the legitimacy of governments. The latter are often both 'strong' and 'weak' at the same time. They are strong when they legislate against the law, but they are weak when forced to resort to 'inflation tax' to cover their costs.

Thus it is relevant to examine the concept of representation in the light of the idea of a 'social contract'. The issue of governability can most usefully be discussed in such a context. Due importance must be afforded to the difficulty of applying the principle of majority rule to a socially and economically heterogeneous population that during most of its history has been submitted to oligarchic, populist, military or monarchical rule. It must be acknowledged that the rule of law and the legitimacy of government are frequently violated under the presidential system of representation, where the government can make as many mistakes as it likes for a predetermined period.

Bearing in mind the specific characteristics of the presidential system, the historical experience of Brazil and the heterogeneousness of its population, it would seem that effective government will be achieved only through a system of representation whereby the government consists as it were of a permanent assembly, as in the parliamentary system. In this kind of system, a succession of attempts to stabilize the economy and reform institutions would serve, as in a process of trial and error, to set up a stable cabinet. Under parliamentary rule, governmental instability is neither frightening nor a threat to institutions – on the contrary, the principle that the government is secure for an indeterminate period makes for stronger institutions.

(São Paulo, March 1992)

4· POVERTY IN BRAZIL:
A Challenge for the Future[1]

José Márcio Camargo and
Ricardo Paes de Barros

Introduction

Between 1950 and 1980, Brazil's growth rate averaged 7 per cent a year; income per capita in the early eighties topped US$ 2,000. Although not a poor country if we take per capita income as the indicator, poverty is a widespread phenomenon. Half of the economically active population earned less than US$ 70 a month in 1989 and all social indicators show very high poverty levels. High infant mortality rates, child under-nourishment and high illiteracy rates are some of these indicators. They show that, after a long period of high economic growth, Brazilian society is still striving to solve the basic problem of the poverty of half its population.

The scenario becomes quite dramatic when we observe that during the eighties not only did per-capita income not grow, but income became further concentrated. The Gini coefficient of the distribution of income of the economically active population increased from 0,580 in 1983 to 0,639 in 1989. Stagnation combined with concentration of income made it impossible for the country to reduce poverty. The result is poverty with economic stagnation, a completely new phenomenon in Brazil.

This article tries to understand why the Brazilian economy generates so much poverty, even with rapid economic growth. There are different factors, linked or not to the labour market, which can generate poverty. We will concentrate our attention on the three which we consider the most relevant: (a) the stock and distribution of human capital; (b) the stock and distribution of physical capital, including land and equipment; (c) the institutions which influence the behaviour of the labour market and their effects on the incentive structures of workers and firms.

Each of these three factors and their interrelation have very important effects on poverty, and we will deal with each one separately later. In the next section we will characterize poverty and make a distinction between the levels and the consequences of poverty; in the following section we stress the point that poverty can have two origins: lack of human capital and under-utilization of available resources. We then analyse how the three above factors interrelate to generate poverty in Brazil.

Poverty and its Consequences

Income insufficiency is the main indicator of poverty in a population. Given a poverty line, we measure the share of the population which lies below it and the average distance of the members of this sub-population from this line. But income insufficiency has different consequences depending on the social infrastructure of the country. The smaller (or less efficient) the social infrastructure, the worse the negative effects of income insufficiency on the population.

In the case of Brazil, poverty is a problem not only because of its size, but also because of its consequences. Table 4.1 shows some important indicators of the consequences of poverty in the country as compared to other Latin American countries.

When compared to any other country in the table, Brazil comes out much worse on almost all the social indicators. In three indices alone – the UNDP Human Development Index, the percentage of households below the poverty line and the infant mortality rate – does Brazil rate above Peru. In other words, being poor in Brazil is a particularly perverse condition because the lack of social infrastructure aggravates the consequences of income insufficiency.

In general, this lack of social infrastructure is itself a consequence of low government expenditure in the social sectors. But that is not the case of Brazil. Table 4.2 shows government expenditure on social sectors for Brazil and other Latin American countries.

Although not particularly high, Brazilian government expenditure in the social sectors is higher than in Argentina, Colombia, Peru and Venezuela, and lower than in Chile, Costa Rica and Mexico. This suggests that the problem is not the amount of expenditure *per se*. Rather, the inefficiency of the transmission process does not allow this expenditure to get down to the poor in the form of reasonable

Table 4.1 Poverty Indicators – Brazil and Other Countries

Country	Infant Mortality Rate (%)	Poverty Rate*	Illiteracy Rate	Early Work (%)	Human Dev. Index (UNDP)
Argentina	32	13 (86)	4.5	3.4	99
Brazil	63	40 (87)	22.5	10.0	80
Chile	18	17 (68)	5.6	1.4	107
Colombia	46	38 (86)	17.7	4.2	86
Cuba	11	–	–	0.1	92
Costa Rica	19	25 (88)	6.4	6.0	103
Mexico	43	30 (84)	9.7	5.0	91
Peru	88	52 (86)	15.2	3.2	74
Venezuela	36	27 (86)	13.1	2.5	89

Source: United Nations, *Anuario Estadístico de América Latina y el Caribe*, CEPAL, 1989. United Nations Development Program (UNDP), *Human Development Report*, 1990, Oxford University Press.
* Poverty rate – percentage of households with income smaller than two times the cost of the basic food bundle.
Numbers in parenthesis show the year of the data.
The Human Development Index is a composite index constructed by UNDP to measure social development. It takes into account life expectancy, literacy rate and (log of) real GCP per capita. For details see *Human Development Report*, 1990, UNDP, p. 109.

Table 4.2 Government Social Expenditures. Per cent

Country	%
Argentina	21.6
Brazil	25.1
Chile	34.4
Colombia	14.7
Costa Rica	28.0
Mexico	27.9
Peru	14.6
Venezuela	21.8

Source: World Bank, *World Development Report*, Poverty, 1990.

social services. Although we will not deal with this problem here, an understanding of the reasons for this inefficiency is very important in minimizing the consequences of poverty.

The second important point is that poverty, as income insufficiency, is a function of average income and of income inequality. If inequality is constant and average income increases, poverty will decline. Similarly, if the income level is constant but inequality declines, poverty will also decline.

In Brazil, the share of the population below the poverty line declined during the sixties and seventies as a result of the rapid growth of average income. In this period, the degree of income inequality increased, being a force in the direction of increasing poverty. During the eighties, the average income stagnated and inequality increased. In 1983, the poorest 50 per cent of the population earned 13.43 per cent of the income generated in the country. In 1989, this share had fallen to 10.94 per cent, while the richest 10 per cent of the population increased its participation from 46.06 per cent to 52.23 per cent of income. As a result of these two forces, not only did the average income of the poorest group of the population not increase, but income distribution also worsened.

Origins of Poverty

The first step towards understanding the causes of poverty is the identification of its origins. Insufficiency of income has two origins, one intrinsic to the worker and the other related to the behaviour of the labour market. On the one hand, society is responsible for the reproduction of the labour force and for the permanent improvement of its quality. On the other, it is also responsible for the adequate valuation of the productivity of its labour force.

Brazilian society has both problems. At each generation it produces workers of very low quality who will be poor regardless of the conditions of the labour market. At the same time, the labour market and the economy as a whole underutilize and, consequently, underpay its labour force. These two problems are very important, but the first is more dramatic since its solution calls for structural changes which are beyond the limits of the labour market.

Poverty and Value of Marginal Productivity

As income insufficiency, poverty is basically a function of household income. This income is determined by the stock of physical and human capital owned by the household and by the value of this stock. Income insufficiency is thus a result of the lack of human or physical capital, and/or of the low value of the capital owned by the household.

In a perfectly competitive economy, the value of the capital stock of a household is equal to the value of its marginal productivity. There are three reasons for the income insufficiency of a household: (a) the insufficiency of human and physical capital; (b) the low productivity value of this capital; and (c) earnings below the marginal productivity value of this capital. In its turn, the value of the marginal productivity of capital can be low either because the marginal productivity is low or because the value of the output generated is low.

In the case of human capital, workers can be poor because: (a) they are not qualified enough (insufficiency of human capital); (b) although adequately qualified, their jobs are of low productivity, possibly due to insufficiency of physical capital; (c) although adequately qualified and in a job with high productivity, the price of the goods produced is low; and (d) although adequately qualified, employed in a job with high productivity and producing goods with a high price, they earn a wage below the value of their marginal productivity.

Thus, the stock and the distribution of the two types of capital, as well as the prices of these stocks and of the goods that are being produced and the capacity of the worker to appropriate the value of his marginal productivity, are determinant factors of the poverty level of a population. Policies directed to solving the problem of poverty are different in each situation, depending on the causes of the phenomenon in each country or region.

Poverty and Human Capital

The literature commonly appoints the insufficiency of human capital as the main cause of poverty in Brazil. As some observers point out, poor Brazilian households are not mainly headed by women, nor are they households whose head is sick or invalid or unemployed or retired. They show that the largest share of poor households are headed by men aged between 25 and 40 years who regularly work 40 hours a week or more.

These data and the high wage differentials between workers with and without basic education are good evidence of the relation between poverty and the lack of qualification of the labour force in Brazil. Thus, it is very important to investigate how the accumulation, or the lack of accumulation, of human capital occurs in Brazilian society.

The accumulation of human capital is associated with three social institutions: the family, the school and the job. Each one plays a fundamental role in the process.

The School

This is the institution in society specialized in the accumulation of human capital and the place where a large share of this process occurs. As the main social and private cost of education is the value of the student's time, it is socially and privately optimum that each person makes his/her investment in education at the earliest and in the shortest length of time possible. This is why it is very important to have an efficient basic education system: a system able to accommodate the universe of children of school age, where the quality of the education is such that the time expended in school is adequately valued by the student, with the minimum of repetition and other inefficiencies.

Brazil has a basic state education system large enough to accommodate the great majority of the school age population (except possibly in remote rural areas and some over-populated cities), but it lacks policies to induce all children to complete their basic education and to minimize repetition. Increasing the quality of state education is no doubt an efficient way to reduce poverty.

The problem of the quality of the education system in Brazil is particularly critical for the poorest groups of the population, which have access only to physically and pedagogically poor state schools with high repetition and drop-out rates. In the 1980s, the average drop-out rate in the first year of school was 25.6 per cent (39.3 per cent in the Northeast) and the average rate of repetition was 26.5 per cent (24.8 per cent in the Northeast). Because of the low quality levels of the public school system, high income groups seek out better quality private schools. The corollary of this opting out is a reduction in the pressure on the state sector to improve the quality of its school system.

Although the low quality of the state school system in Brazil is obvious, we have very little information about the links between this low quality and the high repetition and drop-out rates. But it seems that the problem of evasion is not simply the result of the incapacity of the school system to avoid repetition due to its low quality. In fact some studies have shown that the students who drop out of school are not mainly those who repeat school years and schools are not significantly better in the South than in the Northeast where the education system is less efficient. If this information is correct, we should look for other causes besides low quality for the high drop-out rates from state schools.

In any case, it should be stressed that the universal right to free education and the obligation to attend primary school, linked to an improvement in the quality of education in the state schools and a reduction in the repetition rates, are the most important and sustainable ways of reducing poverty in Brazil in the medium term.

The Family

There are three channels through which the family can affect human capital accumulation. First, the hereditary nature of a part of human capital as, for example, some physical and mental abilities. Second, the social environment created by the family which results in the development of certain individual abilities, habits (discipline, persistence and ambitions) and values. Finally, the family environment by itself can condition the child's access to school, his/her achievement and the value he or she puts on education.

Parents with a lower educational level can limit the access of their children to school, either because the level of education of the parents affects their preferences about the education of the children, or because parents with less education are less informed about the gains from education, or, because they are poor, they do not have access to credit and so are not able to invest in the education of their children. In 1989, 65 per cent of 15–17 year olds who had studied for less than one year had mothers who also had less than one year of study. At the other extreme, less than 5 per cent of those within that age range with more than nine years of study had mothers with less than one year of study (while 35 per cent of this group have mothers with more than nine years of study).[2] School achievement is obviously affected by the family environment since, at least in part, the parents help their children in their home assignments.

A very important point in this context is the effect of the rapid urbanization of the Brazilian economy over the last 40 years. Because it is more difficult for rural families to transmit the values needed for success in the urban environment, this rapid urbanization can affect the aptitudes of the urban population today, reducing its disposition for accumulating human capital and, consequently, its capacity for rising out of poverty.

In addition to these factors, poverty itself is a very important negative influence on the capacity of the population to accumulate human capital. The smaller the household income, the higher the opportunity costs for the family to keep their children in school and out of the labour market. In 1989, 50 per cent of the families with children under 17 in Brazil had a per capita household income of less than US$ 35 a month (half the minimum wage). For 27.4 per cent, the per capita income was less than one-quarter of the minimum monthly wage. For these households, the opportunity cost of maintaining a child in school and out of the labour market, where he/she could earn 50 per cent or even more of the household income, is very high. As a result, even if the school is of good quality there is an economic pressure for the children of the poorest families to abandon school and enter the labour market as soon as possible.

Available data tend to support the above hypothesis. In 1989, 26.1 per cent of 10 to 14 year olds in families with per capita incomes of less than one-quarter of the minimum wage, and 20.7 per cent of those in families with per capita incomes of between one-quarter and half the minimum wage, were in the labour market. Taking all children between 10 and 14 years of age, 46.5 per cent worked more than 40 hours a week. A study by the World Bank on secondary education in Brazil shows that going into the labour market is the main reason for dropping out of school. But, even more important for our objectives here, the drop-out rate is much higher in the Southeast (55.2 per cent), where the quality of education is better and the opportunity costs of being in school are higher, than it is in the Northeast (47.8 per cent).

The above hypothesis suggests that one important reason why evasion from the Brazilian state education system is so high is the opportunity cost of remaining in school. As the best students are those who pass the examinations, these have better opportunities in the labour market and also pay the highest opportunity costs for staying at school. In this case, the evasion rate is high because of both the low quality of education and the low income level of the family. Thus, poverty today can be a very important cause of poverty in the future.

The Labour Market

The third important institution which determines the rate of accumulation of human capital by a population is the labour market itself. Some jobs are good jobs in the sense that they provide permanent training and require a high level of qualification, while other jobs consist of mainly repetitive tasks and do not require any qualification from the labour force.

The problem of accumulation of human capital through the labour market in Brazil is the existence of a large number of low quality jobs in the sense that they offer very few opportunities for training. In 1989, only 10.6 per cent of workers aged between 10 and 14 had a signed contract. All other employed workers in this age range were in the informal labour market.

Workers who start their professional life in a low quality job have less chance of climbing to better positions in the labour market in the future simply because they are not able to acquire the qualifications needed to get employment in a good job. In this sense, their own entry to the labour market can put them in a trap from which it is difficult to escape.

The factors analysed above, relating to the effects of school, the family and the labour market over human capital accumulation in Brazil reinforce themselves, generating a process which reproduces poverty. The children of poor families have very high opportunity costs of being in school due to the high proportion of the family income they can contribute. As a result, they enter the labour market very early, and are employed in low quality jobs which pay low wages. At the same time, the low quality of the primary education system reduces the incentives for staying at school. Thus, for these students, the drop-out rate is very high. As they enter the labour market very early with very few qualifications, they get poor jobs which do not provide any training and with very little opportunity of advancement. As a result, they stay trapped in these low-quality, low-wage jobs. If the economy grows at high rates, the increase in average income induces an increase in the real income of this group of workers to a level above the poverty line. But if the economy does not grow, or grows slowly, the tendency is for the perpetuation of high poverty levels.

In the situation described above, society is unable not only to reduce both kinds of poverty, but also to avoid the reproduction of low-quality workers. This means that if we want to turn human capital accumulation into an important factor for the reduction of poverty and improvement of income distribution in Brazil, breaking the vicious circle described above, we should prevent today's high levels of poverty from inducing the children of the poorest families to enter the labour market prematurely in order to complement family income. In other words, it is important to change the initial conditions of the problem, reducing the opportunity costs of these children staying at school and, at the same time, improving the quality of public primary education.

Poverty and Physical Capital

Poverty and the availability of physical capital are related in three ways: (a) through the amount of capital in existence in society; (b) through the distribution of this capital among families; and (c) through the allocation of capital among jobs.

Poverty and Availability of Capital

An increase in the amount of capital in society reduces poverty in two ways. Firstly, with a given degree of inequality of wealth distribution and assuming that poor families own at least a small share of this capital, the more capital there is in society, the higher the capital income of the poor and the lower the level of poverty.

Secondly, with a given allocation of capital among jobs, the higher the stock of capital available, the higher the endowment of capital for each job. The result is higher labour productivity and a higher wage for each worker, with a consequent reduction in poverty even for those families who do not have any physical capital and do not appropriate any capital income.

As the distribution of physical capital is extremely unequal, the poor will benefit more from the growth of capital stock through the impact this has on productivity than directly from the growth of capital income. For this reason, we should expect the second channel to be more important than the first.

Many authors have suggested that the main cause of poverty in Brazil is the scarcity of physical capital. As a consequence, a large proportion of the labour force is employed in jobs with low capital content resulting in low productivity, low wages and poverty.

Besides the effect of its availability, the distribution of physical capital and, in particular, the distribution of land, are closely related to poverty. With a given stock of wealth, a better distribution will be associated with a lesser degree of poverty.

Land Distribution and Poverty

A redistribution of land in favour of the poor, without affecting productivity, would certainly reduce the degree of poverty in a society. But the redistribution of land can affect productivity, reinforcing or mitigating these direct effects.

Table 4.3 Structure of Land Ownership in Brazil

% of Establishments	% of Land 1920	1950	1980
50% smallest estab.	3.8	3.2	2.8
5% largest estab.	66.1	67.9	67.2
1% largest estab.	41.9	44.6	43.2

Source: *Censo Agropecuário*, FIBGE.

Since the productivity of land tends to be higher when cultivated by its owners, it is generally held that the redistribution of land increases productivity and positively reinforces the direct effects of an agrarian reform over poverty. Factors such as availability of incentives and information can raise productivity further.

Nevertheless, other factors can cause a reduction in the productivity of land, depending on how the land distribution is implemented. For example, if the reform prohibits the commercialization of the land indefinitely, or for a long period of time, or if the reform prohibits the use of the land as collateral in credit operations, it can induce a low degree of utilization and, consequently, underutilization.

The division of property in very small parcels without permission for selling and consolidation can also increase underutilization. Thus, alternative forms of organizing production and remunerating labour can be as important a factor as an agrarian reform in increasing the productivity of the land and, consequently, reducing the poverty level of the population (the case of the Mexican agrarian reform is a good example of these factors).

The importance of agrarian reforms in eradicating poverty has been recognized, advocated and practised in different societies. Japan, South Korea, Taiwan, Mexico and Peru are countries that have used agrarian reforms in this century, with varying degrees of success, as a mechanism for reducing poverty and accelerating economic development.

In the case of Brazil, the problem of the structure of land property is particularly important. The country has one of the most unequal distributions of land in the world. Table 4.3 shows the distribution of land property in Brazil in 1920, 1950 and 1980.

In 1980, 5 per cent of the rural establishments accounted for 67.2 per cent of the land in the country while the 50 per cent of smallest establishments accounted for only 2.8 per cent. This high degree of land concentration is a characteristic of all regions of the country, being more pronounced in the North, the Northeast and the Centre–West.

The unequal distribution of land affects poverty in three different ways: (a) by generating unequal distribution of income and poverty in agriculture itself; (b) by inducing migration to the urban centres, increasing the supply of non-qualified labour and reducing real wages in the urban sector; (c) by reducing the productivity of land.

The level of poverty in the agricultural sector has been one of the factors most responsible for inducing rural-urban migration in Brazil since 1950. This rapid rural exodus has increased the supply of labour in the cities, reduced wages, increased the amount of investments needed in urban infrastructure and increased poverty in the urban centres.

Secondly, there is the effect of property size over productivity. The literature has consistently shown a reduction in land productivity proportional to increase in farm size. In Brazil, land productivity is very low. The contribution of agriculture to total value added is close to 10 per cent, while the average contribution of agriculture in countries with per capita income in the same range, is 18 per cent to 20 per cent and in the more developed countries, 7 per cent. While the industrial sector in the more developed countries contributes 36 per cent of total value added, in Brazil this sector contributes only 23 per cent. Service and commerce are the sectors which make up the difference (67 per cent of total value added in Brazil).

Finally, land concentration induces underutilization. The literature shows an inverse relationship between size and degree of land utilization. A recent survey of this literature reports a land utilization/farm size elasticity of only 0.38. For each 100 per cent increase in farm size, only 38 per cent of the land is utilized.

In Brazil, a substantial share of the land of the largest establishments is completely idle. Data for São Paulo in the late seventies, for example, show that up to the 500 to 1000 hectare range, as farm size increases there is a reduction in the number of farms with value of production of less than Cr$ 3,000.00 (1980). Above this range this relation is inverted. About 41.5 per cent of the establishments with more than 10,000 ha. had value of production below this limit. To complete the picture, 21 per cent of the establishments with more than 10,000 hectares were completely idle.

Idleness of land is directly related to its utilization as store of value and to the fact that as size increases there is a tendency to underutilize capital, labour and fertilizers.

Allocation of Capital among Jobs

Finally, the relation between poverty and physical capital is affected in a very important way by decisions about the allocation of the available capital stock among different jobs. The allocation of capital to jobs can be carried out on considerations of efficiency alone or can be directed through a system of fiscal incentives, generating a bias in favour of jobs occupied by more qualified or less qualified workers.

From the point of view of the fight against poverty, it would be of interest that at least some of the bias was in favour of the less qualified workers. It would be convenient that jobs occupied by less qualified workers were, in comparison with the capital endowment of the Brazilian economy as a whole, relatively overcapitalized, leaving the jobs occupied by the qualified workers relatively undercapitalized. In this case, the productivity of the underqualified workers would be higher than in the case of purely efficient allocation, while the productivity of the qualified workers would be relatively lower. In such an allocation, some efficiency would be sacrificed in favour of a better distribution of income and less poverty.

Yet Brazil's existing bias is exactly the opposite. Fiscal incentives have an allocative bias in favour of the more qualified jobs and more advanced sectors. In these sectors, which employ mainly qualified workers, there is a subsidization of capital and labour is highly taxed. The result is a segmentation of the economy, with the formal private sector as well as the productive public sector overcapitalized and demanding a mainly qualified labour force, and an undercapitalized informal sector which underutilizes its non-qualified labour force.

In other words, not only does a high proportion of Brazil's labour force have very low qualifications, but there is also a bias in the allocation of capital against the jobs occupied by these workers. As a result, the large percentage of the Brazilian workforce which does not have access to qualifications only has access to undercapitalized jobs. The productivity of this labour force is intrinsically low and highly underutilized. The final result is the very high poverty levels.

Incentives in the Labour Market

The capacity to create a large number of jobs has always been an important characteristic of the Brazilian economy, with a lower unemployment rate than other countries. This is true even when we limit the comparison to countries without any social infrastructure for assisting the unemployed, such as Chile or Colombia. The problem of the Brazilian economy is not the number of jobs it can generate: it is the lack of quality of the jobs that are generated. Very few jobs provide on-the-job training or opportunities for occupational upgrading and increasing wages with tenure. Most jobs are not equipped with enough physical capital, and consequently underutilize and underpay much of the labour force.

In contrast to other countries, when workers are laid-off in Brazil they generally only remain unemployed for a very short period of time. They tend to accept jobs of lower quality that demand lower qualifications and pay lower wages, often in service, construction and trade. In these sectors the technology is flexible, permitting firms that use out-dated labour-intensive technologies to compete with firms using modern, capital-intensive technologies. As a consequence, these sectors function as a permanent employment buffer, absorbing the supply of labour that cannot find jobs in the modern sector of the economy. In these sectors, supply of labour generates demand for labour. A causation process which resembles Say's Law.

In this section we investigate the reasons why the Brazilian labour market has not been able to generate jobs of suitable quality. In other words, we investigate why the majority of jobs in Brazil do not offer enough on-the-job training and do not give workers and employers enough incentives to invest in human capital or to improve the quality of the job.

There are a large number of reasons to explain why the Brazilian economy has been unable to generate an appropriate amount of jobs of suitable quality. The low rate of investment during the 1980s is certainly one of the most important and evident causes. None the less, we believe that there are reasons directly linked to the labour market which generate lack of incentives for investment in on-the-job training and firm-specific human capital and encourage the over-exploitation of the labour force.

One of the principal characteristics of the labour market is the existence of asymmetric information. The information on which workers base their decisions is different from the information used by firms in their decision-making process. On the one hand, the workers have a better understanding of their qualifications, their productivity, and how much effort they are planning to put in when working. On the other, the firm has better information about the characteristics of the job being offered and the chances of promotion, for example. In such circumstances, the set of incentives provided by the institutions that discipline the labour market are essential to the behaviour of workers and firms. Hence, it is important to analyse the kind of incentives generated by Brazilian institutions which may influence the behaviour of the economic agents involved in the labour market.

Although there are many important institutions that affect labour productivity in the Brazilian labour market, we will concentrate our attention on the *Fundo de Garantia por Tempo de Serviço* (FGTS), a lay-off compensation proportional to tenure.

The FGTS is the main labour market institution related to the process of laying-off workers. Each worker, once employed by a firm, is endowed with a banking account in which the firm deposits monthly an amount equal to 8 per cent of the worker's wages. This account receives interest and is indexed-linked to inflation. The workers have access to this fund in only three circumstances: (a) when they are fired; (b) when buying a house; (c) when they retire.

When laid off the workers receive, in addition to all funds accumulated during their current job, a premium of 40 per cent over these funds. This premium is paid by the firm. So, the longer the workers have worked for a firm, the larger their own fund and consequently the higher the cost for the firm to fire them.

The system introduced by the FGTS was an important instrument in the development of a flexible labour market in Brazil. It greatly simplified the process of laying off workers, relatively to the system that had prevailed before.

The problem of the FGTS is the incentive it provides for unskilled workers in jobs without clear promotion opportunities to seek to be fired. For workers with few promotion opportunities, being fired means an immediate income flow which can be substantial, depending on how long they have held their job, and which would otherwise only be available on retirement. For a worker with five years in a job, being fired represents a compensation (including FGTS, the 40 per cent premium and other benefits) approximately equal to 3.5 times his/her current monthly wage.

In periods of recession, the probability of getting another job is smaller and consequently the worker has less incentive to seek to be fired. However, as the economy grows and the probability of getting another job quickly increases, the optimum strategy is to seek to be fired, reducing the amount of effort dedicated to the current job and consequently, reducing productivity. The optimum strategy becomes to do on-the-job search, so that the chances of getting another job quickly are maximized. The final result will certainly be a considerable decrease in productivity in the current job.

If the workers have an incentive to seek to be fired as soon as possible, the firm, on the other hand, has all the incentives to exploit the workers as much as possible since no long-term relationship is being sought. In particular, neither firms nor workers have any incentive to invest in firm-specific human capital, since the imminent rupture of the relationship does not make this investment profitable. By the same token, the firms have no incentives to provide on-the-job training for their workers since, due to the expected short duration of the employment relationship, most of the benefits of this training would be appropriated by the worker after being fired. In summary, the optimum strategy for the firm will be to provide the minimal amount of training to workers and to exploit them as much as possible.

Under these circumstances, all worker-firm relationships are expected to be of short duration. Firms have no interest in providing training for workers while workers are not involved with the firms' objectives. Countries like Japan and Germany and large multinational corporations have shown that long-term working relations are an efficient procedure for increasing the productivity of the labour force. The FGTS creates perverse incentives in Brazil, encouraging employment relationships of short duration.

An important consideration in this context is the existence of a social cost associated with laying off workers. Firms that ignore these costs and lay off workers too often should be penalized. Nevertheless, this penalization should not be appropriated by the fired worker. If workers who are going to be laid off receive the penalty paid by the firm, then they will have a strong incentive to seek to be fired, unless they can perceive excellent opportunities for promotion. Since information is asymmetric, firms can neither predict workers' behaviour nor workers predict firms' behaviour. In this case neither workers nor firms will invest in firm-specific human capital. The end results are jobs of low quality, under utilized workers and a low productivity labour force.

Conclusions

Regardless of how we decide to measure poverty or to evaluate its consequences, a substantial proportion of the Brazilian population are to be classified as poor. These people, along with their descendants, are deeply affected by income insufficiency.

In this article we have discussed four causes of poverty in Brazil: (a) the human capital insufficiency of a large share of the population; (b) the physical capital insufficiency and bad capital distribution between jobs; (c) bad land distribution; and (d) a labour legislation which hampers the creation of long-term labour contracts and does not create incentives to maximize productivity.

The low qualification of the labour force is certainly one of the main causes of poverty in Brazil. This is the most obvious mechanism of inter-generational transmission of poverty. If this mechanism is not destroyed, there is no sustainable solution to poverty and improving equality of opportunities. Such an improvement would mean a greater independence of individual development from family environment. This can be obtained through three kinds of intervention: (a) better quality of the basic public education system; (b) financial support to the families of the poor to prevent early drop-out from the school system; (c) incentives for the generation of employment opportunities where on-the-job training and opportunities for occupational upgrading are adequately valued and rewarded.

The accumulation of physical capital is an essential condition for improving the quality of labour in the long term. For this reason, all policies for increasing investment in equipment and machinery which increase the productivity of labour will reduce poverty. It is important to note, however, that these investments will reduce poverty levels only if they reach the jobs of the poor. If they remain concentrated in jobs occupied by highly qualified workers, like today, the result will be an increase in inequality among workers without reduction in poverty.

Land is a very important resource in Brazil, but the very unequal distribution of this resource reduces its degree of utilization. Thus, an agrarian reform can be an important instrument for increasing agricultural production and land productivity, helping in a fundamental way to reduce poverty. An agrarian reform can induce an increase in agricultural production, in labour productivity, in the wealth of agricultural workers and reduce the rural-urban migration. As a result, it can have a very substantial impact on poverty in Brazil.

The creation of new labour legislation which would both protect workers and avoid perverse incentives to the maximization of their productivity is a very delicate endeavour. Because it rewards the laid-off worker, the FGTS generates negative incentives for the development of long-term employment relations.

In summary, agrarian reform, the reform of the basic public education system, financial assistance to poor families with children and a careful revision of the labour legislation are policies which, if implemented, would certainly have a significant effect on reducing poverty in Brazil.

5· DEMOCRATIC TRANSITION AND SOCIAL POLICY IN BRAZIL:

Some Dilemmas in the Agenda of Reforms

Maria Helena Guimarães de Castro

Introduction

The restructuring of the Brazilian social policy system was a central item on the agenda of reforms drawn up during the process of transition, for several reasons.[1] Structurally, as a result of the enormous social deficits which, while present throughout Brazilian history, had deteriorated during the prolonged period of exclusionary economic development adopted by the military regime. Strategically, because of the importance which social programmes had acquired in the daily life of vast segments of the population as well as for influential professional groups, such as public sector workers, teachers, doctors and medical workers, and for the economic groups that had grown up around these social policies, such as civil construction and the pharmaceutical-hospital complex. Politically, because a considerable segment of the political forces opposed to the military regime had grown and coalesced around this critique of the military government's social policy and a corresponding promise of reform and expansion. Thus, even as the political regime and economic policy was transformed during the transition, the critique of federal housing programmes, health and social security policy, education policy, and police and justice systems served as points of mobilization and consolidation for the various forces in opposition to the regime. Out of these critiques and a set of proposals for profound changes, the basic platform for election campaigns and policies emerged and gave substance to the redemocratization movement. On the other hand, the control of social agencies and programmes represents a strategic political resource, both from the point of view of the legitimacy of the regime and government and from the point of view of the political parties and their constituencies.

Many of the reforms proposed by the political and social forces which had strived for democratization were debated in the National Constituent Assembly and included in the 1988 Constitution. Respecting principles which, if effectively implemented, would increase social justice, the new constitution points towards a redistributive-institutional model of the welfare state as described by the classical Titmuss typology[2] (or the social-democratic model according to Esping-Andersen[3]), also characterized by a marked decentralization in the formulation of policies and in participative administration mechanisms. At the beginning of the 1990s, the new system was being implemented simultaneously with the formation of a new agenda of reforms. The difficulties of implementing the institutional measures, given the worsening of the political, social and economic crisis seem to point towards a progressive exhaustion of many of the planned reforms even before their consolidation. Firstly, the neo-liberal rhetoric of the present government has brought about proposals for the privatization of social insurance services, namely health care and social welfare agencies, as well as the public university system. At the same time, even some progressives acknowledge a narrowing of options in the social area, given the economic restrictions foreseen for the decade. The crucial problem is, above all, of a political nature: how to build a new consensus around reforms able to ensure the promotion of more social justice and equality while, at the same time, introducing selection criteria which might affect vested interests and 'acquired rights' in the present conjuncture of recession and crises of the state.

This article discusses the formation of the agenda of social policy reforms within the context of transition, the development of this agenda during the Nova República, and some of the emerging dilemmas.

Social and Political Transformation and the Agenda of Transition

With the crisis of the conservative model of a welfare state challenged simultaneously by the demands for more social justice as part of the democratization process and by the worsening economic situation at the beginning of the 1980s, the question of 'paying the social debt' spread among the Brazilian opposition as a basic element in the process of democratic construction.

Among the perverse effects of the economic development model adopted by the authoritarian regime it is important to stress the striking contrast between the marked spread of poverty – namely of the deprived and the disorganized segments of the population – and the emergence of new collective actors, better organized and oriented towards new forms of political action. In fact, the emergence of new forms of association, the creation of new parties, the revitalization of elections and the mushrooming of voluntary associations, not only made an impact on the process of democratization, but had a significant influence on the political debate about the restructuring of social policies. In the labour sphere, the union movement became more active in strikes and negotiations, basically through the wage question and, politically, through the emergence of a new unionism which broke with the populist tradition and, at the same time, the demobilization of the authoritarian period. Nevertheless, workers' organizations seem to have had little influence on the debates about social policy reforms. With the appearance of the two main labour confederations – Workers' Unitary Central (CUT) and General Confederation of Labour (CGT) – in 1983, their scope was amplified.[4] Agrarian reform and the foreign debt were the main issues taken up by the CUT, although general claims, such as 'free public education', 'health care for all', and so on, were increasingly emphasized in the meetings held throughout the decade. In general, however, these proposals emphasized a state-centred position to counter the neo-liberal stance of the entrepreneurial sectors, rather than becoming a concrete demand directed at the state. An example of this was the absence of the social policy issue in the various attempts at a social pact promoted by the Sarney government.

The growth of the new form of association and of the social movements is important in understanding the emphasis on social policies in the agenda of transition. The expansion of the middle classes, together with the revitalization of the union movement in the private sector and the expansion of the liberal professions, gave birth to an organizational trend[5] which expressed new ways of social and political standing. A 'publicly-employed middle class' – teachers, doctors, technicians and researchers – had emerged and would be affected by the economic crisis at the beginning of the 1980s.

Characteristic of this dynamic was the increasing politicization of strikes in the intermediate sectors: besides labour and wage demands, they emphasized new demands, associated with the increase of political and social rights, which contributed to the dissemination of democratic values and participative practices in the process of transition.

At the same time, a wide variety of grass roots social movements were being set up, greatly encouraged by the Catholic Church. Besides the expansion of the minorities movement, both mass sectors and the new middle classes, articulated either in *ad hoc* movements or in the better-organized neighbourhood groups, started to demand urban services and goods. The very expansion of social policies brought about new audiences and clienteles who usually organized themselves collectively (house mortgage-holders, state pensioners, day-care users, etc.)

These movements expressed the formation of new collective identities related to confronting of the authoritarian order and to the need for the democratization of social relationships. At the same time, they reveal a disbelief in the effectiveness of the traditional mechanisms of representation for policy implementation. At any rate, we can observe a strong tendency to define a schedule of demands for services and goods produced by the State.[6]

In the party political sphere, despite the economic difficulties, the starting point of the discussion of alternatives to the conservative policies was the verification of the immense social disparities and extremely low levels of welfare provoked by the process of economic development. Correctly, the origins of these disparities were identified as lying in the perverse concentration of wealth, resulting from the economic model and fragmented, ineffective and distorted social policies. It also correctly attributed this pattern to the authoritarian rule. Party programmes showed the degree of consensus which this diagnosis achieved in different opposition parties. Also, the demand for 'growth, redistribution of income, and more social justice' appeared as one of the axes for the uniting of opposition forces in the process of mobilization for the 'Diretas Já' movement.[7]

In addition, in a context of recession and intense mass movements, the state administrations, directly elected in 1982, faced an array of demands requiring a response. With the contraction of the federal financial resources and the relative paralysis in the decision-making process, the new state governors sought alternative solutions: they developed low-cost social programmes; they emphasized decentralized management in all social areas; they stimulated popular participation in the production of welfare services (*mutirões*, mutual self-help, and so on); they tried to direct actions towards specific clienteles (children and adolescents, slum dwellers, the unemployed); and they encouraged the municipal administration to act as partners in the process of implementation of social programmes.

In a certain sense, the emphasis on participation and decentralization, already present in the process of democratization, acquired greater relevance with the new ventures developed by the states and municipalities, and began to become a feature in the agenda of the transition.

Thus, the 'agenda of the transition' now had shape and content regarding redemocratization as a necessary condition for the promotion of social reforms. Growth would be combined with income redistribution and social policy reform, within a context which presupposed the prominence of the public sector in the production of goods and services as well as through state regulation. Roughly speaking, the desired strategy would combine development, more jobs, higher salaries, and more effective and universal social policies.

Amidst this intense debate about social policy reform, the following points became part of the agenda of the Nova República government, inaugurated in 1985: (1) the restructuring of the funding system for social spending, especially with respect to a wider use of special funds rather than normal fiscal budgeting, and diversification of funding sources in order to reduce the sensitivity of funding to economic cycles; (2) a reorganization of the administrative apparatus for social services, which had become institutionally fragmented into diverse, competing agencies, with poorly-paid, poorly-trained and disinterested workers who were consequently ineffective and inefficient;[8] (3) the promotion of a major debate, including various groups from civil society, to identify a model of social policy that would be compatible with effective, efficient, equitable and just governmental intervention and would correspond, simultaneously, to the demands for democratization of governmental action itself. Such a model would call explicitly for substantial decentralization of decision-making and execution and for greater community participation in the definition, gestation, and control of the programmes.

It is evident that an agenda of this magnitude would require the command of a hegemonic group, committed to the strategies of reform, with the power to give direction and meaning to state actions. Nevertheless, both by the nature of the heterogeneous and contradictory forces articulated in the Aliança Democrática and the amplitude of the 'generic agreement' around which this coalition was organized, in practice the Nova República government went no further than promoting emergency programmes to fight poverty reduced to social aid actions implemented with politically clientelistic goals. The only exception was the Decentralized Health Care System (SUDS), started in 1987, clearly demonstrating the success of the organized interests present in the Sanitary Reform Commission.[9]

The discussion about structural reforms brought to the Constituent Assembly in accordance with the newly established democratic game, was intensified by the battle between various lobbies.

At any rate, the agenda of transition was to a large extent carried out through the constituent process, in amplifying goals for social rights, restructuring the profile of labour relationships, creating a new decentralized system of government intervention in the social area, defining important changes in the tax structure and in the attributions and responsibilities of the three levels of government. At least in a formal way, the 1988 Constitution expressed the opposition aims.

Constitutional Reform[10]

The innovations introduced with the 1988 Constitution suggest an important advance in the standards of social protection. According to Draibe,[11] such changes indicate a move away from the particularistic-meritocratic model – which characterized Brazil's 'Social Welfare State' from its creation in 1930 up to its consolidation in the 1970s – towards a redistributive-institutional model. That is to say, these changes seem to project a more egalitarian and universalistic format for the social protection system, in that they reinforce the redistributive character of social policies; require greater public responsibility in their regulation and production; define homogeneous social rights, the universalization of access to them and a certain loosening of the contributive link as a structuring principle of the system, besides redefining minimum amounts for social benefits.

In the field of social rights, one of the most important advances was the adoption of the social security concept, embracing the actions related to social welfare, health care, and social assistance.

In the case of social welfare, the most important changes were the equalization of benefits between rural and urban workers, correcting the existing inequities. Moreover, selection criteria were introduced for a greater protection of the low-income insured person and their dependents (family bonus), improvement of maternity benefits and introduction of a leave of absence for the father at the birth of a child. The novelty was the institution of a monthly income for the elderly and handicapped and the definition that social security will be financed by society as a whole, directly or indirectly, a step in the direction of collective insurance against social risks. On the other hand, the principle of individual insurance was retained, guaranteeing welfare benefits paid for by monthly contributions.

The principle of universalization differs most from the previous model in the case of health care: it has introduced egalitarian access for the whole population. The new organizational structure, defined as an integrated, decentralized and hierarchical network, establishes a single system in each level of government, giving priority to state action. A complementary role is granted to the private sector in the delivery of services, by means of contracting out services. Comprehensive care is emphasized, priority given to preventive medicine and community participation in the administration of the system.

In addition, social aid is recognized as a right of the population regardless of previous contribution, and is conceived according to the currently accepted definition of the minimum necessary to live on. In organizational terms, it introduces the municipalization of social aid actions, and the participation of community assemblies in its formulation and implementation. As to education, the universal right to basic education is reaffirmed; 50 per cent of the public resources in the sector are directed towards the expansion of basic schooling and the eradication of illiteracy; the right to pre-school education is assured. It also advocates the municipalization of the pre-school and primary school system.

The chapter dedicated to urban policy assigns to the federal government the responsibility of defining guidelines for urban development, including housing, basic sanitation, and urban transport. At the same time, the states of the federation and the municipalities became responsible for the execution of urban development policy, including the compulsory duty for each town to establish its own Urban Policy Act, to regulate land use, land expropriation and mechanisms for controlling urban growth. It assured the participation of the organized population in local planning.

Finally the new constitution instituted a tax reform, changing the criteria of intergovernmental transference, as well as promoting an important decentralization of revenues, favouring the states and municipalities, besides deeply changing the structure of social policy financing.

While it paid regard to a democratic social and political order in principle, the new constitution transferred the dilemmas of how to put the new social order into practice to a later moment, the implementation of regulating and enabling laws by the Congress. Beyond the difficulties in promoting the conciliation of conflicting and excluding interests in the relations between the executive and the legislative – a process which was aggravated by the chronic fragility of the party system in Brazil – the realization of the new social measures depends upon at least two main factors: the resolution of the economic crisis, which worsened dramatically in the 1990s, and the recovery of the financial and administrative capacity of a state, in permanent crisis over the last few years. In short, the complexity of the process of implementing the reforms is worsened by a set of factors which can explain the present difficulties: underdevelopment and structural inequalities, and political structure and democratic transition. We now turn our attention to these.[12]

Underdevelopment, Structural Inequalities and the Existing Social Policy

First and foremost, there are factors related to the size, complexity, and intensity of the social problems inherited by the Nova República. It is important to remember that despite the high rates of economic growth prevailing in the past decades and the substantial public expenditures in social programmes, the social situation of the country has not improved accordingly. Social injustices are cruel, inequalities (both social and regional) are widening, and poverty and destitution are still rampant. According to recent research by the IBGE,[13] of Brazil's approximately 150 million population, two-thirds are considered to be poor or miserable: 50 million have an income beneath the poverty line and another third slightly above that mark. Only the remaining 50 million can, theoretically, enjoy the benefits of citizenship and participate in the market economy. Despite this picture of social deprivation, preliminary balances of the eighties show that the population's living conditions would have been far worse if the country had not possessed a social policy system. There was an improvement in the indicators of health and education coverage compared with previous decades. It is the poverty issue that poses some dilemmas for the future.

Secondly, there is the perennial dilemma over the short-term allocation priorities for economic development investments aimed at increasing per capita income, raising food production and exports, expanding employment (since the labour force is still growing at around 3.0 per cent annually), as well as supporting research, science and technology on one hand and social programmes on the other. This profound dilemma for a still-poor country becomes particularly sensitive when inflation, public deficit, and stagnation persist for long periods of time.

Thirdly, there are factors related to the existing social policy programmes that restrict the improvement of social assistance for the poor, particularly in programmes expanded during the military regime. Under the military regime, programmes such as housing, social security, health care, urban transportation, education, and food supply were expanded: (1) by creating financing mechanisms that either obstructed the access by the poor to the services provided (such as in the case of the housing programmes) or implied a cut-back in resources precisely at moments of social crisis when demands for services increase (as in the case of social security and health care), or both; (2) by expanding the coverage without providing adequate financing through the fiscal budget, adequate wages for social services personnel, or suitable training programmes, especially in the spheres of education, health care, justice and security; (3) by promoting forms of interrelationship between the public and the private sectors that led to distortions in terms of service costs and other perverse effects, notably in the provision of health care and housing.

One aspect of the structure of social benefits inherited by the Nova República deserves to be singled out for closer attention: the problems of inefficiency, internal inequality and mistargeting. Having developed in a context where clientelistic, patronage, and authoritarian relationships prevail, the Brazilian system of social benefits is marred by internal inequalities and by almost systematic mistargeting.

The benefits provided by the public sector pension funds vary enormously, favouring segments of the public bureaucracy and the formally employed urban groups and discriminating against those working in the rural areas and in the informal urban sector; the housing programme undoubtedly favoured the urban upper and middle classes; the financing of the educational system discriminated against high school education (and consequently against the lower-middle and lower-class children and adolescents); public, preventive, and less expensive health care receives much less attention than private, curative, hospital-based, high-tech medicine. To put it succinctly, there are three forms of mistargeting of social services resources:

i) mistargeting within sectors such as education and health, resulting in relatively high public subsidies for the types of programmes that are not likely to reach the poor;
ii) mistargeting across sectors, with relatively high public subsidies for those programmes, such as social security and housing, that currently serve primarily the middle class and the rich, compared with sectors such as nutrition that primarily serves the poor;
iii) failure within programmes to reach the poorest and neediest groups, such as the rural Northeastern poor.[14]

All this results in a structure of unequal 'acquired rights' (i.e. consolidated rights and job tenure) which is extremely difficult to change and crystallizes a pattern of struggle for social rights that, given resource scarcity, favours the groups with easier access to the political and administrative systems, discriminating against the rest.

The end result of the existing structure of inherited social policy mechanisms is an array of social policy programmes in deep financial crisis, conducted by a vast ill-paid, centralized, and inefficient bureaucracy, and providing a variety of unequal and discriminatory benefits. All this, of course, is a powerful source of inertia and internal tension.

Political Structure and Democratic Transition

There are constraints associated with the Brazilian political system and its past performance that limit the possibilities of developing, in the short term, an adequate welfare system for the poor. The major developments in the system have all taken place either during strong presidential regimes, characterized by populist and corporatist overtones (such as the Vargas presidency), or during periods of authoritarian rule (such as the recent military governments). This has helped to create a distorted perception about the way social rights are institutionalized and about the role played by the state in this process.

Rather than resulting from political conflict and negotiation among political parties, pressure groups and social movements, social rights are perceived as paternalistic concessions granted by the governing élite and the State.

The lack of a long and stable party system capable of creating and sustaining clear-cut party programmes has limited the identification of different political parties with explicitly distinct approaches to welfare. On the contrary, Brazilian politics has been marked by short periods of party development interrupted by long periods of authoritarian rule, curtailing an evolution where alternative political parties could take up social welfare issues posed by distinct constituencies. As a result, these demands are adopted wholesale by generic opposition parties and periodically 'explode' in plebiscitary elections where they end up having little importance.

Furthermore, the interrelated precariousness of both the party system and the democratic political process implies the lack of party or party alliance alternation in the exercise of power. Consequently, on one hand, the commitment of these parties to their welfare rhetoric cannot be tested and, on the other, the experience of dealing with the administrative responsibilities involved in running a welfare apparatus in a still poor country does not feed back into party rhetoric. The governing élites, in turn, may remain elliptical in their welfare platform and manipulate welfare development according to their own convenience.

Finally, the growth of a highly centralized state, controlling a huge amount of resources, and intervening in a wide range of activities, has implied growing pressures for finding privileged connections with the state apparatus.

Therefore, successful participation in the political game has become exaggeratedly dependent upon access to state resources: in the words of the saying, 'there is no salvation outside the state'. Access to the growing welfare machine, as a strategic source of political resources, became indispensable and its control an important basis for political clientelism.

The net result of these structural political constraints for the social policy system – in a society still strongly influenced by a patrimonial and patriarchical ethos – has been the prevalence of populism and demagoguery in political practice and the widespread clientelistic utilization of the social policy state apparatus. The 'catch all' rhetoric of promising to solve all social problems through state-supported programmes and benefits became a generic 'opposition platform' for all political forces outside the governing coalition.

The absence of a long and sustained experience of democratic government has biased perception of the social issues and the public policies required to deal with them for all the players: the citizens; the politicians, their parties, and their constituencies; the government and their bureaucrats. This non-zero sum game could be sustained, more easily, in situations of rapid economic growth. Now that expansion has halted, it is increasingly difficult to operate under these assumptions.

The political movement behind the recent democratic transition raised people's hopes that the structural constraints we have just reviewed would be removed. However, given the deepness and the complexity of the issues involved, it is clear, from an analytical point of view, that global structural changes could not be achieved in the short run. But the particular form that the process of transition towards democracy has been taking in Brazil has enhanced the political difficulties of this enormous and complex task, turning progressively into frustration. Relying upon the analyses of democratic transitions by O'Donnell, Lamounier, and Campello de Souza[15] among others, three aspects of the Brazilian transition are relevant for exploring the restructuring of the social policy promised by the political mobilization.

First, the fact that the military regime in Brazil – when compared to the Argentina dictatorship, for example – was able to sustain high rates of economic growth and to modernize certain segments of the state apparatus, although at the cost of deepening social exclusion. It was also able to expand social policy coverage although using rather perverse financial mechanisms and systematic mistargeting. As a result, a large proportion of the upper level administrative and technical 'cadres' in the state apparatus emerged during this period of authoritarian rule.

Secondly, the transition was a very long one, developing at different paces from 1974 onwards when General Geisel proposed the 'slow and smooth opening of the political system'. Such a long transition, with its ups and downs, allowed time for different political segments to progressively disengage themselves from the military regime and facilitated the inclusion, within the opposition coalition, of an array of divergent interests, loosely articulated and with conflicting priorities.

Thirdly, the ending of authoritarian rule occurred not only as a result of popular mobilization but also from a political pact that encompassed a broad spectrum of political forces, including many of those that had actively supported the military regime. The access to presidential power took place without a general election: it was Congress that elected President Tancredo Neves and Vice-President José Sarney. José Sarney had been the leader of the party (PDS) that supported the military regime and an active member of the forces that, in Congress, voted against the reestablishment of direct elections to choose General Figueiredo's successor. With the dramatic events leading to the death of President Tancredo Neves, Vice-President José Sarney became the incumbent president supported, but not enthusiastically, by much of the broad and heterogenous political front called the Democratic Alliance. This transition coalition included former supporters of the military regime and the centre-to-right forces grouped around the PMDB, but excluded specific forces from the left of the political spectrum, particularly those organized around the Workers' Party (PT) and the Democratic Labour Party (PDT). For better or for worse, this was the political price of the 'negotiated transition'.

The political limitations this 'agreed upon transition' imposed on the improvement of the Brazilian system of social policy became progressively clearer. At the beginning, the more progressive forces within the governing coalition had access to decision-making centres from where the reforms could be launched. However, they had to face resistance, within the state apparatus, from existing interest groups that kept control over second-level, but strategic, decision-making organs. This opposition ended up giving the more conservative political forces control over some important ministries and the inner power circle around the presidency. As a result, structural reforms of the social policy system, with the possible exception of the National Health System, converged towards the National Constituent Assembly.

A strategy distinguishing short-term emergency policies from structural reforms was actively embraced by President Sarney and the more conservative forces coalescing around him, emphasizing the emergency plans. Such programmes were more easily conducted clientelistically and could be manipulated to provide electoral leverage.

The Agenda of Reforms: Some Dilemmas

The democratic transition was completed with the election of the new president of the republic, by universal suffrage at the end of 1989. President Fernando Collor de Mello was elected after an unyielding competition against former union leader Luis Inácio 'Lula' da Silva, of the leftist Workers' Party.

After a year of attempts at an economic adjustment, the worsening recession and rising inflation led the federal administration to suggest some alterations to the social reforms established by the 1988 Constitution. With the so-called National Reconstruction Project of March 1991, together with the present emphasis on the need to reform the constitutional text, the government has taken the initiative in suggesting a number of modifications: the organization of a complementary system of private social welfare; the full privatization of some welfare schemes, particularly work accidents; the broadening of the private social insurance; the elimination of the right to a pension after a certain number of years at work; a new tax partition more favourable to the unions. Many of the proposed measures are not clear. At any rate, political speculation in the press has focused on the trend towards privatization, which is strongly supported by business sectors related to private insurance and by rightist party groups, indefatigable defenders of the success of the Chilean model.

Among the progressives, the worsening of the economic crisis in the 1990s seems to have rapidly led to the drawing up of a new agenda, restating the previous issues while questioning the objective possibilities of achieving the advanced welfare model established by the constitution.

The central axis of the present debate, refers, on the one hand, to the role of the state and of public funds in the provision of social goods and services to the neediest population and, on the other, to forms of decentralization in the operation of these policies.[16]

Yet, it is poverty which is the central question, in particular in the elaboration of proposals which oppose universalistic policy in specific programmes directed at the poor. As Draibe remarks:

> The fact that creates tension and dilemmas is that the present crisis both offers the possibility of broadening social rights, through the universalization of programmes and the multiplication of non-contributive policies, while simultaneously reducing public and private resources available for social expenditures,

> forcing options, selection of policies and the prioritization of certain beneficiaries, which theoretically contradicts the tendency to universalization.[17]

In this sense, the central dilemma lies in the contraposition of the universalistic conception of social rights with the state as principal provider of social goods and services (as established in the new constitution) and the neo-liberal position with its emphasis on the need to restrict expenses, define selective policies, privatize services directed to the less needy classes, decentralize the administration of public services and transfer new responsibilities to the states and municipalities.

There is a great deal of criticism of the insufficient neo-liberal strategy. As it does not contemplate the structural roots of the poverty that strikes two-thirds of the population, it could serve to consolidate the immense social inequalities, as well as exacerbating the aid and clientelistic aspect of state action in Brazil. Yet the definition of specific, decentralized policies involving the profit-making and non-profit-making sectors has also been supported by some progressive sectors, although with a different viewpoint from the neo-liberals.

Considering the gravity of the social situation, some proposals defend a radical (specific) programme of poverty eradication combined with the modernization of health systems and of basic education of a universal type. Decentralization and the involvement of people's participation in the administration of programmes is also advocated, but as a strategy to assure democratization and to break with the excessive bureaucratization of the social policy apparatus consolidated during the authoritarian period. The basic difference from the decentralization proposed by the neo-liberals is in the definition of automatic mechanisms of financing the various levels of government in order to guarantee the continuity of the policies, avoid the risk of misuse of funds, and reduce the degrees of regional inequality, which might be worsened by a process of privatization and decentralization.

The conflict is still intense between these proposals and the defenders of the universal and redistributive model of a social welfare state, countersigned in the constitution. It is enough to recall that the parties which defended the reformist policies approved in the constitution obtained about 46 per cent of the total votes in the first round of the 1989 presidential elections, and presently control nearly 47.3 per cent of the seats of the House of Representatives and 51.7

per cent of the Senate.[18] Nevertheless, they have proved unable to effect coalitions to support the reforms, partly due to the fragility of the Brazilian party structure, partly due to their distance from their electoral bases. At any rate, the paradox of the present situation is that while for the first time in recent history institutional conditions favour the construction of a more egalitarian social welfare state, the economic crisis had already been imposing a new agenda of reforms before the implementation of many of the social reforms established in the constitution.

6· UNIONS, ECONOMIC CRISIS AND HIGH INFLATION

*Maria Herminia Tavares de Almeida**

> Social and political structures help to shape inflation; conversely inflation alters collective social roles. (Charles Maier)

Introduction

In this article, I focus on union responses to the anti-inflationary policies introduced in the 1980s by Brazil's first civilian government. My intention is to discuss the political limitations on union strategies that contributed to confining them within a vicious circle in which their efforts were concentrated on fighting for wage indexation. This struggle was both highly defensive in nature and produced uncertain material results.

Brazil's return to the circle of democratic nations coincided with significant deterioration in its economic performance. The nascent democracy had to deal with an economic crisis of considerable proportions, complex roots and difficult solution. The most visible manifestations of the crisis were: slumps or spasmodic oscillations in the growth rate, spiralling inflation, an immense foreign debt and fiscal deficits which dramatically reduced the state's capacity for exercising its normal tasks of regulating, stimulating and co-ordinating the economy.

Economic problems persisted and worsened throughout the 1980s, contrary to the expectations of those who had opposed the authoritarian regime and struggled for democracy. In Brazil, unions – as well as business associations – were important actors during this period when efforts at democratic reconstruction coexisted with economic deterioration. Not only were their actions profoundly affected by these two processes. They, in turn, influenced them.

The perverse coincidence of the democratization process with the economic crisis gave unions contradictory stimuli. The construction of a new order implied the union movement's full reinsertion into political life. Consequently, unions had to choose forms of action capable of increasing their power or, at least, guaranteeing their recognition by business leaders, the government and other political actors. Yet at the same time, possible solutions to the economic problems required a certain degree of moderation in wage demands and forms of concerted action, together with the willingness to give up immediate benefits in order to attain long-range goals. What was needed was unionism focused on *political exchange*, as understood by Pizzorno.[1]

Confronted by such a dilemma, the Brazilian union movement chose courses of action aimed at achieving short-term wage goals and increasing its power through *confrontation strategies*,[2] characterized by systematic opposition to government policies and by emphasis on mass mobilization and strikes. This strategy did not conflict with collective bargaining between unions and business associations. But, undoubtedly, it was contrary to the negotiation of mid- and long-term policies which implied restrictions on current demands.

During Sarney's government, confrontation was the dominant strategy of active unionism. Yet the same period also saw the emergence of a more pragmatic labour leadership, more inclined to negotiate with the government. The existence of the latter, however, did not significantly change the majority leaning towards confrontation.

Preference for confrontational strategy brought Brazilian unionism many benefits. It guaranteed unions a place among the relevant actors in the Brazilian political arena, as well as bringing about important changes in the labour relations system which strengthened union power. Nevertheless, as the economic crisis deepened, confrontation strategies revealed their limitations as a weapon capable of yielding lasting economic improvements for the wage-earners whose interests unions mediate and seek to represent. The unions were not even able to defend the purchasing power of wages devoured by runaway inflation.

Paradoxically, in the late 1980s, confrontation became a defensive action against economic deterioration. The same was true of the competing strategies. Confrontation had become a *struggle for* indexation,[3] a continued effort with ephemeral immediate results. At the same time, this struggle imperceptibly and involuntarily propelled unions into a form of *inflationary coalition* with entrepreneurs.[4]

Union choices were strongly conditioned by factors of a political nature. In the first instance, the unions responded to the need to confirm their power in an emerging democratic system. Secondly, the very dynamics of union politics, characterized by stubborn competition for power and leadership among groups, influenced their choices. Above all, labour strategies were conditioned by the government's inability to promote policies of economic co-ordination capable of achieving price stabilization. This incapacity resulted as much from the nature of party politics in the first civilian government as from the choice of economic policies adopted by President Sarney, and was rooted in the collapse of a certain pattern of state interventionism. This crisis became evident in the increasing loss of effectiveness of the traditionally available state mechanisms for regulating and managing the national economy.

From Confrontation to Inflationary Coalitions

In 1985, the nascent democracy inherited a gamut of economic problems, of which the most visible sign was increasing inflation. The last military president, General Figueiredo (1979–84), ended his mandate immersed in short-term economic difficulties and political discredit. He had failed in his attempt to confront the problem of economic adjustment.[2] At the time, his failure was attributed to government ineptitude and to the decay of the authoritarian regime, both of which were real and partly explain what happened. They were not, however, the only causes. In addition, we find a process of corrosion of the state's instruments for managing the economy, resulting from the economic crisis as much as from the policies used to combat it. High inflation was the most visible symptom of the state's debility.

This was not, however, generally perceived at the end of the military regime. There was a strong belief that the new democracy would bring an end to economic imbalance and a return to economic growth. The rejection of adjustment policies was deeply entrenched throughout the opposition. Such policies were identified with the authoritarian government and its notorious lack of sensitivity to the social consequences of recessive measures. 'No to recession!' was the rallying call that united all the opponents of the military regime. For its part, between 1978 and 1984, the Brazilian union movement was on the upswing, helped by confrontation strategies. Nor could it have been otherwise. Under an authoritarian regime in crisis, the quest for free collective bargaining had been inseparable from opposition to the government's wage policy; demands for union autonomy had been transformed into opposition to the overall presence of the state in socio-economic relations; and aggressive, mobilizing union action had opened the way for recognition of the political existence of the workers' movement. The strategy of confrontation produced good results and turned the union movement into a political actor of indisputable importance.

Beyond reinforcing the bonds of solidarity and self-identification of a social movement in the making, the strategy based on strike mobilization and systematic opposition to the government had an unmistakable political impact. Union leadership – and the workers they represented – shared society's broader optimism about the benefits democracy would bring. Having emerged during the years of the 'Economic Miracle', they wanted their share of the wealth that had been generated then, not realizing that it had been shrinking for some time.

Fighting inflation without penalizing the poorest, regaining the momentum of economic development, renegotiating the foreign debt – as well as establishing democracy – were set out in the *Compromisso com a Nação* (Commitment to the Nation) signed by the two parties that made up the Democratic Alliance – the Brazilian Democratic Movement Party (PMDB) and the Liberal Front Party (PFL). It sealed the pact between centre-left oppositionists and dissidents of the old regime, which made possible a smooth transition to civilian government with Tancredo Neves' victory in the Electoral College. It explicitly referred to the end of wage containment policies and to restoring union freedom. Above all, it reiterated the PMDB's political platform and expressed belief in the viability of economic development with social justice.

The *Compromisso* was a re-edition, in synthesis, of the principal points of the 1981 PMDB policy document, *Esperança e Mudança* (Hope and Change),[6] which had a strongly developmentalist flavour. Both rested on the assumption that the economy would return to growth and wealth distribution would be improved. Common to both were two tenets that Bresser Pereira[7] considers central to the economic ideology of Brazilian left: income distribution and rejection of adjustment policies – a position that was shared by the two recently constituted union associations. It was expressed in the Workers' Unitary Central's (CUT) 1983 founding document and also in the *Carta de Praia Grande* (Praia Grande Letter), produced by the National Conference of the Working Classes (CONCLAT), which, in 1986, would become the moderate and pragmatic General Confederation of Labour (CGT).

In the climate of negotiated transition, emphasis was placed on negotiation, moderation and national unity.[8] It was in this context that the expression 'social pact' appeared in Tancredo Neves' speeches, before and after his election. Lechner underlined the significance of such pacts in the Latin American democratization processes:

> The bulk of intellectual political debate can be located within the framework of the 'neo-social contract'. In troubled societies, whose political history is characterized by catastrophic stalemates and reciprocal vetoes (Argentina and Bolivia), by great ideological polarization (Chile, Peru) or by traditional mechanisms of domination (Brazil, Colombia and Ecuador), the idea of the pact and strategies of consensus are important innovation. They respond – after the experience of disorder under authoritarian governments – to a generalized aspiration for stable, participatory institutions. We must remember the 1980 plebiscite in Uruguay, the multitudinous mobilizations in Argentina in 1983 and in Brazil in 1984. Counting on massive backing, the idea of the pact expresses the search for a complex yet bewildering agreement in which restoration of the fundamental 'rules of the game', the negotiation of a timetable and a minimum outline for transition, and the establishment of mechanisms for socioeconomic agreement, are the essential ingredients. Even though we can analytically distinguish between the constitutional pact (and the respective debate today about the validity of a kind of 'social contract'), a political pact for transition (as in the case of the multi-party alliances in Argentina and Uruguay or the Democratic Alliance in Brazil) or a social pact in its strictest sense (business-union-State agreement), in situations of transition the three levels are in fact necessarily intertwined.[9]

In the newly elected president's discourse, references to the social pact were especially addressed to union leadership. They meant that, rather than impose new wage rules, these would be discussed and agreements would be reached with the unions. Such references were also a way of calming unions faced with the prospect of a basically orthodox economic policy, a prospect made tangible given the choice of minister of finance. With Vice-President José Sarney's ascension to the presidency, calls for a social pact disappeared, giving way to an economic policy that combined highly orthodox principles with major concessions to heterodox ideas. The point of departure for the finance minister Francisco Dornelles' policy was that inflation had to be overcome first in order to later achieve growth and that inflation would be combated by liquidating the public deficit. This would be done through cuts in public expenditure, tax increases, control of currency issue and an increase in the public debt. Concessions to heterodoxy came through private sector price controls and a freeze on the prices of goods and public services. Contrary to what had occurred under authoritarian rule, there was no attempt to discipline wages. In the private sector, these could be freely bargained. In the public sector, they were subordinated to the general effort of expenditure containment.[10]

As had happened at the outset of General Figueiredo's government, enormous resistance in and outside government brought Dornelles and his policy down in six months. The Democratic Alliance, transformed into a government coalition, quickly lost substance, deeply divided by internal conflicts which affected the relations between the executive and Congress, the president and the PMDB leadership, and within the government itself. The result was a governability crisis that was not the result of excessive pressure by society.[11] It was induced by the incapacity of the government – lacking a loyal and stable parliamentary base – to make decisions on themes on which full consensus did not exist, be they fighting inflation, agrarian reform or the law defining strike rights.

In this context, the labour movement found no reason to drop the confrontational strategy that had turned it into an important political actor during the authoritarian regime's twilight. Among the unionists affiliated to CUT – which grouped the principal unions responsible for strike activity – the choice of confrontation was reinforced by links with the Workers' Party (PT). Recently formed, the PT defined itself as the party of the mass of the population who were excluded from élitist politics and, consequently as intransigent opposition to a government born out of an élite compromise. Confrontation in the labour sphere reinforced the image of intransigent opposition in the political arena.

The previous success of confrontation, the government's lack of political definition and the conservative nature of the Democratic Alliance, on one hand, and renewed economic growth, mounting inflation and expectations of higher wages, on the other, reinforced the union's preference for mass mobilization and collective conflict. The latter escalated along with prices.

Inflation in 1985 was 235.1 per cent – compared with 223.8 per cent the previous year (See Table 6.1). Work stoppages leapt from 492 to 619 and the number of working days lost multiplied 6.8 times.[12] In the mobilization, CUT strengthened its command over the union movement.

As prices increased, demands to increase the frequency of inflation adjustments for wages multiplied. The active labour movement put all its weight behind the struggle for indexation. Real wages rose, partly because of strike mobilization, and partly due to reactivation of the economy. Nevertheless, exacerbation of strikes, a successful strategy from the union point of view, helped speed the inflationary spiral.[13]

Strike mobilization created particularly complex problems for public sector management. Pressure was particularly acute in the case of direct public administration, where budgetary resources were committed to the public workers' payroll to an extremely high and increasing degree. This made the government specially sensitive to wage demands from civil servants. And these demands accompanied the trend of price increases.

The participation of public sector employees in strikes was significant. They were responsible for 31.2 per cent of work stoppages and 73.6 per cent of working days lost during the year.[14] At the end of the year, it was clear that the government could not do without an anti-inflationary policy. In the New Republic, there seemed to be little room for an economic policy negotiated with society's organized interests. Concerted income policies were not systematically pursued by the government. However, calls for a social pact had not completely disappeared from government rhetoric, especially in the Ministry of Labour. They surfaced with every new wave of strikes, each broader and more threatening than the one before,[15] or when the business community protested against government passivity in the

Table 6.1 Joint Brazilian Economic Indicators

				Real salary (3)		Employment	
Year	GNP (1)	Industrial GNP (1)	Inflation (2)	Public Administration	Manufacturing	Public Administration (4)	Manufacturing
1979	6.8	6.80	77.2	100.00	100.00	100.00	100.00
1980	9.2	9.25	110.2	106.30	116.08	105.60	102.60
1981	−4.4	−8.85	95.2	103.01	120.24	112.09	95.53
1982	0.6	−0.02	99.7	109.70	135.03	119.15	92.01
1983	−3.4	−5.85	211.0	91.88	112.77	122.49	85.72
1984	3.3	6.61	233.8	83.23	109.86	132.13	90.63
1985	7.9	8.27	235.1	105.81	120.74	140.28	98.75
1986	7.5	11.76	65.0	123.80	124.74	150.86	109.62
1987	3.6	1.06	415.8	103.11	106.78	160.18	106.26
1988	0.1	−2.59	1037.6	105.46	112.52	167.02	107.57
1989 (5)	3.3	3.00	1782.9	89.04	95.00	167.75 (6)	113.94 (7)

(1) Annual indices in variation in real product
(2) General price index – IGP
(3) Deflated by the INPC/FIBGE (1979 = 100.00)
(4) Personnel in direct public administration and autonomous entities
(5) Estimates:
A) Nominal salary, supposing the same growth by the FGV's IGP-DI
B) Employment, supposing growth observed in information taken from the General Register of Employment and Unemployment (law 4.923)
(6) Through the month of October

Sources: Foundation of the Brazilian Institute of Geography and Statistics – FIBGE
Conjuntura Econômica – Getúlio Vargas Foundation – FGV
Annual Report on Social Information – RAIS
CHAHAD (1990:555)

face of union pressure. But the government did not adopt it as policy. Nor was it a solution that attracted union leaders, whose power and prestige appeared to grow with confrontational behaviour.[16] In fact, unionists tended to underestimate the risk of an uncontrolled acceleration of inflation and the impact that more frequent wage adjustments had on escalating prices.

In the end, the Sarney government opted for a shock policy, similar to the one that seemed such a success in Argentina. In late February, it issued the Cruzado Plan, an attempt to escape the vicious circle in which it was entangled and fulfil the hopes of a society anxious for stability, economic growth and individual improvement without great sacrifices. Contrary to the orthodox view, the government recognized that stabilization required some type of co-ordination of wages and prices. At the same time, it did not seem to believe in a cooperative and pact-based solution. It chose, therefore, the solitary road of heterodox shock policy.

The Cruzado Plan involved a freeze on prices and foreign exchange, monetary reform with de-indexation and *tablitas* for conversion of cruzeiros to the new currency, a freeze on wages previously readjusted by the preceding six months' average real salary, with an additional bonus of 8 to 12 per cent for the minimum wage, a wage trigger for when inflation rose by 20 per cent, and unemployment insurance. Its implementation was accompanied by an expansionist monetary policy and low interest rates. The Cruzado Plan not only surprised ordinary citizens, distant from the world of politics. It also caught off guard well-informed public opinion and the leaders of political parties – including that of governing parties – of the unions and other organized interests. As in Argentina, the new anti-inflation policy was hatched in secrecy, in a technocratic style similar to the decision-making procedures of the authoritarian regime. Despite this procedural similarity, there were significant differences which gave the new economic policy an altogether non-conservative stance.[17]

The Cruzado Plan confirmed the government's disposition to honour its commitment to pursue stabilization of prices without compromising economic growth. It also indicated that the government had not lost its capacity for defining policies and resolutely putting them into operation. After wavering for a year, the New Republic finally seemed to have begun. Enthusiasm for the shock policy was testified in public opinion polls. One month after, 80 per cent of those interviewed considered the Sarney government 'excellent' or 'good', compared to 33 per cent that had said the same thing three months earlier.[18]

Like the vast majority of the population, the business community's first reaction was to praise the plan. The most influential business organizations gave public support to the stabilization policy, as did individual entrepreneurs, as shown by the opinion polls.[19]

Running against the tide, union leaders at first condemned the stabilization policy. Immediately after it was decreed, the rival labour confederations, CUT and CONCLAT, denounced it as a new form of wage squeeze, warned of its recessive impact and threatened a general strike. Union opposition to the stabilization plan was rooted in political and economic arguments. The former were based on a study by labour's advisory institute DIEESE and emphasized the new policy's negative impact on wages and its recessive consequences for the economy. Political arguments stressed the technocratic and authoritarian decision-making procedures. They also alerted against the wage freeze's demobilizing effect on union struggles.

The unanimity of union positions was soon broken. In the first week, CONCLAT's confrontational stance gave way under the weight of the Cruzado's popular support. When CONCLAT became CGT, in late March, it totally adhered to the Sarney government's stabilization policy. Without retreating from its opposition posture, CUT's leaders were, nevertheless, unable to carry out the proposed general strike against the plan. Protest was reduced to rhetoric. Indeed, while objecting to the economic 'package', they did not fail to support the price freeze. Without saying so, the CUT unionists – like the CGT, political leaders of the government coalition and the entrepreneurs – looked favourably upon the new policy's effects on reactivating economic activity, which soon became apparent. The Cruzado Plan seemed to have buried the conservative idea that the struggle against inflation would require sacrificing economic growth.

Just as CUT's opposition consisted more of words than action, support manifested by business groups and by the CGT did not signify a major commitment to the prevailing stabilization policy. Its initial success was undoubtedly due to the popular support it inspired. But continued price stability depended exclusively on the government's capacity to guarantee that they would remain frozen. The price freeze aggravated conflicts between clients and suppliers. Attempts to get around it characterized business behaviour from the very beginning. Very early on, statements surfaced about the need to limit the period during which prices would remain under government control.[20]

In the same fashion, unions, regardless of their affiliation with CUT or CGT, took advantage of the new opportunities to negotiate better wages. These opportunities arose in the middle of the year, when growing consumption brought about by the plan – and stimulated by generous fiscal and monetary policies – heated up economic activity. Defenders of the freeze on prices but not on wages, unions attempted to wrestle wage increases from businesses working at full steam.

In 1986, there were more than twice as many strikes as in the previous year, in spite of a significantly smaller number of work days lost.[21] Except for the month of March (the first after the freeze), the number of stoppages, month by month, was consistently higher than those registered in 1985. On the other hand, business ceded to the demands more readily when they could discretely get around the freeze and pass at least part of the adjustments on to prices.[22]

The government did not attempt any form of negotiation with organized interests that would have made them share responsibility for the stabilization policy's success. Lulled by the immense popular support the package brought, the government trusted, first, that the pressure of that support would force respect for the freeze and, afterwards, believed in the precarious legal instruments and state organs of control which were hardly up to guaranteeing that thousands of prices would remain frozen.

Moreover, during the first few months of the plan, the government attempted to use the freeze as an awkward exercise in populism. Going over the heads of institutions, parties and interest organizations, the president of the republic seemed to seek confirmation of his political leadership through a direct relationship with the mass of consumers. The way the stabilization policy was administered did not help create active solidarity from organized interests or from individual citizens who benefited from it. Nor was it capable of dealing with accumulating tensions that were beginning to give the first indications of just how precarious victory over inflation was.[23]

In July, the government made its first correction to the course of economic reform. Nicknamed the Cruzadinho[24] (Little Cruzado) plan, its aim was to increase revenue available to the government for investment and slow down aggregate demand. The measures were taken in the midst of secret discussions amongst members of the economic team and against a background of public debate between orthodox economists and those who defended the Cruzado Plan. The Cruzadinho was a reaffirmation of the developmentalist nature of the reform, banking on renewed investments as the solution for its emerging problems and rejecting higher interest rates and fiscal discipline.

Because of the manipulation of the Consumer Price Index (IPC), the unions linked to CUT saw the decreed measures as another form of penalizing the working class. The CGT president criticized a policy that, attempting to contain consumption, was 'based on a recessive philosophy.'[25] Having made their customary statements, unionists from the two confederations continued to seek benefits for their members through strikes and decentralized bargaining.

The business sector received the new measures cautiously and with little confidence, and attempted to negotiate compensation from the government for the sacrifices demanded. From that point on, they began to call on the government more frequently to play its part in the economic stabilization efforts. Statements in favour of containing the public deficit, through administrative reform and privatization multiplied. But as Diniz observes, that was a veiled way of pressuring for the realignment of prices, if not for an end to the freeze.[26]

In spite of business pressure and the now visible distortions the freeze provoked, the government did not consider ending it. The price freeze was transformed from an inflation-fighting measure into the trump electoral card for the PMDB, the majority party in the government coalition, which was disputing state governorships and seats in Congress and state assemblies.

The course of the reform was changed in a brusque and surprising manner with the Cruzado II, decreed one week after the elections, which had delivered an overwhelming victory for the PMDB. The aim was to align some relatively important prices, adjust the notoriously out-of-line exchange rate and partially reintroduce indexation, abolished in February.[27]

Reactions to the measures were immediate and almost totally unfavourable. The press and opposition politicians denounced the 'electoral fraud' committed by the government, which had altered the stabilization policy after using it as a banner in the campaign. Business leaders protested and demanded realignment of all prices.

Unions condemned the increase, manipulation of the price index and changes in the wage trigger. Opposition to the government's policy brought rival unions together, and they jointly called for and launched preparations for a general strike to protest against the measures. Opinion polls showed the populace's dissatisfaction. This materialized dramatically in a large demonstration in Brasília organized by unions and opposition parties, which flared into an open and violent conflict with the military police and the army.

In response, the government promised that subsequent steps in the stabilization policy would be negotiated. Thus, the social pact returned to the political agenda. It was destined to disarm violent reactions to Cruzado II, particularly the general strike engineered by CUT and CGT.

From the beginning, the attempt to re-establish a pact for the solution of the economy's impasses floundered in a sea of uncertainty: in terms of the scope of negotiations and their concrete guidelines, in terms of its interlocutors and their degree of representation; in terms of the government's proposals and orientations. The main problem was to be found within the government itself. Once over the general strike, which was only partial, and with the alarmist expectations of social upheaval defused, the pact was no longer the Sarney government's chosen policy for solving the political and economic dilemmas resulting from the Cruzado Plan.

In late January, when the minister of labour was attempting to put together an accord that would include orderly realignment of prices, some readjustment of wages, a policy for the minimum wage and an acceptable solution for the wage trigger, the minister of finance announced readjustments in the prices of electrical appliances and raw materials of around 25 per cent. Negotiations were broken off. The minister of labour's attempt at a social pact and the Cruzado Plan sank together.[28]

The first half of 1987 was a turbulent period. In February, the country, racked by a deficit in the commercial balance that was rapidly devouring hard currency reserves, declared a moratorium on foreign debt payments. That month, the minister of planning resigned and, in April, the minister of finance was replaced.

A disorganized effort to realign frozen prices pushed inflation upwards.[29] The increase in interest rates, meant to eliminate the threat of hyperinflation, provoked a fall in production and employment levels and stimulated a rush on indexed financial assets. Wages lost their buying power in spite of the trigger which was itself one of the factors that contributed to inflation. The escalation of prices swallowed gains obtained with the Cruzado Plan. Between December 1986 and April 1987, the average real income of workers fell around 30 per cent, dropping back to the same level as before the heterodox shock.[30]

Economic deterioration and the absence of a government policy erased the differences between the principal union groups. They all took up the rhetoric of confrontation and embarked on struggles for indexation, driven by strikes. The volume of work stoppages and work days lost in 1987 was the highest for nine years.[31] The number of strikes doubled in relation to 1986, rising from 1,004 to 2,193, while the number of work days lost increased 2.7 times. The majority of the conflicts (76 per cent) took place during the critical months of the first half year, in the vacuum left by the collapse of the Cruzado Plan.

In the private sector, growth in participation by low wage-earners – building workers and unqualified workers in the service sector – was significant, a reaction that can be explained by the drop in their real income, following the rise induced by the Cruzado.

However, it was the public sector workers, especially those employed by the state, who were most responsible for the growth in strikes. In 1987, the number of strikes in the public sphere was 3.7 times higher than the preceding year. The principal cause of this intense strike activity was the application of the wage trigger to the public sector. In some state-owned companies, the dispute was bitter and the government's reaction was violent.[32]

Strike mobilization in the state sector further strengthened public sector union organization, which was already on the increase, as we have seen. Most public employee unions belonged to CUT, reinforcing that confederation's option for confrontation strategies. For direct administration employees, strikes and confrontation were resources for forcing recognition of social rights denied by law, such as collective contracts, union membership and the very right to strike.

In June, the new minister of finance issued another stabilization plan, which bore his name. The Bresser Plan made use of experience prior to the Cruzado and attempted to combine a freeze on prices, wages and the exchange rate for a pre-set period, rules for later ending the freeze and greater monetary and fiscal discipline.[33] The stabilization policy was to be complemented by mid–term measures summarized in the Macroeconomic Consistency Plan, released one month after the beginning of the freeze. It was intended to untie the knots that prevented the national economy from returning to growth while maintaining price stability.

The proposal was innovative, not so much in its goals, which were basically consensual, but in terms of the proposed means. It abandoned the idea, so dear to the coalition that had made the New Republic possible and to the public at large, that it was possible to gently stabilize prices and recover a form of sustained growth without some type of fiscal adjustment.

The Macroeconomic Consistency Plan rested on two pillars: fiscal adjustment and renegotiating the foreign debt in a way to recuperate conditions for growth with price stability. It proposed a strict monetary policy and reduction of the public deficit by containing expenditures, maintaining real wages at their end-of-the-first-half year levels, a better commercial balance, and higher tax rates in a way that would allow growth in levels of savings and investment.[34]

In spite of the price freeze, Minister Bresser's stabilization policy represented an important rupture with the Cruzado Plan's suppositions and practices, and, consequently, with the developmentalist conceptions that moulded the thinking of the opposition during the military regime, especially the PMDB. The new policy intended to reject 'economic populism', which the minister identified in his predecessor's policy and in his party's ideals.

The Bresser Plan did not spark the same enthusiasm that had surrounded the Cruzado Plan. Polls taken immediately after it was decreed showed that public opinion was divided between caution and pessimism. Forty per cent of those interviewed expected their lives to worsen, 20 per cent imagined that they would improve, while 37 per cent believed that nothing would change.[35] Business leaders, deeply sceptical, gave it reticent support.[36] They hardly welcomed the new freeze and did not trust the government to discipline its own spending.

Debates in the press showed that intellectuals who influenced public opinion were equally divided between meek applause, prudent expectation, and criticism of the new policy's real or supposed recessive and socially regressive effects. The latter group especially reproached the fact that the new plan consecrated wage losses verified in the first half of the year, and aggravated them with a proposed formula for restructuring the wage trigger.[37]

Unanimous and intransigent opposition to the stabilization policy characterized labour's reactions. In unison, labour leaders expressed vehement opposition to the new policy. The CUT and CGT decided to organize a general strike to protest against the Bresser Plan. Successively postponed, the attempt at a general strike made patent the confederations' limited ability to mobilize support for a political act and showed up the fissures between the principal union groups. Finally held in August, its organizers recognized the strike as a failure. Those organizers did not include the followers of the moderate current, *unionism of results*, that had recently been set up in opposition to CUT and distant from the CGT.

The labour movement, represented by the confederations, was unable to combat the stabilization plan through political pressure. However, the unions helped undermine it in the area of collective bargaining, where business leaders were reasonably receptive to its demands. While the confederations were preparing the general strike, there was intense negotiation between business associations and unions about anticipating residuals from the moving scale. They involved important regional business federations – the State of São Paulo Federation of Industries (FIESP), Rio de Janeiro Federation of Industries (FIRJAN), Rio Grande do Sul Federation of Industries (FIERSG) – as well as the principal national federations – National Confederation of Industry (CNI) and National Confederation of Commerce (CNC) – not to mention decentralized negotiations involving factories or specific sectors of production.

In this climate, attempts to create mechanisms for reaching a pact between interested organizations of businessmen and workers – more lasting and independent than the government's – blossomed. These initiatives did not get as far as becoming institutionalized, but the anti-containment consensus – which united business leaders and unionists in opposition to the minister of the economy's efforts to control inflation, which they saw as excessively orthodox – remained alive. In the following months, that consensus bore fruit in labour agreements and collective agreements that assured wage hikes well above those stipulated by government policy. Nor did price increases keep to the limits established by the government during the thawing-out period. Price control was politically complicated and administratively unworkable. Friction between the government and business leaders over prices became more and more frequent.

The private sector was not, however, the only front of resistance to Minister Bresser Pereira's stabilization policy. While unions and businesses negotiated agreements circumventing the official norms, public sector unions confronted the government. In 1987, 59.8 per cent of work stoppages in the public sphere took place after the Bresser Plan was decreed. Many of them were clearly confrontational. Violence marked at least two strikes in public enterprises. Information in Table 6.1 suggests that a significant fall in wages in the public administration in 1987 provided the fuel for exacerbating strike activism.

Strikes in the public sector contributed to imploding the economic team's containment goals and eroding its authority.[38] Pressure to loosen the reins on public spending not only fed labour conflicts in the public area. It was also a constant from state governors in the midst of their own fiscal crises. And it came gushing from congressional representatives with whom the Sarney government attempted to form a majority in Congress in order to guarantee approval of its most cherished projects, among which was the extension of the presidential mandate by another year.

Minister Bresser's last battle was fought when prices began to rise again. It consisted of an attempt to promote a vigorous fiscal adjustment, based on spending cuts obtained by closing public organs and increased revenues through tax reform. It contemplated a tax on capital gains and on net assets. Bureaucratic opposition to the liquidation of public organs, violent reaction by business leaders to tax innovation and the presidency's unwillingness to defend its minister's austerity policy provoked Bresser Pereira's resignation in December.[39] That month, inflation was 14 per cent.

From that point on, the Sarney government abandoned its aspiration to lastingly stabilize prices, even though combatting inflation would continue to dominate presidential rhetoric. The new minister of the economy took office confirming his intention to abandon shock policies, substituting them with daily combat by conventional arms. However, this new orientation did not mean endorsing mid- and long-term pacts with political actors and organized interests. Throughout 1988, the so-called 'rice and beans' policy attempted to administer price increases in order to impede an explosion of hyperinflation. Negotiations, which were multiplying, were always attempts to prevent exorbitant rises in prices or a large-scale labour conflict. At the end of the year, this policy of muddling through revealed its limitations for containing the precipitous price race. Annual inflation was more than 1,000 per cent for the first time in the country's history.

In January 1989, the government once again turned to heterodox shocks, in the form of the Summer Plan. Once again, monetary reform, devaluation, and subsequent freezing of the exchange rate, prices and wages and de-indexation of the economy were used. The government also committed itself to maintaining rigid fiscal discipline, cutting costs through closing public organs and ministries and beginning privatization of a group of public companies in the steel and petrochemical sectors.[40] In practice, the new policy was restricted to monetary reform and an attempt at a wage and price freeze that quickly melted. With the return of inflation, generalized indexation of the economy also reappeared.

In the government's final months, economic policy was once more reduced to the administration of price increases, and the only aim was to avoid hyperinflation. Once more, mechanisms of economic administration were resorted to, the reiterated use of which slowly and inexorably reduced the government's room for manoeuvre: containment of tariffs for public services, delaying paying suppliers, delays in currency exchange, retaining already budgeted moneys, an open-ended moratorium on servicing the foreign debt and, especially, a policy of elevated remuneration of treasury bonds with ever shorter redemption periods, which, in turn, pushed prices upwards.

At the end of the 1980s, the hopes that democracy would soon bring about a return to growth with greater equality had disappeared. The lack of horizons for the future, especially after the Bresser Plan, increased the unions' lack of confidence in the government. It also exacerbated defensive, short-term union conduct, focused almost exclusively on the struggle for the indexation of wages.

In the private sector, strike mobilization revealed a more or less stable pattern in the number of strikes and work days lost: work stoppages tended to be short term, decentralized, quickly leading to negotiations, which were frequently favourable to the workers. Strikers in the private sector, in general, did not have to confront great resistance from management. Businesses absorbed the impact of wage increases, passing them on to prices. This process happened in an evidently uneven fashion, related to each union's bargaining power and the particular sectors' strength in the market.

By the end of the Sarney period, monthly indexation of wages had become a generalized practice, at least in the more solid businesses, and was relatively independent from strike pressure. The understanding between unions and businesses which presupposes a growing spiral of prices is what Maier called a *de facto* – or implicit – inflationary coalition between organized labour and business, in detriment to non-organized labour, those living from rents and small businessmen.[41]

In the public sector, the struggle and, consequently, the intensity of the conflicts, continued to be more intense, judging by the number of working days lost. However, in this case, the exacerbation of inflationary fever also seems to have contributed to a more conciliatory attitude on the part of the government. Figure 6.1 shows the rate of meeting strike demands in the public and private sectors. Even though they also include demands other than wage increases, the results can be taken as a good indicator of wage concessions, given the weight of this type of demand among the motives stated for work stoppages.

Still, the successful struggles for indexation of wages constituted truly Pyrrhic victories. If we return to Table 6.1, we can see that, in 1989, real wages, whether those of private sector or public administration workers, were slightly less than they had been ten years earlier. During the 1980s, workers and unions had run hard to remain in practically the same place. During this time, the Brazilian labour movement's institutional, organizing and political gains had been significant, but material benefits were sparse.

Unions' behaviour remained the same throughout the one-and-a-half years of the Collor administration. Intransigent opposition to government economic policies and efforts to sustain high levels of strike activity especially characterized the CUT unions. The results were not brilliant. At present (March 1992), the union movement seems to have come to a deadlock and to be losing the political grip it had previously gained.

Conclusions

Events during Sarney's term seem to lead to the conclusion that the range of choices available to the Brazilian union movement was indeed very limited.

At first, the adoption of confrontation strategies was closely related to the experience of opposition politics during the lengthy and complex crisis of the authoritarian regime. Since the degree and rhythm of the political opening depended on a complex interplay of pressure by organized social forces and initiatives by the military government, confrontation became not only a recourse for obtaining

Figure 6.1 Rate of Strike Demands Met

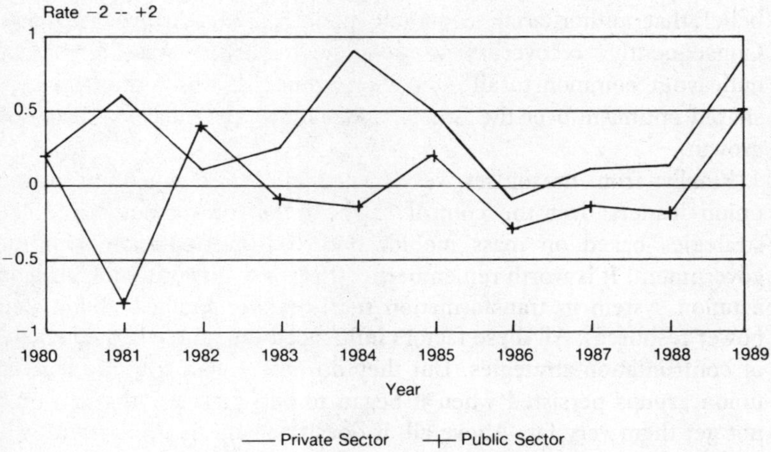

According to Major Sectors, 1978–1988

Source: Eduardo Noronha, NEPP/UNICAMP

Observation: The results of each strike's demands are classified in four groups:

a) Demands totally met
b) Principal demands met
c) Secondary demands met
d) Demands not met

The rate presented here is calculated as follows: The sum of the two times the frequency of 'A' and the frequency of 'B', minus the sum of the frequency of 'C' and two times the frequency of 'D'. This result is then divided by the sum of 'A', 'B', 'C' and 'D'. Therefore, the rate can have a variable from −2.0 to +2.0.

Or rather $R - \frac{(2\ \Sigma^a{}_1\ A - \Sigma^a{}_1\ B) - (\Sigma^a{}_1\ C - 2\ \Sigma^a{}_1\ D)}{\Sigma^a{}_1 - A - B - C - D}$

wage increases, but, above all, a way of imposing recognition of basic civil and union rights.

The choice of confrontation also resulted from the intimate link the larger unions had with a party opposing the first civilian government. New unionism and its most outstanding leaders formed the directive core of the new Worker's Party (Partido dos Trabalhadores) and were the most powerful symbol of its clearly popular character and its rejection of the traditional politics of conciliation among élites.

On the other hand, the opposition's predominant perception of the social consequences of the military government's economic policies justified, to some extent, aggressive union strategies. It was a shared belief that authoritarian economic policies had penalized workers. Consequently, recovering workers' wage losses was a political endeavour common to all opposition groups. It was reinforced by a shared optimism over the Brazilian economy's potential for sustained growth.

Finally, from the outset, very heated internal competition among union leaders over the control of the union movement reinforced strategies based on mass mobilization and confrontation with the government. It is worth remembering that these disputes took place in a union system in transformation that was attempting to build new power resources. All these factors influenced the unions' initial choice of confrontation strategies. But they do not explain why the leading union groups persisted when it began to become clear that it would not get them very far. Above all, it does not help us understand why groups more open to dialogue with the government also failed.

The large body of literature about experiences of high inflation (which some authors prefer to call hyperinflation) identifies one of the consequences as the narrowing of the time span available to the principal actors in the socio-economic arena for decision-making. Business, business associations, unions, consumers and investors all chase after short-term gains, based on their expectations of vast uncertainty and great instability in the future behaviour of prices. Collective behaviour based on such expectations spills over into more or less institutionalized forms of indexation and itself fuels the process of disorderly price increases.

This perverse and persistent dynamic, characteristic of high inflation situations, has been identified with the typical structure of non-cooperative games, whose solution tend to be *sub-optimal*, implying losses for all those involved.[42] Similarly, Franco recognized in the obstacles to price stabilization, the Olsonian problem of collective action to provide public goods.[43] And he pertinently observes that when the economy is more heterogenous, society less organized and a greater number of relevant actors is involved, the tendency towards the non-cooperative behaviour typical of the *free-rider* becomes even more marked. Consequently, when inflation runs out of control in a democratic environment, price stabilization seems to create problems of political co-ordination[44] and requires intervention to broaden the time span for relevant actors and to create incentives for co-operation. These challenges can only be confronted and undertaken by government initiative and presumes that the government has the intention and the capacity for it.[45]

In Brazil, heterodox shock policies were a specific effort to solve problems of economic co-ordination and reverse the expectations about price behaviour that nourished the quest for indexation. They excluded income policy pacts and placed responsibility for the success of stabilization entirely in the government's hands. To this extent, they falsely presumed the government was capable of exerting control over the economic system and its actors.

There is a lot of controversy about the reasons why governments in Latin America resorted to shock policies. At one extreme, Torre attributes them to the 'logic of economic emergency' which makes 'intervention by an agent who quickly and imperatively coordinates the response to the crisis' possible, desired and even desirable.[46] At the other extreme, reflecting on the Argentinian experience, O'Donnell[47] associates them with the more permanent features of an authoritarian political culture, with the illusion of technocratic omnipotence, and with the conception, also authoritarian, of politics as a zero sum game.[48]

The Brazilian experience seems to indicate that there is a grain of truth in these seemingly contradictory explanations. The gravity of the crisis and the urgent need to find a response to it undoubtedly made room for technocratic solutions produced by economists from the academic élite. Their intervention was favoured by political circumstances that seemed to make pacts with political parties and/or organized interests very difficult. Or, at least, that was the dominant perception of the principal actors both within the government and the opposition. Sarney's appeals for a concerted effort, with the poorly disguised intention of buying time, only increased the lack of confidence in the viability of economic policies agreed by the political opposition, the more aggressive labour unions and, indeed, business leaders.

But the shock policies also turned out to be non-viable. In the first place, they presupposed an ability to control the economy which the Brazilian government did not have. Fishlow,[49] reflecting on the experience of the last military government, was the first to call attention to an apparent paradox: the Brazilian state was both big and weak. It participated directly in the economy to a high degree and engaged in extensive regulatory activity, but was not strong enough to promote adjustment to new international economic conditions. It did not have stable control of real resources, was confronted by growing fiscal problems, was losing its ability to reactivate the economy through public investment and was capable of neither controlling nor co-operating with the public sector. Above all, its weakness did not result from lack of political support or legitimacy, as those who opposed the authoritarian regime had supposed. It had a more structural foundation, resulting from the state's own inability to create non-inflationary mechanisms for financing the public sector. The new democratic government inherited a state on the verge of bankruptcy and administrative structures incapable of giving material support to the political authority that the shock policies aimed at reconstructing.

In the second place, by averting the idea of negotiation and exalting the government's interventionist impetus, the shock policies did not inspire mechanisms of commitment to the official initiatives. Instead of creating incentives for co-operation and institutions to help promote it, they permanently encouraged *free rider* behaviour.

Finally, when the initial illusion about the efficiency of shock instruments in achieving lasting stability was dispelled, the government's insistence on this type of policy undermined its authority, corroding the already precarious mechanisms of economic administration, and facilitating the return – with redoubled virulence – of non-cooperative behaviour by individuals and organized interests.[50] At this point, confrontational unionism ceased being a question of choosing from available strategies. It became the only course of action possible, though with decreasing effectiveness.

7· INSTITUTIONAL STRUCTURE AND GOVERNABILITY IN THE 1990s*

Bolivar Lamounier

Introduction

More than just historically correct, it is theologically comforting to admit that Brazil is being punished for old and deep-seated vices. In fact, sin must be atoned for. If in five decades of accelerated industrialization all we managed was to fall back into cartorialism, into inflationary unruliness, and into wealth concentration, we would clearly pay a price sooner or later; and in fact we are paying in the form of economic retrogression, superinflation and the intensification of social conflict. Unfortunately, seen from a politico-institutional viewpoint, our problems are even more severe. If we hope to avoid losing yet another decade, we must examine as of now one more theologically disagreeable possibility, namely, that Brazil may eventually also be punished for its qualities.

This article argues that we have come to the nineties carrying a politico-institutional structure which is full of generous democratic intentions but is probably unsuitable as a solution to the challenges posed by modernization and, moreover, dangerous from the perspective of governability. The institutional model to which I refer combines fragmentation and a multiplicity of counterweights appropriate to the so-called consociational democracies[1] with the somewhat illusory expectation that the resulting blockades can be controlled or neutralized by the plebiscitarian nature of the presidency. It is therefore possible that we may be falling into a dangerous double error. On the one hand, there is the exacerbation of the consociational component in electoral procedures, in party structure, and in the federation. This component, developed originally in the thirties in historically relevant circumstances, has become more accentuated over time by a variety of impulses and even by the unexpected consequences of actions intending to eradicate it. Today, given the structural complexity and the social inequalities of the country, it is more than evident that the high consociational component in the Brazilian institutional organization has surpassed the limits of advisability, stimulating political fragmentation and making broad and stable governmental compositions more difficult.

In Brazil the remedy for the fragmentation of political forces has always been sought in the strengthening of the federal executive power. Since 1930, in both authoritarian and democratic periods, the global decision-making capacity of the system has been defended or restored by means of material and/or symbolic accretions to the presidency. The main ideological inspiration underlying these attempts has been the plebiscitarian presidency: the belief that mass support transforms the republican presidency into a powerful centre of decision-making, capable of constantly and efficiently overcoming the risks inherent in such a fragmented political process. This perception too must be re-examined in the light of certain historical weaknesses of Brazilian presidentialism and the new difficulties generated by recent changes.

Towards a Consociational Democracy?

Most analysts of Brazilian political history would probably react with disbelief at the suggestion that our institutional structure has anything even remotely comparable to that of the so-called consociational democracies. This term, in contemporary political science, usually designates a subgroup of stable democracies in hyper-developed Europe, such as Switzerland, Belgium, and Holland, countries which have both consolidated representative democracy on the macro-political level and offset it with detailed counterweights and rights designed to protect minorities against the majority. It may seem absurd, at first glance, to claim that an institutional structure of this type may have been implanted in a country which, in the last sixty years, has undergone two long dictatorial regimes, in which ethnic and religious claims do not project themselves forcibly on the political arena, and in which the distribution of wealth is notoriously one of the worst in the world. A country, moreover, whose political culture allegedly reflects the sub-political or proto-political authoritarianism of a patriarchal society. Applying the concept of consociational democracy to such a reality is similar to imagining that generous or wisely pluralist institutional qualities could be harvested from a field long fertilized by authoritarianism and social inequity. This, however, is precisely this article's thesis. I will attempt to show that the Brazilian political system, on one of its axes, has become excessively consociational and that, at the same time, there seem not to exist, within the democratic mechanism, adequate counterweights for dealing with the ensuing fragmentation and blockades; and, therefore, that the final result may well be a perverse and unstable polyarchy exhibiting a strong tendency towards ungovernability.

The experience of two authoritarian regimes (the Estado Novo and the military regime emerging from the 1964 coup) and the hypertrophy of the executive still evident today prevented, during various decades, the recognition of an opposite, but no less basic, characteristic of the Brazilian political system: the fact that the backbone of the representative subsystem, under democratic conditions, tends more towards blocking than taking and implementing decisions. The image of the concentration and verticality of power, if not of the truculence emanating from the executive's actions, distinctly contrasts with that obtained from an analysis of the electoral process, party system, the functioning of parliament, the federative structure, the new organization of the judiciary power, of certain governmental councils, and even of the internal structure of some private associations. If one examines these mechanisms individually and in their mutual interrelationship, one perceives clearly that the Brazilian political system is today much closer to the 'consociational' pole than to the 'majoritarian' one, according to Arend Lijphart's terminology (see note 1). That is, it is closer to the understanding of democracy as a system which blocks the power of the majority than to the opposite concept, more concerned with identifying an electorally authorized majority capable of implementing a governing programme.

As mentioned above, the consociational model of democracy configured itself in some small European countries as an institutional response to the division of society along ethnic, linguistic, and religious cleavages. Clearly, then, I am employing the concept of consociational democracy somewhat analogically. It is not a material similarity between the constitutional mechanism of those countries and ours that I speak of, but a similarity in the functioning and aggregate effect of the political-institutional machinery, a similarity more in the 'spirit' than in the form of laws, as Montesquieu would probably have said in this context. With one noted exception – the composition of the Federal Chamber – our political legislation resorts neither to quotas nor to guarantees of representation for specific regions or social groups. *Et pour cause:* while differences and eventual tensions in the relationship between ethnic and religious groups may exist in Brazil, there has not been to the present an explosive projection of cleavages of this type in the political arena warranting special or privileged treatment. The basic divisions of Brazilian society are essentially socio-economic and, to a lesser degree, regional and ideological. Despite this fact, and despite the enormous economic and cultural differences between Brazil and the European countries I referred to, our party-parliamentary sub-system has developed, since the thirties, more in the direction of institutionalizing blockades than of facilitating the aggregation of interests and the implementation of a majority's will.[2]

We must at this point consider a possible objection to my argument, namely, that Brazil's is not a deliberately planned consociational structure but the result of a consociational 'situation', that is, of a momentary dispersion of power resulting from the recently-ended political transition, from the somewhat fluid jurisprudential profile of the 1988 Constitution or still from the present crisis itself, which temporarily dilutes or weakens some of the traditional pillars of power. I will show, however, that the electoral-party sub-system has been evolving in a consociational direction for a longer period. In any case, this hypothetical objection serves only to reinforce the argument I wish to develop. With the existent normative framework, in effect, it will increasingly tend towards producing the effect of multilateral blockade to which the concept of consociational democracy refers. This model, in fact, is characterized by, on the one hand, the low cost of access to party and parliamentary power and, on the other, by the virtual veto power given to minorities – small parties and ethnic, religious or linguistic minorities – with the explicit intent of preventing majority groupings from dominating through sheer number.

If my assessment is correct, we will sooner or later have to inquire whether a structure which induces fragmentation and blockage is suitable for a society lacking the cleavages characteristic of the European consociational democracies, which need to ensure a high level of productivity in decision-making and which would scarcely be able to do so through a plebiscitarian presidency. Generically considered, our risk is that the institutional organization which began to assume definite form with the 1988 Constitution leads us to a perverse polyarchy, with a multiplicity of poles which mutually annul one another or which markedly increase the cost of decision-making. This does not mean, naturally, that we should go to the opposite pole ('majoritarian' according to the terminology I am employing). To attempt to revert the pluralism existent today by means of an imposed dual-party system or other such means, as did the recent military regime, is not only authoritarian but non-viable and naïve.

Let us emphasize the differences between the consociational and majoritarian models, understood here as global and contrasting models ('ideal types') of democratic organization. In the classic model of majoritarian democracy, Great Britain, the basic rule is that the elected majority governs while the minority forms an opposition. That is, the minority vote is temporarily neutralized as far as participation in government and decision implementation is concerned. The electoral system (districtal and majoritarian) permits the polarization between majority and minority within the area of each district. The party structure, essentially bipolar, reinforces the polarizing effects of the electoral system. By controlling parliament, the victorious party controls the cabinet, and is consequently responsible for all or almost all ministries and important executive posts. Parliament's sovereignty is virtually unopposed, be it on account of the judiciary's weak revisional role or the fact that it is not limited by a written, rigid and detailed constitution. The generic character of the constitutional precedents makes up for the eventual exiguity of the governing majority, avoiding political wear and tear in the search for a qualified quorum to support difficult and frequent constitutional reforms. Clearly, each step up this ladder of authorizations signals the formation of a potentially broader authority. With respect to the British model one must also consider the unitary character of the state. Although existing subnational distinctions are important, central power is not formally submitted to the blockages proceeding from the political, administrative, and financial autonomy of federal states.

The British institutional mechanism combines 'majoritarism' (again according to Lijphart) with a parliamentary system of government, but the vertical concentration of power to which we have already alluded occurs more easily in presidential systems if the majoritarian ingredients are well configured. Argentina, for instance, has a dual-party system even though some of the provinces exhibit multi-party features; parliamentary elections occur with rigid lists tied to the opposing presidential candidacies; presidential prerogatives include the nomination of such important figures as the mayor of Buenos Aires; the judiciary is incomparably weaker than the Brazilian in its role of checking the executive; and, given its evident archaism, the operative constitution, dating from 1853, lacks normative force in crucial points. Within such an institutional structure the president can at times correspond to the expectations of a plebiscitarian doctrine, accelerating structural reforms and giving coherence to the whole system; but his contribution to an effectively democratic inter-institutional relationship depends largely on the objectives and tendencies of the incumbent and the group surrounding him at the apex of power. In Great Britain, as in presidentialist Argentina, parliament and the resulting cabinet are invested with a theoretically extensive mandate, converted or not into unilateral power according to circumstances, the specific character of the leaders and of the dominant coalition, the expectations of public opinion, and society's capacity for resistance.

In the consociational model, on the other hand, democracy is understood as a means of safeguarding the minority from being completely excluded from power; of making certain that it will always be represented in the governing coalition and that it will have effective veto power over a wide range of decisions, starting with those basic cleavages which themselves gave rise to this model. It is, therefore, an institutional model which seeks above all to prevent the indiscriminate application of majority rule throughout the system, from the heights of national legislation to specific administrative areas. The Swiss Federal Council, the executive power of that nation, necessarily multi-party in its composition, is a distinct example of the apportionment of power at the highest level; the Belgian requirement that even the lowest-level public servants be bilingual is another on the other end of administrative implementation.

It is not difficult to understand the preference for this model of democracy in pluralist societies, where ethnic, religious, or linguistic groups coexist in permanent tension; or, for that matter, in situations such as those existing in the former Soviet Union, in Czechoslovakia, in Yugoslavia or in South Africa, where national survival depends on reducing the conflict between groups which constitute real subsocieties. Yet it is not always the case that typically consociational models are always adopted by countries marked by strong internal cleavages. After independence, India, exceedingly fragmented in all these senses, chose an institutional model characterized by very definite majority components (a conscious decision reached after explicit rejection of consociational proposals, such as that of multi-ethnic executives inspired by the Swiss model).[3]

In Brazil, on the contrary, the institutional model built since 1930 contains strong consociational elements despite the fact that cleavages of this type are recognizedly of little importance. Among the main pillars of this model are proportional representation; a multi-party system from which ministries are selected; the federative regime, a bi-cameral system in which both houses of Congress are strong, and a rigid and detailed constitution. Detailed examination of each of these mechanisms would reveal that the evolution of some of these have extended the consociational principle by facilitating minority access to important power resources. Our pluri-party system, for example, combines an extreme easiness of party formation with an almost automatic concession of access to national channels of radio and television. Moreover, dating from the 1988 Constitution, parliamentary representatives may legitimately and directly file claims of unconstitutionality in the Supreme Federal Court. As concerns the electoral system, a model based on the principle of proportionality was partially implanted by the 1932 Code and improved in 1950. Although the mathematical results are only imperfectly proportional, benefiting the larger parties, it is also true that the weakening of this key element of the consociational model is in part counterbalanced by another: the enormous amount of power which the smaller states hold in Congress. This is an issue which gives rise to frequent misconceptions in the present institutional debate. Those who criticize the over-representation of the smaller states in Congress on the principle of 'one man, one vote' frequently forget that this distortion was legally constituted in the thirties as a reaction against the situation in the First Republic, when the two largest states, São Paulo and Minas Gerais, in effect controlled the whole country. Despite evident casuist manipulations and the alleged ideological archaism of this favouring of the smaller states, it was originally a means of attenuating the economic power and electoral strength of the large states; an explicit reinforcement, therefore, to the consociational model already underlying federative organization.[4]

In the preceding paragraphs I have not only compared the majoritarian and consociational models as 'ideal types,' but have also argued that Brazil's institutional development in the last 60 years seems to have consolidated an important consociational mechanism within the larger political system. The Constitutional Congress of 1987–8 both incorporated some older elements of this mechanism and introduced new ones. Inter-parliamentary relations frequently have connotations of this type, in any country, due to the rules of coexistence and the internal organization of legislative proceedings. It is important to note, however, that our Constitutional Congress, perhaps because of the special circumstances in which it met – after 21 years of military regime when most political leaders still felt manifestly insecure as to their own legitimacy – unequivocally reinforced the consociational 'style'. This fact was evident from the beginning in the extremely decentralized and participatory character of the process of constitution-writing, a fact without parallel in recent history.[5] This tendency was visible, however, in the style of inter-parliamentary relations itself. Under the banner of 'transition', of the spirit of the Constitutional Congress and the wish to maximize the legitimacy of the new constitution, Congress, informally and most probably unconsciously, mapped what could be termed a parity model of representation in which the personal authority of a member or the special representativeness of a position sometimes took precedence over the number of votes which could theoretically be mobilized for the opposing interest. We can thus understand, on the basis of this inter-parliamentary process, why the Constitutional Congress chose to strengthen the consociational character of the system while discarding a more minute analysis of its global impact.

From the Original Tripod to the 1988 Constitution

If it is true that we have evolved towards consociationalism, how did this occur? What is this model's origin? To what other elements, some eventually contradictory, is it associated? Very simply, one can affirm that the model which has been consolidated in the last 60 years has three distinct components. Although elaborated at more or less the same time, as from the revolution of 1930, each resulted from an independent and quite specific political and ideological setting. The first, which we will not discuss extensively in this article, was corporatism, designed to annul the conflict between capital and labour in the competitive political arena by imposing a compulsory format for interest representation subject to strong administrative controls. This first element developed, it is known, under the influence of ideologies connected to protofascism and the doctrinaire ideal of a 'third way' between capitalism and socialism.[6]

The second element was the consociational accommodation imprinted on the representative sub-system, that is, on the group of provisions relating to the electoral process, the political parties, the internal structure of the legislative, and the federation. The ideological underpinning was essentially liberal. Despite its roots in the *castilhismo* of Rio Grande do Sul and a shared rhetoric of the 'strong state', the 1930 revolution brought also to power some important liberal dissidents, starting with those from Rio Grande do Sul whose origins went back to the old Federalist party. In other states, notably São Paulo, a rapid radicalization of the political élites, frightened by the 'permanent revolution', occurred to counter the centralizing trend of the new governing coalition. To this one must add the practical force of demands for electoral reform which accumulated during the Old Republic and spread to larger social segments.[7]

The third element was developed *pari passu* with the growing personal power of Getúlio Vargas and probably owes more to his personality and style than to explicit juridical concepts or ideological inspirations: the transformation of the oligarchical presidency of the Old Republic into the plebiscitarian presidency we know today. The latter developed gradually as the presidency became a focal point for a national constituency, that is, a more numerous and anonymous electoral mass. In the Old Republic the presidency was little more than an extension of regional oligarchies. After 1930 it underwent a significant broadening of its independence from these traditional bases of power as the executive began to demand a legitimacy which was both distinct from and superior to that of the legislative and the judiciary, calling upon the plebiscitarian foundation which was slowly taking shape.[8]

In the sphere of politico-electoral legislation, the consociational tendency manifested itself soon after the revolution of 1930 in deliberate and explicit fashion. This decision reflected itself mostly in the inclusion of Assis Brasil (a representative of the Rio Grande do Sul opposition) into the ministry and specifically into the commission responsible for drawing up an electoral code. Although historiography emphasizes the small number and mental narrowness of the traditional political élite and the way authoritarian sectors mimicked fascism, the fact is that, from the beginning, the objective of the new politico-electoral legislation was to bury the state parties of the Old Republic, by undermining their bases of governing power and by creating conditions for the peaceful exercise of opposition. Whole libraries have been written about the restrictive and oligarchical character of that political system but most studies have minimized or completely ignored the Electoral Code of 1932. It has not been recognized that it was precisely this fact which made the increasingly consociational formation of the representative sub-system possible. Up until then electoral practices had been notoriously fraudulent and only a very small portion of the population voted, even in presidential elections. Whether or not we use the apparently archaic and élitist term 'conciliation', it was only after this initial milestone that a modern institutional construction was able to develop with reasonable coherence. Even admitting that the chief objective of the 1932 Code was to enable subgroups of the political élites of the period to coexist in legislative chambers and party leadership, the fact is that from this time the representative sub-system began to be bounded by clear pluralist mechanisms and intentions. The accommodation of these micro-interests was as or more important to the preservation of national unity than the centralist fixation because it was necessary for the pacification of conflicts within the élite itself. This consociational embryo permitted the development in Brazil of what Robert Dahl has called 'peaceful contestation' – even at a moment when totalitarian clouds were gathering on the horizon.

The establishment of the Estado Novo did not fall specifically upon the consociational embryo mentioned above, but upon the whole of the representative mechanism whose operation was suspended at the three levels of government. As far as the redemocratization in 1945 and the institutional reforms of the following years are concerned, Brazilian historiography tends to underscore the 'inauthenticity' of the new pluralism and ignore or minimize democratic or consociational advances. In this sense, it emphasizes the persistence of *coronelismo* in the interior of the country, the exclusion of Marxist parties and the denial of the right to vote to the illiterate, all of which remained in effect until the 'New Republic'. In retrospect, however, one can see that these restrictions did not annul the general trend previously delineated, one which was increasingly democratic and embryonically consociational.

The liberal and minority oppositions in the thirties wished to avoid *governismo* and the uni-party regime of the Old Republic – thus the demands for electoral reform. The post-Estado Novo period was a dictatorial development along the lines of Getúlio Vargas – which explains the insistence on a short presidential mandate, on non-reelection and on state autonomy to counter the central power. In the 1980s, one must add a three-fold rejection: of the recently-ended military regime, of the compulsory two-party system, and of electoral casuistry. One must also consider the vital impulse represented by the enormous expansion of the electorate (from 16 to 85 million between 1960 and 1985), and the broadening of participation and pluralism at the very base of society, a result of resistance to the military regime and of national and international behavioural changes. Consequently, the doctrinaire input brought to the Constitutional Congress of 1987–8 by politicians and opinion-makers was founded on unequivocally consociational premises. That which stimulated pluralism and diluted power was seen to be intrinsically good; that which contradicted this trend was deemed 'authoritarian debris'. All cautionary reflections on party volatility went into the category of 'debris', as did the need to stimulate a more ample aggregation of political interests and the need to make the choices clearer in order to reduce information costs for the individual voter. In other words, the predominating climate of opinion, before and during the Constitutional Congress, was abstractly doctrinaire. There was greater evaluation of the abstractly democratic character (or not) of each proposal, considered in isolated form, than of the trade-offs implicit in the institutional mechanism.

With respect to political parties, there was a further crystallization of the old assumption that the Brazilian problem lay in the 'artificiality' of the associations. There were, the assumption meant, highly relevant social and/or ideological differences, but these were latent and repressed and could only manifest themselves with totally permissive electoral and party regulations. Instead of limiting the access of inexpressive parties to Congress by means of percentage barriers, a diametrically opposite course was advocated; namely, that the formation of new parties and their access to representation should be encouraged and that the political market would, on its own, select the survivors. The very fact that it was a political transition – some argued, perhaps with some grounds for reason – meant that it would be wise to adopt more flexible rules so that no one sector alone would be tempted to contest the legitimacy of the new democracy. Thus, the reforms of the 1980s and of the Constitution of 1988 took the consociational model to its final consequences. Without going into the question of the merits or demerits of Collor de Mello's government, only in the light of the above can one understand how a candidate, launched by a party set up only a few months prior to the elections and counting on no more than 3 per cent of Congressional support on the eve of inauguration, could come to power.

There are two moments in the 1945–64 period (sometimes called 'populist democracy') which are especially important for comprehending the excessive consociational trend in Brazil. The first was the failure to implement voting in blocked lists (that is, previously prepared order of party list), despite the provision in Decree 8.566 of January 1946 which regulated the 1947 elections. According to Costa Porto, 'for the first time the proportional list system was going to be used in Brazil, as in other countries, with plurinominal choice and the voter accepting a list prepared by the party'.[9] The rejection of this provision at a critical moment for the organization of a modern party system gave rise to the belief that choosing an individual from a party list, in a proportional regime, was, if not perfection itself, the only true democratic practice. Almost 50 years later, any change in this system is generally perceived as an attempt to curtail the voter's freedom of choice. The fact is, however, that the so-called blocked list is accepted in practically all democracies which adopt the proportional system. If in some Latin American countries dissatisfied sectors question it as an instrument of 'partycracy' (as, for example, in Venezuela and Argentina), it is because blocked lists decisively contributed to the consolidation of present-day party structures. We come to the 1990s with half a century of practice in the preferential (individual) vote, a fact which by itself determines high inter-party individualism in Brazil. More serious, however, is the fact that this mechanism pulverizes parties internally within a party framework which is itself fluid in its borders as a result of the permissiveness of laws concerning the formation of new parties, the ease with which members can switch from one party to another, the ease of electoral coalitions, the speed with which new members can rise to superior legislative functions and the accessibility of means of communication.

Another crucial moment in the exacerbation of the consociational trend came, paradoxically, in 1965 with the extinction of the existent multi-party system and the imposition of a dual-party system by the military regime. Although the essence of the consociational model to which we refer had already been established between 1945 and 1964, its fragmentary effects were attenuated by a still modest level of urbanization and of political mobilization and by a reasonably strong party structure which seemed at the time to be in the process of consolidation. The extinction of this system by decree, in 1965, could be compared to an ecological disaster in that it eliminated the associations which, for better or worse, ensured a precarious balance without replacing them with any another reasonable viable system. Without mentioning the irrealism of attempting to create a stable dual-party system by authoritarian decree, the text of Complementary Act No. 4 itself reveals the nascent military regime's hesitancy as to the route to follow, for it spoke of replacing the 13 then-existing parties with two 'temporary organizations' and not of an explicit intention of restructuring the political system along a bi-polar model. For 15 years, up until 1979, party diversity was reduced by the combined effect of the exile of many leaders, of the coexistence of conflicting groups under the shield of sub-parties, and later, in the phase of 'opening,' by the plebiscitarian character of the confrontation between government and opposition.[10]

With the return to democracy, the promulgation of the new constitution and the presidential election of 1989, we evidently face serious party fragmentation. Under the combined effect of the suppression of pre-1964 parties, the permissiveness of party legislation, the increment of social diversity and the corporative interest lobby, Congress is undoubtedly practising a conceptually perfect consociationalism, the essence of which is the coexistence of multiple fragilities.[11]

How could one, at the apex of the political system, reconcile or reunify this party and parliamentary base which suffers continuous fragmentation from the diverse social interests, from corporatism and from a legislative which is exaggeratedly consociational? Where can one find the leadership and the power resources capable of lending coherence to this diverse group with so many entry points and independent focuses of power? Until recently, the answers to these questions were sought in generic sociological and cultural categories rather than in politico-institutional factors. At times it was proposed that unity would be supplied, for better or worse, by society's structure itself – that is, by the 'natural' or 'historically' congruent character of hegemonic interests; at other times, the opposite was said, that political stability was necessarily illusory in a country subject to clear 'hegemony crises'. In both cases, the institutional structure was merely an irrelevant formalism. The conflictive diversity of the political system was either illusory (a matter of appearances in a society which, in its essence, was effectively controlled by hegemonic interests) or incapable of being channelled through institutional engineering. Again, in both cases, the economic structure would automatically establish a possible and necessary level of political reconciliation by different means: by *patrimonialista* co-optation, by the converging actions of a dominant class around common interests, by, finally, the depoliticization or behavioural deference of the oppressed. Whatever the merits of these interpretations with respect to the first decades of this century, it is evident today that they were less useful after 1930 and even less so after the 1950s when industrialization and urbanization accelerated in Brazil. It was at that time that a certain politico-institutional hypothesis began taking shape: the belief that a plebiscitarian presidency could be the great unifying force, the alfa and the omega of the political system.

The Plebiscitarian Presidency

The plebiscitarian radicalization of presidentialism occurred after the revolution of 1930 and, specifically after 1935, when repression of the *Integralista* and communist movements created the conditions for the expansion of Getúlio Vargas' personal power. The utopia of plebiscitarian presidentialism was thus progressively created: the belief in the unifying power of an institutional charisma, the president of the republic. Elected by direct vote, representing the great national constituency, possessing privileged access to the means of communication and charged with a highly symbolic centrality, the presidency can impress a coherence on the political system, a coherence which would otherwise be unattainable.

Clearly, a plebiscitarian element exists in North American presidentialism and even in parliamentary regimes, albeit in a less virulent form, personified in these cases by the leader of the victorious party who becomes a natural candidate for head of government. In Brazil, and perhaps throughout Latin America, the plebiscitarian doctrine is more radical. The president of the republic is viewed as a great stabilizer, the powerful force which could deter and discipline particularities; and simultaneously as the constructive de-stabilizer, pointing out directions and dictating the rhythm of great social reforms, overcoming resistances and mobilizing the necessary support for the consolidation of these advances. In this conception of authority lies the presidentialist proposal of a solution to what is Brazil's most evident institutional dilemma: how to reconcile respect for the rules of democracy, the balance between powers, and the necessary decision-making efficacy with the very high probability that presidents, within this reigning consociational poliarchy, will almost always be in a position of parliamentary minority? How can one avoid, in a media-intensive society such as ours, in a party system without stable contours and with internal divisions, that freelancers gain decisive advantages in presidential elections, with or without double-balloting?

The belief in the presidency as a unifying and stabilizing force is not altogether far-fetched in presidential regimes which drastically reduce the consociational component of the institutional system. On this point one is reminded of Venezuela, where the party system is clearly bi-polar and where the election of congressmen, occurring simultaneously with that of the president, is based upon hierarchical party lists and excludes the voter's choice of individual candidates; or of Argentina, where the provincial multi-party system is clearly subordinated to the bi-polarity of *peronistas* and radicals on the national level and where voting in blocked party lists also predominates. A detailed comparison of Argentina and Brazil would show not only that the former tends clearly towards a 'majoritarian' pole but also that a greater integration of the political process available by this means is counterbalanced by a high potential of confrontation between the two main political forces.

In such clearly bi-polar situations the gains in decision-making effectiveness are offset by a greater risk to democratic stability as a result of face-to-face antagonism and its association with the zero-sum game characteristic of presidential elections in a presidentialist regime; contrarily, in Brazil, following my proposed interpretation, the risk stems rather from the president's parliamentary anaemia and ineffective decision-making. For the Scylla of face-to-face antagonism corresponds the Charybdis of consociational fragmentation.

More than 60 years after the revolution of 1930 and after a first test of the double-balloting mechanism established by the 1988 Constitution, we possess some important elements for examining the unifying potential of the plebiscitarian presidency. It is true that the existence of authoritarian sub-periods prevents our considering these 60 years as a unity. In any event, the first comment to make is that a primary requisite of this supposed stabilizing leadership is lacking in that the presidents themselves lack stability. Among the popularly-elected presidents of the period, only two – Dutra and Kubitschek – concluded their terms of office. One could also evaluate, indirectly, the plebiscitarian capital and the authority exercised by the presidents during their mandates on the basis of the influence they exerted over their own succession. Considering all the presidents from 1930 until today, including the military, everything indicates that only one, General Ernesto Geisel, significantly influenced the choice of his successor. The image of a safe and exemplary magistrate cultivated by a certain presidentialist ideal vanishes when considered in this light, leaving in its place the lame duck of North American political folklore. In fact, if presidents had little or no influence on their succession, even in the recent military period, it seems unreasonable to suppose that they would exercise a continuous and broad influence over the political system during their mandate, as the theory of plebiscitarian presidentialism presupposes.

Another suggestive angle for the examination of the plebiscitarian capital of presidents is offered by public opinion polls, whether of élites or of the masses. If presidents effectively dispose of power resources and symbolic capacity as this vision of authority implies, this potential should find correspondence of some sort in indexes of popular approval of their performance. One should approach this type of evaluation with caution given the strong dependence of poll results on economic conditions and inflationary fluctuations; on the other hand, this idea sustains our argument, which tries to demonstrate the vulnerability of presidentialism in these circumstances. If a context of economic adversity strongly affects indicators of presidential unpopularity, then we should urgently emphasize the risk of institutional instability that this type of authority erosion presents to democracy.[12]

One of the approaches to this problem, in the methodology of public opinion polls, consists in asking citizens which political leaders they 'most admire' and which were, in their view, 'the best presidents'. This question was asked by IBOPE to a national sample in 1989 at the beginning of the presidential campaign. Spontaneously answered, 'the most admired' leaders were Getúlio Vargas (16 per cent), Tancredo Neves (13 per cent), and Juscelino Kubitschek (8 per cent). Not only the fact that the three were dead but also the modesty and dispersion of the numbers suggest that the plebiscitarian connections may well be more tenuous than generally thought. In the induced question about the 'best presidents,' again Getúlio Vargas was in first place with 33 per cent, followed by Juscelino Kubitschek with 17 per cent and João Figueiredo with 11 per cent.

If this data suggests a probable insufficiency of positive feeling, the indexes of (non) confidence in President Sarney in the last year of his mandate indicate the risks of instability which can arise from negative feelings. IBOPE polls, in effect, demonstrated a stabilization of the levels of confidence in the president, during the year of 1989, at a dramatically low level: between 20 and 30 per cent in the total sample and between 10 and 20 per cent of those interviewed receiving an income higher than ten monthly minimum salaries. The numbers referring to Sarney's performance as president were even more perturbing. Those who believed he was excellent or good amounted to 16 per cent in February/March 1988 but were reduced to 8 per cent on the eve of the 1989 presidential elections; among the high-income interviewees these numbers were 12 per cent and 4 per cent respectively. In other words, Sarney's presidency met an agonizing end as regards prestige and popular approval. This fact is undoubtedly well-known and is mentioned here only in order to counter the underlying belief in the assured security of the plebiscitarian presidentialist premise.

It is true that the failures of Sarney's economic policies after the Cruzado Plan weighed on his presidency, but there was also the added weight of reservations concerning his form of inauguration (he was elected through an Electoral College as the vice-president of Tancredo Neves) and his political origins. President Fernando Collor's situation is rather different. Elected by direct vote with an absolute majority as a result of the implementation of the double-ballot system, the erosion of his prestige in the first two years of his mandate was a direct reflection of the economic situation, that is, of the continued inflationary process and of the high social cost of measures taken to stabilize the country. Without discarding the hypothesis of an eventual recovery, my argument is that a fully democratic inauguration, such as that assured by the election of 1989, would not prevent the president, during a good part of his term, from losing plebiscitarian support.

Although officially denied, the executive's popularity is an important political resource in any country and in any government system. It indicates the degree to which members of Congress, on the basis of their support for government programmes, can feel favoured or damaged in their efforts to be re-elected. Coming to power as a freelancer, with little experience and practically no support in Congress, Fernando Collor knew from the beginning that he needed popularity and sought it assiduously through his recognized communication skills. Despite this, his popularity suffered a speedy decline. A poll made by IDESP between September and November 1991 showed that the erosion of his credibility with respect to Congress was even greater than the decline of his popular support. Only 6 per cent of the 406 interviewees (federal deputies and senators) described his government as 'excellent' or 'good'. As a corollary, most were sceptical as to the chances of success of some hypothetical initiatives which the president might take in order to overcome the crisis. At the beginning of 1990 Congress was isolated by Collor's electoral victory, by the imminence of hyperinflation (leading public opinion to demand drastic action), and possibly by the tempestuous style of the president himself. Eighteen months later our research verified that only a handful of congressmen saw any chances of success in a hypothetical attempt to mobilize public support in order to obtain greater collaboration from Congress. As shown in Table 7.1, positive evaluation of this hypothesis was under 50 per cent even among the governing parties (PRN, PFL and PTB). In other words, the president's plebiscitarian capital was no longer considered a relevant factor in overcoming the impasse between the executive and the legislative. This data only confirms directly what could otherwise have been deduced by the data customarily collected from the public by specialized institutes.

Conclusion

The problem, of course, is that in a presidentialist regime there are no institutional incentives for the formation of a viable parliamentary base (a stable majority, or at least a substantial minority to which other supports can be added at a reasonable political cost). This base can exist or not depending on various factors, such as the greater or lesser fragmentation of the party system and the intensity and duration of the president's eventual erosion of credibility with respect to public opinion. Since there is a fusion between the heads of government and of state, there is also the likelihood that the negative incidence of these factors may compromise decision-making effectiveness and endanger the stability of the democratic system. As I have argued throughout, these risks are augmented in the Brazilian case by the precarious and contradictory combination upon which our institu-

Table 7.1 Congress's Evaluation of Hypothetical Political Initiatives which the President Could Take in order to Overcome Crisis (*)

Initiatives	Total	PMDB	PFL	PDT	PDS	PRN	PSDB	PTB	PT	Others
Social Pact	62	57	78	68	79	71	69	66	20	49
Coalition Government	52	43	56	41	45	67	51	79	47	51
Anticipated Plebiscite	52	61	51	29	69	29	81	51	40	42
Government of National Unity	44	42	61	26	26	57	45	63	10	51
Popular Mobilization for obtaining support from Congress	25	17	46	19	21	48	9	41	6	26

Source: Poll conducted by IDESP in the National Congress between September and November 1991 (406 interviews with federal deputies and senators).

(*) The percentual points in the table refer to those who believed that the political initiatives, if taken by the president, would have 'some' or 'much' chance or would 'almost certainly' be successful.

tional structure is based: on the one hand, the excessive consociational character of the representative sub-system, comprising the electoral process, the party structure, certain aspects of the internal organization of Congress and the existent federative organization; on the other, presidentialism, and chiefly the perception of plebiscitarian support as a rotative capital of authority to which the president can resort at any time.

The election of Fernando Collor has taught two important institutional lessons. The first is that the risks inherent in the fragmentation of the party system do not refer to the inter-parliamentary process alone. With easy access to the means of communication, individuals or parties lacking parliamentary ballast can be hoisted to the republican presidency. In this hypothesis, only those presidents endowed with extraordinary personal qualities can exert the necessary influence to overcome the impasses resulting from a fragmented legislative, which in effect is only the tip of the great consociational iceberg. The second lesson is that two-round elections are a far from adequate solution to the problem. The mistake, in this case, is the intention of restoring central decision-making capacity to a fragmented political system through renewed investment in plebiscitarian capital. If the problem is an exacerbated consociationalism, reconstruction must be more encompassing and gradual. The introduction of strong plebiscitarian elements would produce tremors and would give rise to anxieties, but it would not alter the reality of the problem. The last sixty years' experience and the singularity of Brazil within Latin America suggest that Brazilian presidentialism could scarcely be reformed in this way. At least in this first experience it seems evident that the resentments resulting from the two-round elections lasted longer and affected political compositions to a greater degree than the subsequent increase in plebiscitarian capital.

If the institutional reform of the coming years is to be fruitful, it is necessary to consider as of now the fact that the alternative is not merely a matter of choice between the present system and an abstractly conceived parliamentarism. Whatever the result of the plebiscite expected to be held in 1993, the questions which must be answered refer, firstly, to the practical model of parliamentarism or presidentialism, and secondly to the desirable or necessary degree of consociationalism in a country such as Brazil. Among the four possible combinations between presidentialism/parliamentarism and consociationalism/majoritarism, there is no doubt that, in respect of governability, ours is the worst. In this case, if presidentialism is chosen, subsequent reform of electoral and party laws would be essential to reduce the consociational component in the system. In this hypothesis, our development would be similar to that of Argentina or Venezuela. If parliamentarism is chosen, party fragmentation in Congress would have to be compensated for in the short term by specific rules, particularly the motion of constructive censorship (article 67 of the German Constitution and article 113 in that of Spain); that is, the requirement that, in the same act of disavowing one government, the legislative immediately approve another by absolute majority. The revision of the current electoral system and an adaptation of the German model should both be equally examined, whatever the choice of system of government. Parliamentarism does not necessarily require the implantation of a pure districtal system (majoritarian/uninominal), but it would probably be more difficult in the present proportional system.

Although legal reforms are important, a great deal more is necessary for rebalancing the Brazilian institutional structure. A new party structure may develop from the present one, moulded by the great economic and institutional debate now being held in the country. Along the economic axis this debate is centred around the redefinition of the public sector, that is, the magnitude and composition of entrepreneurial presence in the state as well as the scope and *modus operandi* of its social policies; along the political axis, the core of concern is to define the institutional identity of the country on the basis of a definite choice of government system. In the medium term, everything indicates that ideological and power coalitions resulting from these choices will be highly relevant.

8· CONSOLIDATION OF DEMOCRACY:

Governability and Political Parties in Brazil*

Maria D'Alva G. Kinzo

Introduction

One of Brazil's greatest challenges in the present decade is consolidating democracy in the face of the current social and economic crisis. Since the onset of civilian rule in 1985, governability has represented the main crisis for Brazil's new democracy. While it is not a crisis emerging with democratization – the state's capacity to govern had actually been deteriorating since General Figueiredo's government – it certainly worsened after the re-establishment of democratic politics. Democratization was bound to lead to an intensification of pressures caused by the increase in social and political demands, coupled with discontent arising from the accumulation of unresolved problems.[1]

Policy ineffectiveness is the manifestation of this crisis. However, its hidden face lies in the political actors' enduring incapacity to reach a basic consensus capable of accommodating the diverse interests of Brazilian society, as illustrated by the government's unsuccessful attempts to promote a social pact. The problem seems to be related, to a large extent, to the absence of arenas for effective political negotiation against the growing disjunction between the main economic actors and the government embodied in the executive, and between those entities and the parties represented in the legislative.[2]

Consequently the political system (the state structure in particular) has become incapable of reacting effectively to a crisis which is mainly political. In this sense, the question of the state's capacity to govern, that of creating conditions for governability, is largely related to the country's ability to strengthen its democratic institutions. This applies in particular to the parliamentary arena and political parties, institutions that are supposed to function as locus for political negotiation and mechanisms of consensus-building.

Due to the importance of political parties as intermediary institutions between the state and society – and hence as mechanisms facilitating the accommodation of social demands – this article concentrates on the problematic state of the party system in Brazil, questioning the political parties' role (if there is one) in creating the conditions for governability and consolidation of democracy.

Political Parties in Brazil

Instability, fragility, fragmentation, non-differentiation, lack of cohesiveness and representativeness, are the words commonly used to depict Brazilian political parties. In fact, Brazil is one of the rare cases of democratic transition where the party framework which emerged with the end of military rule retained little trace of the previous democratic party system. At the same time, the new party system has yet to be effectively consolidated. What has prevailed is an unsettled and unstable situation marked by party dissensions, often leading to splits and the creation of new parties. Changes in party affiliation in Congress have been so frequent that an accurate picture of party representation in the legislature is almost impossible. A brief look at party composition in the National Congress in the last seven years clearly indicates the transitional character of party politics since the inauguration of the New Republic. As Table 8.1 illustrates, party representation has been altered every year, even though legislative elections took place only twice during this period. Also remarkable is the growing fragmentation in the party system. Between 1985 and 1991, there was a considerable increase in the number of parties not only sitting in Congress but also having at least a 5 per cent share of the seats.

Thus, any analysis of the state of the party system in Brazil would firstly be concerned with its weakness, fragmentation and instability, particularly when the intention is to assess its role within government politics. It would also be concerned with the other recurrent criticism levelled at the parties: their lack of cohesion and representativeness and consequently the absence of linkage with society. It is generally accepted that political parties are channels whereby demands from

Figure 8.1 Political parties in Brazil

Parties supporting the Government:

PDS (1966)	–	Social Democratic Party (ex-ARENA, ex-pro-military government)
PFL (1984)	–	Party of the Liberal Front (PDS dissidence)
PTB (1980)	–	Brazilian Labour Party
PRN (1989)	–	Party for the National Reconstruction
PDC (1985)	–	Christian Democratic Party
PL (1986)	–	Liberal Party
PSC (1986)	–	Social Christian Party
PST (1989)	–	Social Labour Party
PTR (1989)	–	Renovating Labour Party
PSD (1989)	–	Democratic Social Party
PRS (1990)	–	Party for Social Reforms

Parties in the Opposition:

PMDB (1966)	–	Party of the Brazilian Democratic Movement (ex-MDB)
PDT (1980)	–	Democratic Labour Party (PTB dissidence, Brizola's party)
PSDB (1988)	–	Party of the Brazilian Social Democracy (PMDB dissidence)
PT (1980)	–	The Workers' Party
PSB (1985)	–	Brazilian Socialist Party
PCB (1985)	–	Brazilian Communist Party
PCdoB (1985)	–	Communist Party of Brazil
PMN (1989)	–	National Mobilization Party

* Date in parenthesis refers to the year the party was created

society are expressed and may be translated into public policy.[3] It is for this reason that parties are agencies of linkage, that is, a means of connecting citizens to the state. As K. Lawson asserts, 'the political party is the one agency that can claim to have as its very raison d'être the creation of an entire linkage chain, a chain of connections that runs from the voters through the candidates and the electoral process to the officials of government'.[4] It is on the basis of this conceptualization that some analysts have shown much concern with such questions as grass-roots participation and internal democracy within the party – aspects that, it should be said, are largely over-emphasized in the criticisms of Brazilian political parties.

This analysis will therefore focus on two aspects: first, assuming that there is no intrinsic constraint in Brazilian political culture

Table 8.1 Changes in Party Representation in the National Congress (Senate + Federal Chamber) – 1985–1991

Parties	1985	1986	1987*	1988	1989	1990	1991*
PMDB	41.1	44.9	54.6	42.0	36.7	26.8	23.1
(1966)	225	246	305	235	209	153	135
PFL	13.3	27.2	24.0	22.4	18.3	18.1	17.5
(1984)	73	149	134	125	104	103	102
PDT	4.4	4.7	4.7	5.0	5.4	7.5	8.9
(1980)	24	26	26	28	31	43	52
PSDB	–	–	–	8.6	10.5	12.6	8.0
(1988)	–	–	–	48	60	72	47
PDS	37.2	14.8	6.6	6.1	5.4	6.1	7.9
(1966)	204	81	37	34	31	35	46
PTB	2.6	2.4	3.4	5.2	4.0	5.6	7.4
(1980)	14	13	19	29	23	32	43
PRN	–	–	–	–	3.9	6.0	7.4
(1989)	–	–	–	–	22	34	43
PT	1.5	1.1	2.9	2.9	2.8	3.0	6.2
(1980)	8	6	16	16	16	17	36
PDC	–	0.7	1.1	2.3	4.9	3.9	4.5
(1985)	–	4	6	13	28	22	26
PL	–	0.9	1.3	1.3	4.0	2.3	2.4
(1986)	–	5	7	7	23	13	14
PSB	–	0.9	0.2	1.1	1.4	1.8	2.1
(1985)	–	5	1	6	8	10	12
PCdoB	–	0.4	0.5	0.9	1.1	1.1	0.9
(1985)	–	2	3	5	6	6	5
PCB	–	0.5	0.5	0.5	0.5	0.5	0.5
(1985)	–	3	3	3	3	3	3
Others	–	1.5	0.4	1.8	2.6	4.7	3.4
	–	8	2	10	15	27	20
Total	548	548	559	559	569	570	584

Source: Câmara Federal, Senado Federal and *Folha de São Paulo*, 21.09.88.
* Composition resulting from the 1986 and 1990 elections, respectively.

against the institutionalization of a party system, this article will point out the factors behind the problematic situation of party politics within the framework of earlier party developments. Secondly, in order to examine the question of party linkage, a discussion of both the parties' relation to the electorate they represent and their action at grass-roots level will be presented. In other words, this analysis will be concerned with the two contexts in which parties are expected to operate: (1) the social and electoral – their role in connecting citizens to the state; and (2) the state context – their governing function, namely their role in the decision-making process.

Obstacles to Party Consolidation

At least three sets of problems have hindered party development in Brazil. The first stems from the country's history of discontinuity and the low institutionalization of previous party systems.[5] Although Brazil had, during the 1945–64 democratic period, an important experience of party politics, that experience did not evolve towards a consolidated party system. Twenty years were insufficient for the parties to put down enough roots to survive the military interregna.[6] Moreover, most of their problems stem from the functioning of a highly centralized government structure built in the 1930s and re-enforced during the military regime. The presence of an executive power centralizing decision-making left the parties and the system itself with little control over the resources necessary for their participation in the formulation and implementation of social and economic policies. The political parties were consequently unable to develop into effective channels of representation and expression of social demands. Although they had been in national politics since the mid-1940s, the party system never had the relative autonomy needed by political institutions to operate effectively in the political system. Since they have not developed as independent organizations for political representation they ended up as minor partners in the political process or instruments of clientelism and patronage.[7]

The second set of problems constraining party development is related to Brazil's specific experience of military regime, particularly the way in which the military intervened in party politics. Under military rule, the old parties were dissolved and replaced by a two-party system – the pro-government ARENA and the opposition MDB. The continuing functioning of this system throughout the long years of military rule resulted in the effective death of the previous party system. As ARENA and MDB competed for votes in every election, new party identifications were created, and memories of the previous experience of party politics faded. Moreover, in 1979 the military intervened once again, dissolving the two-party system which had become an obstacle to its control over the political process, particularly with the policy of gradual liberalization. These interferences were certainly obstacles to party consolidation, as the party structure had no time to achieve stability.[8]

New changes occurred in 1985, as civilian government lifted restrictions on the creation of political parties. Notwithstanding its democratic character, the full freedom for party organization established by the 1985 political reform ended up making party development more difficult. Party law was so permissive that it functioned as an incentive for indiscipline and splits, rather than strengthening established party organizations. This leads us to the third set of factors that contribute to the instability and fragility of party politics in Brazil: the institutional framework.

It is widely recognized that Brazil's electoral system has a disruptive effect on party development. This article does not intend to provide a full account of the complexities of the electoral system, but would like to point out two problems. The first is the method of proportional representation used in the election for the Chamber of Deputies (as well as for the state assemblies and municipal councils). The most problematic aspect of this is the use of the open list. This means that the candidate's position in the party list (which will determine whether or not he/she is elected) is not previously fixed but results from the number of votes he/she individually receives, measured against others competing under the same party label. As a consequence, the election for the legislative houses becomes a fierce competition among hundreds of candidates, in some cases within the same geographic area and under the same party label. Moreover, the parties as organizations have hardly any responsibility for financing their candidates, who have to raise the huge amounts of money needed for an election campaign themselves.

In addition, as previously mentioned, the current party law has undermined party development since it does not restrict the creation of parties. In Brazil a political party is allowed to operate under a provisional status for the period of a year provided that its founders (a provisional national party committee of seven to eleven members) apply for its registration at the Electoral Tribunal by issuing the party manifesto, programme and statute, followed by the signature of 101 founding members. It is true that in order to acquire permanent registration this party must have carried out, within the period of a year, party conventions to elect state and local directories in nine states and one-fifth of their respective municipalities. However, for a year it will be allowed to run for elections, have access to free television time to publicize its programme and to campaign for its candidates.[9] Moreover, there is no rule regulating electoral alliances, neither are there provisions restraining party indiscipline and change of party affiliation. In this context, the creation of party identification, development of party loyalties – not to mention political accountability – become extremely difficult.

The second problem is the negative impact of the presidential election on party consolidation. Firstly, it should be emphasized that presidentialism by no means helps develop strong party links. As Epstein remarks about the US case, 'the very fact that the voters are asked to choose individuals for the presidency (. . .) encourages personalized campaigns'.[10] When the case in consideration is Brazil where autonomy and centralization of power in the executive is quite prominent, the relevance of political parties in the presidential election is even more limited. In addition, substantial political resources are needed for a successful strategy towards presidential election based on the majority system within a nationwide constituency. Given Brazil's huge area and its political diversity, a presidential candidate would need to seek electoral alliances with the regional forces, often in different parties, to maximize his/her electoral gains and increase the chance of victory. If this situation is aggravated by an unsettled party structure where there is no restriction on changing party affiliation and political pragmatism seems to be the norm, then party instability is bound to increase.

The 1989 presidential election is a good illustration. In the months preceding the election, party representation in the legislative houses changed almost every day. Furthermore, that election was the best example of the disconnection between presidentialism and the party system as illustrated by the dissociation between the electoral competition and relative strength of the parties. Table 8.2 shows the parties' place in the 1989 presidential contest and their electoral gains in the gubernatorial and legislative elections in 1990. If the future development of the main parties were to have been predicted on the basis of their performance in the presidential election, a rather misleading scenario would have depicted the virtual disappearance of the two major parties – PMDB and PFL – and the ascension of the PRN, PT and PDT (the parties of Collor de Mello, Lula and Brizola, respectively). What the 1990 elections showed, however, was a different picture, with the PMDB and PFL keeping control of most of

Table 8.2 Position of the Parties in Executive and Legislative Offices. Per cent.

Parties	President[1] 1989	Governor[2] 1990	Senate[3] 1990	Fed. Chamber[3] 1990
PMDB	4.4	25.9	33.3	21.5
PFL	0.8	33.3	18.5	17.3
PDT	15.5	11.1	6.2	9.3
PSDB	10.8	3.7	12.3	7.4
PDS	8.3	3.7	3.7	8.5
PTB	0.5	7.4	9.9	7.0
PRN	28.5	0.0	3.7	8.0
PT	16.1	0.0	1.2	7.0
PDC	–	0.0	4.9	4.4
PL	4.5	0.0	0.0	2.8
PSB	–	0.0	1.2	2.2
PCdoB	–	0.0	0.0	1.1
PCB	1.1	0.0	0.0	0.6
Others	3.2	14.8	4.9	3.2

1 Percentage of the election results in the first round presidential contest.
2 Percentage of state governorships won by each party.
3 Percentage of seats in the Senate and Chamber of Deputies.

the state governorships and the largest representations in Congress, while the PT and PRN resumed their position as small parties.

The important element to be emphasized here is that the presidential and congressional elections have different dynamics whose results are bound to affect the relationship between the president and the Congress. A presidential election held within the context described gives the president considerable autonomy in relation to the political parties because, regardless of strength of links with his/her party, the winner always goes beyond this party base. In other words, the electoral support responsible for the victory is larger than his/her original party base, a trend which is even more pronounced under a two-round election and within a more fragmented party system, as in Brazil's case. In this sense, a natural distance – not to say a gap – exists between president and party, particularly as regards governing matters and the relationship between the executive and the legislative powers. This is certainly more problematic when the president is elected without the support of any party organization, as was the case of Fernando Collor de Mello. The relationship that the Collor government has developed with Congress since taking office in March 1990, is worth mentioning as an illustration of the complex problems involving the interaction of the executive and the Congress.

The major concern dominating political and academic circles from the moment Collor's victory was known, was related to the difficulties he would certainly have to face as a consequence of his very precarious parliamentary basis. The small party – the PRN – that provided the label for his running for the presidential office had only 22 representatives in the Congress. While Collor might expect that the parties (i.e., PFL, PDS, PL, PTB and PDC) that had rushed to give him support in the second round of the election would help him in Congress, this basis could not be taken as a safe and stable majority. Thus it was anticipated that Collor's lack of substantial party support in Congress would result in difficulties for his government.

There is little doubt that Collor's faltering party base has been one of the constraints confronting his administration. However, what is still to be proved is the extent to which Congress has been an obstacle to the government's attempts to deal with the economic crisis. What in fact has been seen so far is that, in spite of his unstable parliamentary basis in Congress, Collor was able to put forward a drastic economic stabilization plan – the Collor Plan I – which affected a large range of interests. For that, the president counted, not only on his power of veto to cope with any unwanted legislation passed by Congress, but mainly on a constitutional mechanism – the *Medidas Provisórias* (provisional measures) – which entitled him to enforce all the measures of his economic plan without previous approval by Congress. Even though *Medidas Provisórias* are subjected to parliamentary approval within a month after their decree, none ended up being rejected.[11] Yet, in spite of Congress's 'co-operation', Collor's plan failed to produce positive results. Consequently, it may be asked whether Congress and the political parties have actually been a major problem. It seems, in this case, that neither have they put up obstacles to decision-making, nor have they, by providing parliamentary approval, contributed to the effective implementation of the government's economic plan. In fact parliamentary support is essential only in a context where the parties do have a say in the decision-making process, either in the role of ruling party or as partners in the process of negotiation.[12] This does not seem to be the case in Brazil.

To affirm that the party system has not been a relevant actor in this context does not mean to suggest that the parties and the party system are regarded as having nothing to do with the crisis of governability. They certainly have. But this is mainly because of their fragile position in the political system and because of the fragmentation of the party system which make it difficult to build definitive political interlocutors. Without clear partners for political negotiation it becomes difficult to seek not only a minimum consensus but also compliance with any of the terms that may be agreed.

In a situation where many unfavourable conditions for party development are evolving, it is quite difficult to envisage any significant change unless determined efforts are made to modify at least those conditions which it is possible to reverse. Prior to discussing this point, the analysis will deal with party linkage with society, namely the question of representation and participation.

Political Parties in Society

As mentioned in the introduction, Brazil's political parties are commonly regarded as lacking representativeness and participation. In fact, a look at the experience of the 1945–64 democratic period would show that 'seasonal' organizations were the dominant feature, that is, parties emerging during one election and then vanishing until the next. The connection between party candidates and voters was so weak that deputies often moved to a different party even before the inauguration of their legislative term.[13]

For obvious reasons during the 1964–85 military rule, a significant change in this style of politics was not expected. In spite of the fact that a two-party system was kept in operation and elections were held periodically, the military imposed so many constraints on political participation and party activities that the emergence of a new pattern would have been surprising.

With regard to the current experience, it is too early to predict a new trend for the future. As far as the present situation goes, it is difficult to foresee the development of a participatory and representative style of party politics, considering the low indices of party identification, high electoral volatility in recent elections, and, as already pointed out, the common practice of party hopping among parliamentarians.

Paradoxically, however, Brazil has been the stage of an important experience of party linkage for more than a decade. Firstly, the experience of the MDB (Brazilian Democratic Movement) should be mentioned. In spite of the artificial and restrictive conditions of party politics during the long period of military rule, the first attempts at grass-roots work actually date from that period and were carried out through the MDB local organizations. As the only legal channel of opposition, an umbrella for the most diversified political groupings, the MDB was a useful agency for those groups interested in developing grass-roots work. While it is true that this was not widespread throughout the country and did not result in an effective linkage agency, nevertheless the attempt was certainly an important beginning. In any case, working at grass-roots level was a hard task taking into consideration the fact that this new experience started only in the mid-1970s with the beginning of the political relaxation. Moreover, it was a political action directed towards a population that had been demobilized for a long time or had never experienced political participation at all.

While reservations exist concerning the MDB experience as a case of 'effective party linkage', the work developed by the PT (Workers' Party) is widely regarded as an authentic example worth discussing. The importance of the PT's emergence is widely recognized. Brazil may be the only recent case of democratic transition where the re-establishment of competitive party politics brought about the organization of a new party, not only created externally – in Duverger's term – but also largely inspired by social movements. In other words, what was new in the creation of the PT was not only its mass party features and close links with the trade union movement, but particularly its concern with grass-roots participation, an aim which became the party's pillar. Thus, a close link between the PT and the urban popular movements, particularly those influenced by the Catholic Church (Comunidades Eclesiais de Base), was established from the party's formative period. As a result, the PT is perhaps one of the few parties where social movements are organically linked to the party's structure. As Meneguello[14] remarks in her study on the formation of the PT, the structure of its organization is based on the principle of participatory democracy. Aiming at promoting its members' participation in party decisions, the PT established the so-called *nucleos de base* (base nuclei), a mechanism designed to make the connection with the party's rank and file more effective. As defined in the party statute, the *nucleos de base* are the locus of democratic party organization as well as political education for the rank and file and comprise affiliated members either from a neighbourhood, professional group, work place or social movement. The aim is to establish permanent activity based on regular meetings, encouraging grass roots militancy. What is apparently new in the PT experience, according to Meneguello, 'is the fact that it effectively established mechanisms in its organization that can strengthen the link with its grass-roots organization, thus giving priority to the social struggle, rather than to electoral and parliamentary politics as has been the main concern of other parties'.[15]

There is no doubt that the PT's experience is important. It has certainly had an impact on party dynamics and the political system at large. However, its experience also underlines the complexities involved when the question is party linkage. The problems of reconciling the needs and functioning of grass-roots organization with the ends and functioning of the party (which, above all, is a political organization participating in elections, in the parliament and in government) seems to be one of the party's most serious difficulties. It is worth noting that the relationship between parties and social movements is always tense because of their intrinsically different nature. While social movements are expressions of specific social demands and therefore aim to maximize benefits for a particular group,[16] political parties are supposed to deal with wide-ranging objectives which can, in some cases, counteract social movements.[17]

Apart from that, the extent to which the PT has an effective and extensive linkage with grass-roots associations is still unknown. Data collected among 700 state deputies (1987–90 legislature) indicate that the party representatives' connection with associations from civil society, even in the case of PT, is not as extensive as expected. Table 8.3 leaves no doubt that the PT has the largest proportion of deputies linked both to trade unions (30 per cent) and neighbourhood associations (15 per cent). However, 51.5 per cent of its state deputies have no link at all with associations from civil society. Obviously, less can be said about the other parties: in the cases of the PMDB, PDT and PSDB, the percentage of state representatives having no connection with grass-roots associations are 71.5, 74.5 and 67.9 respectively.[18]

Yet, it should be stressed that participation in associations is far from being a widespread practice among Brazilians. Indices of participation have not been noteworthy. According to the IBGE national survey (PNAD), only 4 per cent of the Brazilian electorate are affiliated to neighbourhood associations, a percentage rising to just 10 per cent regarding trade-union membership.[19]

If all these aspects are taken into consideration, then the problems of party linkages are far more complex than the simple question of building up grass-roots organizations and practising democracy within the party. The problem becomes much larger when taking into consideration the fact that political parties whose fortunes are decided by elections are supposed to be related to their overall voters rather than to their active supporters. To assess whether there is a linkage involving the voters will only be possible if there is, in a polity, reasonable stability in voting patterns and some cleavage in relation to which the parties can be channels of expression and representation for their voters rather than for their active members only. This hardly exists in the Brazilian party picture.

Thus, in spite of the existence of social movements and grass roots participation (at least in parties such as the PT), it is difficult to assess the extent of party linkage when taking into account the fact that, lately, elections in Brazil have not shown a clear pattern to allow an analysis of the parties' social bases. In this context, the PT is a good example. While it is characterized as having participatory and representative features, it is still difficult to identify a linkage between the social base this party theoretically represents and its electoral constituency.

The 1989 presidential election was a good indication. The opinion polls carried out during the election period showed that the PT's candidate – Luis Ignacio Lula da Silva – was not the candidate supported by the low strata of the electorate. That was Collor de Mello. In fact, those opinion polls as well as other surveys on electoral behaviour, show that the lower the voter's income and schooling, the greater his support for Collor, while the reverse occurred in Lula's case.[20] These are facts that raise the question of the relationship between parties (and candidates) and the electorate and, more specifically, the consideration that electoral strategies with a clear programmatic-ideological appeal do not necessarily affect the social sectors they are aimed at and whose electoral support is sought.

Table 8.3 Party Representatives at State Level and their Links with Associations

				Type of association			
Party	None	Union	Professional/ employer	Community Neighbourhood	Sport/ recreational	Religious	Others
PDS (68)	68.8	–	10.9	1.6	6.3	12.5	6.3
PDT (53)	74.5	3.9	5.9	–	7.8	3.9	7.9
PT (37)	51.5	30.3	6.1	15.2	3.0	6.1	–
PTB (30)	69.0	–	3.4	3.4	17.2	6.9	3.4
PMDB (269)	71.5	2.0	10.8	3.2	8.0	5.2	7.2
PFL (143)	64.7	1.4	10.8	2.9	10.1	10.1	2.9
PSDB (30)	67.9	3.6	14.3	3.6	3.6	7.1	7.1
PL (19)	78.9	–	5.3	–	10.5	–	5.3
PDC (33)	56.3	3.1	18.8	–	6.3	18.8	–
PRN (14)	83.3	–	–	16.7	8.3	8.3	–
Other Left (14)	71.4	7.1	7.1	14.3	–	–	–
Others (16)	66.7	–	13.3	–	6.7	20.0	–
TOTAL (726)	68.5 (469)	3.2 (22)	10.1 (55)	3.5 (24)	11.5 (79)	7.7 (53)	4.7 (34)

Source: The author's own data collected for the research project 'A Estrutura Partidária Brasileira'.

Final Remarks

A set of factors that warrant discussion in the analysis of political parties in Brazil has been pointed out. The first relates to the fragility, instability and fragmentation of the party system, underlining the difficulties met by Brazil's new democracy in consolidating party politics. It was suggested that those difficulties stem not only from a history of discontinuity and lack of institutionalization but also from an institutional framework that, in several aspects, has hampered the development of party politics.

Although some structural problems of Brazil's political development persist, thus making the emergence of strong parties difficult, there are still grounds to believe in the possibility of improving the present situation by changing the institutional conditions that determine political competition and the power structure. If matters of institutional engineering are accepted as having relevance, this is an area where much can be done to counteract the negative effects caused not only by the present electoral system and party law but also by presidentialism.

The second aspect discussed in this article relates to representation and participation, pointing out the complexities involved in the consideration of parties at grass-roots level and as agencies of linkage. Problems of representation and participation in regard to political parties are certainly more serious in Brazil's political system than in most other cases. However, they are not a Brazilian peculiarity. The crisis of representation facing political parties has been identified everywhere, for more than two decades. Trends such as the transformation of mass parties into catch-all or professional-electoral parties, loosening their links with their traditional social bases, the political parties' process of marginalization from their traditional functions, the emergence of alternative movements and organizations, have been widely debated in the literature.[21] But it has also been argued that there is no substitute for parties; that is, in spite of the emergence and growing importance of the so-called alternative organizations, these have not been able to replace the traditional political parties as agencies for gaining power and of governing. For this reason, to discuss the complex functions and dynamics of party politics in new democracies such as Brazil's, is not just a question of assessing whether or not the present parties are genuine channels of representation and means of participation. It is also a question of examining the limits of their role in the much more complex environment in which they presently operate. In this regard three other considerations should be made.

The first refers to the role of mass media as a factor constraining party development. In the era of television when the electoral campaign through the media has become so powerful and effective as a means of catching votes, it is much more difficult to consolidate party organizations since they are no longer the fundamental instrument for a successful electoral campaign.

The second refers to the question of regional politics. The diversity of regional interests and internal dynamics of party competition among Brazil's states works naturally against the development of cohesive national parties. In other words it is very unlikely that Brazilian parties will ever be highly cohesive and disciplined.[22] And this is certainly a problem for party development. However, part of this could be avoided if parties were not obliged to be nationwide organizations as required by the constitution. If a political party were allowed to exist just as a regional organization it would not be bound to attract highly heterogeneous state or local groupings from areas where it has little chance of creating its own base.

The third refers to the type of party that is likely to predominate in Brazil. Considering present party developments in western democracies as well as Brazil's previous experience, it is very likely that the catch-all party type will become the dominant feature of the Brazilian party system. In other words, organizations pragmatically oriented towards election rather than towards political principles may become the rule. In this context, the orientation and behaviour of politicians are guided by the calculus of costs and benefits, rather than by questions of ideology. This makes the question of institutional crafting essential. If fragmentation and lack of cohesion are the main problems, then it is necessary to create institutional mechanisms that would encourage party discipline and responsiveness while discouraging excessive fragmentation of the party system.

Parliamentarism is also an essential change. Obviously the establishment of a new system of government will not cure Brazil's ills. It should be noted that parliamentarism has not prevented India's political system from developing a very centralized and personalized power structure. Neither did it prevent the weakening of its institutions (particularly the Congress Party) nor, as Kohli argues, the emergence of a growing crisis of governability.[23] However, it is possible that it is parliamentarism which has prevented India from having a major institutional crisis since independence in spite of its highly divisive polity, eruptions of discontent and the assassination of two prime ministers.

Institutional crafting can help change the circumstances under which political competition and government can develop. However it will not solve Brazilian economic and social problems. In this respect it is worth quoting Huntington who remarked 'what determines whether or not new democracies survive is not primarily the severity of the problems they face or their ability to solve those problems. It is the way in which political leaders respond to their inability to solve the problems confronting their country.'[24] The establishment of institutional mechanisms that can help prevent the emergence of uncontrollable crisis should be seen as part of the way political leaders could respond.

9· DEMOCRATIZATION AND POLITICAL CULTURE*

José Alvaro Moisés

Introduction

Democracy has become one of the most important issues of our time. Everywhere we see the defence of liberty, equality before the law, the rights of the individual and institutional legality. To the surprise of certain exponents of democratic theory, millions have mobilized to resist threats to democracy, or simply to demand the rule of law. This has been the case, for instance, in the last few years in countries as different as Spain, Argentina and the Soviet Union.[1] As if reacting against a long sequence of reverses, this new democratic spirit is bent on universalizing the principle of the autonomy of the governed. But, in contrast with key historical events in the pursuit of democracy, just when libertarian principles seem to be fulfilled, democracy appears to be abandoning the egalitarian tradition from which it also sprung. There could be no greater and more cruel historical irony than that, at the end of a century that began with egalitarian revolutions proclaiming a new beginning in the history of humanity, we should see libertarian revolutions taking their most radical form in those cases where they seek to sweep away the remnants of the very regimes which started out in search of egalitarianism. On the threshold of the twenty-first century, we discover that liberal democracy – and not socialist revolution – has been the prime mover in the century that is now ending.[2]

At the same time, when the 'festival' of democracy that has usually accompanied recent democratic transitions is over,[3] the real problems begin to appear. However desirable they may be, the new democracies (just like, although in a different way, those which were born two or three centuries ago) are characterized by inequality in terms of distribution. This is not just the case of material goods, but symbolic ones too, such as the power resources available to different sectors for confronting the basic conflicts in society. Certainly preferable to authoritarian or totalitarian alternatives – if only because competition for material goods can be conducted peacefully – these democracies nevertheless exist alongside enormous social, racial and gender inequalities and, equally, a huge gulf between the 'governed' and the 'governors'. In fact, far from disappearing, these inequalities tend to become more visible as democracy becomes established. So the initial enthusiasm for democracy may turn into disillusionment, apathy and even hostility towards the democratic regime. The reversal of expectations and the slowness of the political process in delivering substantial benefits can lead to frustration among the majority of citizens; it can also lead to reactions that undermine democratic institutions and provide the pretext for action by those who seek to destroy the new democracies.[4]

In fact, achieving a democratic order is a lengthy, difficult and painful process. Creating the institutions to handle the plurality of objectives that characterize complex societies, turns on a long and often contradictory process of collective effort. The procedures that have to be adopted presuppose difficult negotiations between competing groups with different interests, outlooks and expectations of the democratic order. In addition, even when they are fully established, institutions and procedures do not always mean the same things to different political actors. Thus, though dispensable as a precondition, the creation of a basic normative consensus that is capable of allowing democracy to evolve and not break down every time a fundamental social conflict arises is just as important for establishing a democratic regime as the formation of a party system or the institutionalization of political representation.

This consensus, sometimes referred to as the concept of political culture, involves, among other things, the general acceptance of a set of basic values, political procedures and attitudes among the various different segments which constitute a polity. It is both the result of socialization and the political experience of those who form that entity.[5] It is something that becomes important once the process of democratization gets under way. Key questions include: (1) To what extent does the mass of a population have attitudes and patterns of behaviour which are compatible with the way in which the new political system works? (2) To what extent are the minimal requirements for participation seen as providing channels through which different segments can meaningfully pursue their demands on the political system? (3) Do differing conceptions about democracy among different sectors open up the possibility of changes in the political system?

This article looks at some of these questions as they relate to Brazil. The line of argument adopted involves two stages. Firstly, it looks at the importance of mass democratic culture for the consolidation of a democratic regime. Without casting aside some of the more important counter-arguments, it affirms that this needs to exist in order for democratic stability to be assured. Secondly, taking as given both the impact of social and economic modernization on Brazilian politics over the last 20 or 30 years and the inertial effects caused by the survival of anachronisms in the political system,[6] it asserts that important changes are taking place in mass political culture in Brazil.

Preliminary Considerations

In much of the recent literature on political transition, democratization is seen basically as the result of a strategic choice by the élites involved. This tends to discount the importance of creating a democratic culture.[7] The premise explaining this choice follows the well-known axiom of Robert Dahl in his deservedly famous *Poliarchy*.[8] The central idea is that democracy becomes a preferential option among élites when the costs of suppressing opposition (or the suppression of basic social conflicts) exceed those of tolerance. The assumption is that changes of political regime take place *if* and *when* the élites concerned become conscious of the negative effects of the 'war of every man against every man'. At that point, some sort of combination of repression and representation becomes a preferable option.[9]

Not all who follow this view reject, however, the importance of the conversion of the élites concerned to democratic values, but the nature of the argument over transition and democratic consolidation is clearly 'minimalist'. This means that the democracy can flourish and stabilize even in the absence of favourable structural and cultural conditions as long as (1) democratic structures geared towards institutionalizing political competition have been established by the élites, and (2) when the political loyalties and passive consent[10] of the élites shift from the old to the new regime as the advantages of the new regime outweigh those of the old. The problem then, it is said, is not one of political legitimacy, rather one of a choice which – institutionalizing the uncertainties arising from conflict – provides at least the minimal conditions for the élites to achieve their aims. It is a calculation that is at once rational and instrumental.[11]

In my view, there is no reason to doubt that a decision by the élites to opt for a democratic regime is a key factor in starting the transition from authoritarianism or totalitarianism. A review of recent examples shows that when this was possible, democratization got under way and advanced with greater impetus than when this was not the case, or when – as shown by events in the Soviet Union in 1990 and 1991 – it was insufficient. Whether in prompting the crisis of authoritarianism or guiding it towards new alternatives, the role played by the élites in the emergence of democracy is crucial.

But whether or not this is sufficient to ensure that democracy is taken to heart by other groups in society, or indeed that the new regime is capable of consolidating, is a different matter. The issue which I want to address in this article is the lack of a theoretical or practical basis for the 'minimalist' argument in relation to the role played by mass political conditions in situations where a democratic government has replaced authoritarian rule, but where a real democratic regime is still not established. In much of the literature on democratic transition there is an almost total absence of analytical treatment of the importance of the commitment by non-élite groups to basic democratic values.[12] The fact that this has been overlooked possibly stems from the way in which research has tended to apply itself to a 'genetic' approach to transition rather than to addressing vicissitudes in the development of democracy once established. But this can no longer be justified. Most of the original cases of transition analysed previously are now countries where democratic regimes are in the process of consolidation; the issue of whether or not the population has become accustomed to, and indeed supports, democratic practices is now a matter of concern.[13] But the consequence of not giving sufficient consideration to the spreading of mass values when looking at key issues such as equality before the law, its importance in reducing social conflict, tolerance towards those who think or act differently, the right to dissent, the need for public controls over what governing groups do, and so on, is shown by the frequent lack of attention to the creation of mechanisms which separate public life from private interests. In societies that have gone through a democratic transition, the survival of archaic ways of practising politics, where public order is dealt with as if it were a private matter, shows up these problems, and greatly increases the strategic difficulties facing the democratic elites and others who support the consolidation of democracy.[14]

Some examples highlight the practical importance of this matter. They refer to some of the *new democracies* which are emerging from what O'Donnell termed the 'second transition'. With representative systems of government insufficiently established, these are leading to what has been called 'delegative democracies'.[15] On the one hand, these are popularly-elected governments, but on the other, the results of their electoral victories have tended to weaken the already fragile party systems. This is the case in Argentina, Brazil and Peru where popular support is combined with a strong plebiscitarian component; charismatic leaders like Collor, Menem, and Fujimori feel they are authorized to interpret their democratic mandate in accordance with their own particular political designs. Similarities with populism in the 1950s and the 1960s are more than just coincidental. Frustration arose from overly ambitious electoral promises, with their enormous repercussions on the expectations of those who believed in democracy: indeed it is difficult to know how mechanisms might be set up in such conditions which would make such regimes attractive to all competing interest groups. The presidential system of government in Brazil is a case in point here. It concentrates enormous power in the hands of the executive, irrespective of the rules which give the legislature and the political parties the capacity to oversee its activities. The president has a strong armoury of weapons at his disposal when it comes to political bargaining. In such circumstances it is virtually impossible to stop or correct abuses, whether through the legislature, the judiciary or through private institutions in civil society.

But if it is clear that in these 'delegative democracies' the usual instruments of representative democracy do not disappear, they tend to work in a very precarious way. They are impinged upon by charismatic leaders who are continually looking for greater freedom of manoeuvre in decision-making; they have to face stinging criticism from an electorate dissatisfied with the methods by which politics are conducted and with the lack of efficacy in everything that has anything to do with state institutions.[16] In this context it is easy to see how structures of clientelism and patronage, methods by which certain élite groups achieve their objectives, live on. Complementing the way in which the presidential system works, these serve to exacerbate the 'private' aspects of the way in which the political system works and undermine the 'public' dimension of democracy. The political parties in this setting become virtually redundant, losing their sense of representativeness and, in the words of one analyst 'the idea of accountability to those institutions or to other private or semi-private organisations appears as an unnecessary impediment to the full authority that the President has been delegated to exercise'.[17]

The question therefore is not whether delegative democracies are essentially anti-democratic; they have democratic attributes – some even go as far as to think they are more democratic than the representative system. The issue is the extent to which, in these conditions, they become 'semi-democracies' which work only for a section of the actors concerned. The rest, the 'outsiders' who wish to come within the system, find their way blocked if they try to impose public control over the way in which power is exercised, thus entering into political competition on very disadvantageous terms. The key question then is whether, in such circumstances, they see any reason to continue with their initial support for democracy.[18]

This and other examples[19] show that to look at the internal dynamics of authoritarian regimes does not exhaust the question. Neither does analysis of the way in which 'moderates' or 'hardliners', 'minimalists' or 'maximalists', 'progressives' or 'traditionalists' (both in power or in opposition) provoke or deepen the crisis and choose democracy as the 'second-best alternative' on offer.[20] The specific way in which the mass public influences this process – as it becomes 'accustomed' to democracy, it begins to put pressure on democratic institutions or eventually comes to support those who threaten it – has to be considered as a factor in itself, which can tilt the élites' allegiances towards a change of regime.[21] This should not be underestimated, still less ruled out, in the analyses of the democratization process.

In fact, examination of the classic processes of democratic consolidation shows that the values, attitudes and proper procedures of a democratic culture are reinforced by a complex interaction between behaviour and the ways in which political structures function. This implies both processes of political socialization and resocialization and necessarily the passing of time. But it would be hard to argue that the building of democratic institutions in Britain or the United States, for instance, did not go hand in hand with, and did not benefit from, the spreading of basic democratic values among the citizens of these countries.[22] It is not a matter of a simplistic dialectic between political structure and democratic values; these examples show that when democratic institutions are lacking, it is very difficult to develop democratic practices and customs such as tolerance towards those who think and act differently. At the same time, if political tolerance or the rule of law to resolve conflict are taken as contingent instruments and not things of permanent value, institutions may lose their *raison d'être*, fall into decline and ultimately either disappear or become dysfunctional.[23]

More recent examples also confirm the importance of the interaction between political culture and structure for regime changes. The first is that of West Germany itself, which Almond and Verba's book *The Civic Culture*[24] described as having a political culture that was parochial and insufficiently participatory or democratic. Here the question of the convergence between values and political structure would tend to show the relevance of the experience of Nazism and Fascism and explain the way in which mass political attitudes were congruent with the authoritarian structure of that regime. However, two decades later, research shows that the defence of democracy by the political parties and the exemplary way in which democratic institutions have worked, have resulted in basic democratic values becoming generalized amongst the German public. But much of the literature also underlines the deliberate effort made both by the occupation forces in the immediate post-war period and by German national parties and governments to use education and persuasion to teach the superiority of basic democratic values.[25] Similarly, Spain after Franco also shows that a pre-existing majority democratic consensus is not indispensable for the establishment of a democratic regime. But as well as the need for the transition process (involving the behaviour and the choices of the relevant political actors) to promote the diffusion of these values, the existence of an initial basis for democratic adherence is important.[26]

However, on the basis of the empirical evidence available, it is difficult to reach a definitive conclusion as to the direction of causality: i.e. whether democratic institutions produce a political culture that is favourable to democracy, or vice-versa. Even so, as Lijphart and Kavanagh[27] recall, even conceding that the political structure has great influence over the creation of a democratic culture, it is impossible to completely separate the activity of building institutions from the overall values of the relevant actors involved.

There is no need to fall back on psychological explanations to see that the decisions taken by those actors in relation to political structure are coloured by contextual circumstances – i.e. the nature of political conflict, the way in which the actors interpret them and current and inherited patterns of political behaviour. Perhaps it would be most appropriate to talk, as Rustow does, of the 'reciprocal influence between action and political beliefs'.[28] A good example seems to be the process by which political identities are formed. These lead the actors concerned to take decisions on the best strategies for attaining their objectives, but do not stop them reacting either to impulses from objective conditions (including the strategies of others) or to the stimulus of beliefs, ambitions, desires and values.[29] Even though it is true that in this process the 'internalized norms' through different processes of socialization can be reaffirmed, reformed or rejected, it is difficult to argue that this takes place outside the context of social interaction.[30] To speak of a rationality that is defined outside (or prior to) the context of objective influences that blend with traditions and values, would imply a rationality outside social life – or, in other words, of social actors who are formed prior to them becoming a part of society.

So, if it is true that political culture is insufficient by itself to generate a democratic regime – and if the process of constructing this regime involves in addition what some writers have recently termed the 'crafting' of institutions[31] – this is not to say that it is not a necessary condition. Just as this 'crafting' ultimately depends on how the democratic institutional 'package' is presented to those élites who previously supported the authoritarian regime and who have shifted to supporting the democratic regime, it becomes impossible to distinguish strictly rational intentions from specific choices which arise from a context of social values.[32]

Political Interest and the Commitment to Democracy in Brazil

The Brazilian case provides a good example of the difficulties with which the democratic option of the élites interacts with the formation of a democratic consensus among the masses. The democratic transition in Brazil took more than a decade, generating a broad and complex movement opposed to authoritarianism which helped redefine the élites' commitment to the political regime as well as to propagate the virtues of democracy among the masses. The key factors which contributed to this were various. Firstly, as Weffort has suggested (1984), experience of state terror prompted a profound shift in political attitudes amongst different social sectors towards what are usually called 'formal' democratic rights. Secondly, the beginning of the democratic 'opening' coincided with moments of crisis in the international and national economy (1972–3) and helped 'socialize' dissatisfaction – which up to that point had been limited to popular sectors – among the business élite which became progressively more disenchanted with the authoritarian regime. Thirdly, two decades of economic and social modernization not only changed the social morphology but caused a large degree of socio-political mobilization, triggering in turn new and more complex patterns of social expectations and greater demands on the state. Last, but not least, as Lamounier recalls on a number of occasions,[33] the authoritarian regime in Brazil coexisted with the survival of a semi-competitive political system which provoked not only splits and political mobilization among the élites but led to a permanent de-legitimization of authoritarianism. Even in a system of only semi-autonomous political parties, periodic elections inevitably led to widespread public discussion about the problems of the regime and possible alternatives to it. The consequences are well known: the deepening of divides among the élite; plebiscitarian elections which take on clear anti-regime characteristics; and widespread social mobilization which frequently turned into movements for democracy. This is the context in which change in the political beliefs of Brazilians took place.

Indeed, at a specific moment in time, it became clear that the country was on the way to becoming a democratic regime. That moment was the reintroduction of direct elections for state governors in 1982. It was a turning point which prompted some analysts to begin talking about a 'diarchy' in Brazil. Opinion polls showed mass opinion in Brazil growing increasingly critical of the regime.[34] In spite of this, it then took nearly a decade for a democratic consensus to emerge to the level at which the transition could be completed with direct presidential elections in 1989. By that time, the population had already experienced almost two four-year periods of elected state governments, which in many cases led to a dashing of the expectations of political, economic and social change which had grown up in the transition period. At the same time, the country had witnessed a

Table 9.1 Attitudes and Opinion Changing on Democratic Institutions and Political Participation in Contemporary Brazil: 1972, 1982, 1989 and 1990. Per cent.

	1972	1982	1989a	1989b	1990
Institutions					
Favourable to military involvement in politics	79	52	46	42	36
Favourable to political parties(a)	51	71	50	49	53
Against government control over unions/strike activity(b)	7	42	62	60	70
Participation					
Favourable to direct elections/participation in elections(c)	57	82	61	66	71
Favourable to right to vote for illiterates(d)	38	60	58	59	56
Favourable to the idea that 'the people know how to vote' or 'should give its opinions on how the laws should be'(e)	50	47	49	52	–

Sources: Data for 1972 and 1982: Rochon and Mitchell *The Withering Away of the Authoritarian State? Social Bases of the Transition to Democracy in Brazil.* Data for 1989a/b and 1990: Research project 'Cultura Política e Consolidação Democrática no Brasil' CEDEC/Data-Folha, Dept. of Political Science, USP. cf. Appendix for further information.

(a) In 1972, the question referred to whether 'to give more power to the parties'; in 1982, to parties' ability to 'fulfil a useful role in society'; and in 1989 to whether 'one sole party would be better for the country'.
(b) In 1990, the question referred to whether or not the government had the right to repress strikes using troops.
(c) In 1972, the question referred to direct elections for governors, while in 1982 it was for president; in 1989 and 1990, whether the interviewees would or would not vote if it was not obligatory to do so.
(d) In 1989 and 1990, the question referred to giving the vote to 'people that have not attended school'.
(e) In 1989, the question referred to whether 'the people know how to express their opinion on how the laws should be'.

spectacular and unprecedented mobilization in defence of democracy with the campaign for direct presidential elections.[35] No nationwide research exists to measure the effects of one or the other of these experiences, or whether they both played a role in the formation of mass political outlooks. But it is possible that the problems facing the opposition state governments as well as the political parties (up to 1982 widely seen as vehicles for change) and Congress (which had to decide on the direct elections amendment in 1984) caused a great deal of frustration, if not among the majority then at least among a goodly part of those who had been mobilized.

It is tempting to conclude that such experiences of new institutions did not provide a good starting-point for democratic convictions to take root among the Brazilian masses. But the evidence does not suggest this; rather it shows that the interaction between the process of institution building and the formation of political culture had a greater margin of autonomy than the above-mentioned hypothesis would have led us to suppose. Indeed, although it is necessary to be careful about making comparisons – since the figures in 1989 and 1990 are nationwide, while those for 1972 and 1982 are only for the south-east and some state capitals – some aspects of Table 9.1 are striking. Firstly, we see that between 1972 and 1990, the numbers who saw the military as an option for resolving the country's problems fell notably, even though six years after the authoritarian regime ended they still accounted for more than one-third of the electorate. Secondly, although the data are not strong enough to allow us to talk of significant change throughout the 20-year period, the oscillation in public opinion towards the role of political parties is remarkable, especially in the middle of the period, which in turn made it more difficult to stabilize mass convictions. Even so, about a half of those interviewed saw the parties as having some importance. Thirdly, the data also show that the democratic phase – in the late 1980s – coincides with the period in which the rights of those who are most socially excluded (i.e. illiterates) became an issue. However, this trend tails off slightly in the most recent period. The data then show how the political outlook of the mass of the Brazilian population has changed over these 20 years.

Table 9.2 shows that up to 1989 and 1990 a second step towards the consolidation of mass democratic values may have occurred. This conclusion is also backed up by the dramatic developments of the final phase of the transition period. On the one hand, the 1989 presidential elections came to represent the end of the transition. The conquest of direct elections had a strong symbolic significance, as the majority took them as signifying the end of the authoritarian regime.

Table 9.2 Summary Distributions of Attitudes and Opinions on Democracy, Political Institutions and Political Participation in Brazil: 1989 and 1990. Per cent.

	1989a	1989b	1990
1. POLITICAL REGIME			
'Democracy is always a better form of government than any other.' AGREE	52	64	68
'In some circumstances, a dictatorship is better than a democratic regime.' AGREE	22	17	19
'It does not matter whether the regime is a democracy or a dictatorship.' AGREE	26	19	19
2. DEMOCRATIC VALUES			
'Democracy is dangerous for it allows disorder.' DISAGREE	56	63	–
'Minorities should have the right of influencing the political life.' AGREE	53	–	45
'To keep order, the laws should always be obeyed, even if unfair.' AGREE	48	38	–
'It is not worth it to change the law in Brazil for it is not taken seriously.' DISAGREE	40	–	47
3. POLITICAL INSTITUTIONS			
Repression of strikes. DISAGREE	62	60	70
Governmental intervention in unions. DISAGREE	66	65	–
Executive right to shut parliament. DISAGREE	68	86	–
Press/Electronic media censorship. DISAGREE	73	77	–
Suppression of political parties. DISAGREE	78	80	–
4. POLITICAL PARTICIPATION			
'Politics influences your life'	63	72	–
'You influence politics'	35	55	–
Interested in politics	63	40*	–
Very interested in politics	–	–	19
Interested	–	–	58
Not interested	–	–	23
Read or view news about politics	68	81	78
Talk to others about politics	44	61	51

Table 9.2 *continued*

Try to convince others how to vote	31	47	35
Go to meetings of associations	23	–	25
Participate in electoral campaigns	8	28	24
Sign petitions	19	–	25
Take part in street demonstrations	15	–	16
Take part in strikes	14	–	13
Would vote even if it were not obligatory	61	66	76
One-party system – DISAGREE	50	49	53
Have party preference	44	54	48
Only parties should register candidates. AGREE	38	60	–

Source: Cultura Política . . .
(*) Only percentages for 'interested' and 'very interested'.

On the other hand, the elections marked the end of a very ambiguous period – the first civilian government of the post-authoritarian rule (1985–9). Indeed, under President Sarney the PMDB was the main party in government, but it had also been the main opposition force against the preceding regime; while the president and many other key figures of his government were examples of the continuity between the past and the nascent democratic regime. The problems this government had in demonstrating its capacity to govern stemmed in part from its ambiguous nature. This frequently immobilized a government that was divided and only had precarious legitimacy. At times, it resorted to strategies of framing policy decisions around expected electoral outcome.[36] Its problems were also related to the institutional crisis itself. When it came to revising the constitution, there was paralysis every time the Constituent Congress, in fulfilling its mandate, sought autonomy from and clashed with the preferences of the executive. The results are well-known. Once again popular expectations of a solution to economic and social problems were not fulfilled. Frustration with the way institutions worked grew and signs of disenchantment with the new political institutions became increasingly evident. As the 1989 electoral campaign showed, the demise of the authoritarian regime and the introduction of democracy converted itself into disillusionment.[37]

It is extraordinary that under these conditions, a little more than two-thirds of those interviewed in 1989 and 1990 recognized the impact of politics on their lives, but only around half registered some interest in politics. It is also symptomatic that barely one-third (in 1989) believed that they had the capacity to influence politics. But the data that relate to their political involvement – i.e. the ways in which they get a basic knowledge of public life – do not suggest isolation from sources of information; between a half and two-thirds of the public watch television or read newspapers or magazines. Still, the following points in Table 9.2 are striking: two-thirds of the people in the sample say they would participate in elections even if it was not legally compulsory to do so; around a half declare a preference for a party; and more than 30 per cent say they were prepared for political participation even if it involved personal costs, i.e. 'to try to convince others to vote' for their preferred candidates.

But what is more important, the data in Table 9.2 also show that Brazilians clearly prefer democratic government to dictatorship or to an attitude of indifference about the political regime. The indices vary from a little more than half in September 1989 to a little more than two-thirds in March the following year. In addition, the data show that rejection of a return to military rule increased; while the attitude of deference towards the legal order was still higher than two-thirds. A majority was not only against repression of civil, social or political rights, but the margin was above the two-thirds level, and sometimes considerably higher. Meanwhile, although those who said they favoured the system upholding minority rights remained close to a half, this diminished slightly between September 1989 and March 1990.

Do the Masses have Democratic Convictions?

As to the difficulties of interpretation that arise from the inconsistencies encountered in some replies, two complementary analytical procedures were taken. The first is to look at the patterns we have observed in a broader context by comparing them with other data from a longer time-sequence, and where possible with results from other countries which are experiencing (or have experienced) a similar process of democratization. The second verifies the consistency of the answers in themselves; basing them on factor analysis of the political questions in the September 1989 survey, it takes groups of opinion on two key topics for this discussion: the position of those interviewed on a scale aimed at measuring levels of political sophistication at the mass level; and their position in a continuum of democratic/authoritarian support.

Table 9.3 sets out the data for the first of these exercises. In general terms, the data confirm the consolidation of the democratic opinions mentioned above. Attention to politics increases after the initial democratic phase just as do the indicators of participation and freedom. But, just at the moment of most acute crisis for the Sarney government – the collapse of the Cruzado Plan – clear signs emerge not of a reversal but of a slow-down in the process of consolidating mass democratic convictions. The rates fall for those who declare a party preference; they increase for those who doubt the capacity of the illiterate to vote, and they fall for those interested in participation. However, it is worth noting that these indices shift slightly in the opposite direction towards the end of the decade, i.e. when the end of the transition period becomes self-apparent. Parallel to the poor performance of the first democratic government and especially of those parties which made up the Aliança Democrática (the political coalition that led the transition), democratic convictions fluctuate. But even so, the results do not indicate a rejection of, or even hostility towards democracy, which continues to command support.

Table 9.4 sets out preferences for political regimes in a comparative perspective. Two things are immediately apparent: firstly, adherence to democracy is lower in Brazil than in Chile or Argentina; secondly, the data suggest that the time sequence is a variable that is worth taking into consideration, a point which the German experience also suggests. At the same time, and taking into account that any comparison has to be seen in terms of different historical conditions and in relation to the different connotations of the indicators used, it is important to consider the two following points. Firstly, there is a longer and more deep-rooted democratic tradition in Chile and Argentina than in Brazil. When Brazil was trying to consolidate a party system, parties that had already appeared in Chile and Argentina at the end of the last century played a key role in democratization; secondly, contrary to the experience at least of Argentina, authoritarianism in Brazil brought relative success in the economic sphere and with it significant social and economic modernization. It also involved less brutal forms of repression. These circumstances, called by some authors the 'paradox of success', made the experience of dictatorship less traumatic and memories of it less long-lasting in Brazil. But the data clearly suggest that, with the

Table 9.3 Political Attitudes and Opinions in São Paulo and in Brazil 1974–90. Per cent.

	1974	1978	1982	1986	1987	1988	1989a	1989b	1990
High interest in politics	11	12	11	21	20	13	38[b]	19	–
High interest in government activities	–	30	–	49	53	–	–	–	–
Favours direct elections	62	76	69	–	–	80	–	–	–
Favours electoral participation	–	–	–	–	–	–	61	66	71
Favours legalisation of the Communist Party	–	–	15	47	–	57	–	–	–
Agrees with strikes	–	59	45	55	–	77	62	60	70
Would not vote unless obligatory	–	–	32	30	35	42	39	36	29
Illiterates do not know how to vote/ should not vote	–	34	41	31	41	–	42	41	44
Has no party preference	19	24	25	35	–	60	56	46	52
Does not favour parties[a]	23	–	23	25	–	39	–	–	57

Sources: Data for 1974–88: J. Muszinski and A. Mendes (1990) 'Democratização e Opinião Pública no Brasil', in B. Lamounier, *De Geisel a Collor: o Balanço da Transição.*
Data for 1989–90: *Cultura Política*
(a) Includes those who think parties 'useless' and consider they make 'participation more difficult'.
(b) The data for 1989a refer to interest in 'national politics'.

Table 9.4 Preference for a Democratic Regime in Brazil and Other Countries. Per cent.

	BRAZIL				CHILE		ARGEN-TINA	GERMANY		
Statement	1988	1989a	1989b	1990	1986	1988	1988	1962	1972	1976
'Democracy is always better than any other form of government'	43	44	55	56	56	62	74	74	90	90
'In some circumstances dictatorship is better than democracy'	21	19	15	17	15	10	13	4	7	6
'Immaterial whether democracy or dictatorship'	26	22	16	17	26	23	10	22	3	4
Do not know/No reply	10	15	14	10	4	5	3	–	–	–

Sources: Brazil: 1988: J. Muszinski and A. Mendes (1990) 'Democratização e opinião pública no Brasil', in B. Lamounier, *De Geisel a Collor: o Balanço da Transição*; 1989 and 1990: *Cultura Política*.
Chile: 1986: FLACSO-Chile; 1989: J. Muzinski and A. Mendes (1990)
Argentina: 1988: Muszinski and Mendes (1990)
Germany: O. W. Gabriel (1990) *Cambio Social y Cultura Política – El Caso de la República Federal de Alemania* (Barcelona, Gedisa Editorial).

passage of time, a majority of Brazilians formed with a preference for democracy.

There are nevertheless some reasons for raising the question of whether the mass public in Brazil is really qualified in a general sense not only to reach definitions in relation to democracy – which understandably became a matter of widespread public interest due to the stimuli of the mid-1980s – but also on a series of aspects of the political system like participation, assessment of input and output mechanisms, party preferences and the ability to place individuals, actors and the parties themselves in a left-right continuum, and so on. Indeed, first and foremost, there is the importance of a populist tradition, which, while coexisting with a certain degree of popular participation, involves large-scale political manipulation. Part of the problem resides here: manipulation is indicative of the existence of socio-political factors that detract from mass political participation. For this reason part of the literature treats populism as being a phenomenon in which the masses make themselves available.[38] In the second place, there are the hypotheses which, as Schmitter[39] suggests, stress the depoliticizing effect among the masses in view of the demobilizing effect of authoritarian regimes. Since it destroys public life, authoritarianism implies political inaction and disinformation. Thirdly, there are the arguments, like those of Cohen,[40] that are a combination of these two. These talk of the depoliticization of the mass public, both as a result of the factors that generate populism, and those that stem from its persistence, which just accentuate the tendency. In the case of authoritarianism, the problem is not so much one of depoliticization caused by a destabilizing government, but of the factors that prolong and accelerate the pre-existing conditions of depoliticization and which prevent the public learning how to participate and defining itself politically. For Cohen this explains why in 1972, during the most repressive phase of authoritarianism in Brazil, over 80 per cent of Brazilians said they were favourably disposed to the military regime. Barred from registering an opinion on something on which he or she is not mobilized, the average person has no way of relating to a political regime as an idea. For this reason (although this was only partially the case among the élites) a person's support for the military government was irrelevant. His or her views were simply expressions of support for a government which was seen as supplier, not as being authoritarian.[41]

In view of this, it was necessary to create a scale to measure degrees of political sophistication among the mass public. The initial hypothesis stems from what Neuman and others termed the 'theory of the three publics'.[42] This is the notion that mass publics in complex societies divide up, on the basis of economic, social and political differentiation into three basic segments: an élite of around 5 per cent (in some circumstances this might be a bit higher) composed of the most active, best informed and most articulate members of society; an intermediate public of 75 per cent, moderately articulate and politically informed, but which shares a reasonably homogeneous pattern of opinion and behaviour; and lastly, the remaining 20 per cent which remain apathetic, uninformed and disinterested, both about political participation and public life in general.

This theory is backed up by extensive empirical evidence encountered in societies with consolidated democratic systems of government, but in which there is greater economic and social homogeneity and much less inequality than in Latin America. For this reason, we have to take into account the large differences in socio-economic structure (it is enough just to remember the differences in educational standards, one of the main variables of sophistication, between the United States and Brazil). Thus, the hypothesis has to take into account the proportion of the 'uninformed, uninterested and least active' in Brazil being at least double that for developed countries. The 'intermediate' public would represent around 50 per cent. Given some global characteristics of the way it is formed, the élite – those who live from politics, are involved in it and form opinions about it – would probably vary less, perhaps between 5 and 10 per cent – a similar sort of proportion as in developed countries. Two aspects of this theory, however, make it useful in analysing the Brazilian case. On the one hand, it is analogous to the concept of politicization as it relates to the basic conditions for political participation. Those social sectors lacking intellectual or informational resources are similar to those classified as 'apathetic' or 'inactive'; their inconsistent behaviour stems from this apathy, alienation and inaction. At the same time the theory holds that those in the 'middle' segment, though much better equipped intellectually to develop their perception of reality than those in the 'inactive' segment, are still very far from being comparable to those mobilized by the activists who, by definition, tend to manipulate basic political concepts to 'undertake, debate or diffuse' politics. Indeed, although able to follow politics and define themselves politically, these intermediate groups are not sufficiently equipped to make logical relationships between their points of view, nor do they necessarily do so in a homogeneous way. Even though politics may be something important for them, this does not stop their outlooks and views reflecting the unequal distribution of intellectual resources, information etc.[43]

A scale to measure, where possible, these differences in levels of sophistication in Brazil has been created (see the Appendix for more information about this and other scales). The three criteria used are the degree of mobilization of information, the salience of politics for the interviewees and the capacity and precision of those interviewed in conceptualizing certain phenomena in political life. Starting with this conceptual framework, it was possible to elaborate a scale that was not only additive but cumulative. In other words, those who were able to respond positively to a more exacting question are also able to do so for a less complicated one which, for instance, only tests his stock of information on the world of politics. Inversely, it is most unlikely that an interviewee who fails to get beyond the elementary stage will reach the levels required for a more sophisticated response, i.e., being able to conceptualize what is 'the left' and 'the right' in politics. The advantage of this sort of measure over that used, for instance by Converse,[44] is that the more sophisticated concept will bring in not only the segments of the élite or groups close to it (because of the inequalities in access to education), but also different segments among the mass public which, despite their lack of resources, feel the impact of politics in their lives, become interested in politics and experience the effects of the resulting political resocialization. It is a notable feature of countries like Brazil, that this comes partly from the mobilization and organization of the poorest sectors in pursuit of a less unequal distribution of the resources (like education) needed for social integration. Now, there is no reason to exclude the possibility that this experience – though probably not a factor assisting the articulation of concepts – plays some role in shaping the differentiated patterns of political sophistication among the less privileged, thereby influencing their political convictions.

The data in Table 9.5 come both from Cohen's work for 1972 and the survey of September 1989. Although not strictly speaking comparable – they use different methodologies to measure the same thing and they relate to different universes (the first to the south-east and the second to the country as a whole) – they provide useful pointers to the type and degree of change that has taken place in the

Table 9.5 Levels of Politicization and Political Sophistication among Brazilians, 1972 and 1989a. Per cent.

	1972	1989a				
	Just South East		South East	Brazil	Rural	Urban
Types		Sophistication				
Ideologues and non ideologues	4	High	13	11	4	14
Group benefits	10	Medium	45	43	33	46
Unpoliticized	86	Low	42	46	63	40
	n = 1.147	n = 749		n = 1.685		

Sources: 1972: Cohen (1979) 'Popular Support for Authoritarian Governments: Brazil under Medici'.
1989a: *Cultura Política*

mass public's capacity for perception over nearly 20 years. In sum, two observations can be made. Firstly, there are good reasons to believe that the immediate political context had a strong influence on the 1972 results. Those interviewed may have felt inhibited in expressing their real feelings and their more deeply-held political convictions. This does not refer to the methodology used, but reflects on the utilization of the survey as an instrument for measuring opinions in a political context which, by definition, induced reticence. In the conditions of the Medici period, the most repressive phase of military rule in Brazil, the public may not have felt entirely willing to be interviewed, particularly about their political opinions. It is difficult to evaluate the extent to which this distorted the results, but it is highly probable that it did so to some extent: two years later, in conditions of less political pressure, large numbers of the same public inflicted a severe electoral defeat on the military regime. In addition, the 1974 elections introduced a crucial factor which, practically up to the end of the transition, played an extraordinarily important role in what we are considering: public debate over the destiny of the authoritarian regime and the possibility of a democratic alternative to it.[45]

Secondly, the profound changes prompted by economic and social modernization in the 20 years between the two surveys have to be taken into account. Although it is impossible to deal extensively with this matter here, it is necessary to take into consideration the two types of effect which, as Santos[46] points out, result from the changes that have been taking place since the mid-1950s in Brazil, which were at their strongest during the military governments. On the one hand, these caused profound alterations in social morphology, giving new dimensions to the size and importance of different social groups, expanding wage labour, incorporating new sectors (like female labour and youth) and deepening capitalist relations. On the other, they redefined the relationship both between these social groups and between them and the state. They gave rise to large-scale mobilization in defence of their interests and to greater economic and social demands on the state. Thus they helped to break down the corporatist structures through which workers, business groups and governments had previously related to one another. Important consequences of this process of modernization have been: (a) the fact that today Brazil is essentially an urban society, with more than three-quarters of the population living in cities; (b) although a pattern of highly unequal income distribution persists, the educational system has expanded a great deal, and has oriented itself to the needs of the poorer and unprivileged; and (c) the media and cultural industries have effectively integrated the whole of the population in an enormous information market. Whatever may be said about the political orientation of this market, it cannot be denied that it has had an effect in increasing the availability of information about political life. Among the most significant of these changes are the emergence of social movements and the formation of new political parties.[47]

Tables 9.6 and 9.7 show, meanwhile, that even if modernization helped to educate the population as a whole to deal with reality, it did not annul the effects of economic, social and regional inequality; in some cases it even accentuated them. Indeed, confirming the evidence presented in the massive literature on this topic, the tables show that the mass public's political sophistication is that much greater when the population is concentrated in middle-ranking or large cities. This level of sophistication is connected with the variables that form the 'tripod' of political participation – income, education and occupation. It would be fanciful to think that the 'conservative modernization' put into practice by the military governments in Brazil would have profoundly altered the pattern of inequality which lies at the root of the paradigm in which those with higher incomes are those with better education and with non-manual jobs, and who at the same

Table 9.6 Levels of Political Sophistication among Brazilian voters by size of Municipality, Income and Education. (1989a). Per cent.

	Size of Municipality			Income			Education		
	Small	Medium	Large	0–5	5–10	10	G1	G2	Higher
Sophistication									
Low	59	35	38	51	30	18	56	28	10
Medium	35	52	46	42	54	51	39	55	47
High	6	13	16	7	16	31	5	17	43
Qui2 =	92.691			167.061			330.17		
DF =	4			4			4		
Sig. =	.000			.000			.000		
Gamma =	.29			.50			.62		

Source: *Cultura Política*
Note: Income figures are given in multiples of the minimum wage; Education grades as follows: 1st grade, 2nd grade, higher education

Table 9.7 Levels of Political Sophistication in the Brazilian Electorate by Levels of Education and Position in the Occupation Structure. (1989a). Per cent.

Sophistication	Non-manual				Manual			
	0	G1	G2	Higher	0	G1	G2	Higher
Low	6	60	27	7	17	76	6	1
Medium	1	30	41	28	6	78	15	1
High	0	10	30	60	2	60	28	10
Marginals	(2)	(36)	(35)	(28)	(12)	(76)	(11)	(1)
Qui2 =	141.831				115.451			
DF =	6				6			
Sig. =	.000				.000			
Gamma =	.63				.52			

Source: *Cultura Política*

time are those who participate more in public life. But, inasmuch as they influence the general conditions in which these changes take place for the public as a whole, the contradictory effects of modernization confirm the relevance of the theory of the three publics.

Democracy, Authoritarianism and Commitment to Political Values

Sophistication, however, is but a prerequisite for the formation of political convictions. On its own it does not resolve the problem of the consistency of opinions about democracy. This requires specific treatment. There are at least three points of departure for interpreting the preliminary evidence set out here. Firstly, some classic versions of democratic theory would tend partially to reduce the significance of the commitment to democracy of the mass public in Brazil because of the inconsistencies found in certain responses. But this implies a supposition that, even in the uncertain conditions of political transition, such commitment would have to be complete – that the public would 'buy' a single package of beliefs and democratic values, and that it would extend its convictions into all spheres of social life in a uniform way. As Converse and others have shown, this is not realistic, not even in consolidated democracies.[48]

Secondly, while those with a 'minimalist' vision of democracy, as criticized above, would admit that political culture may be useful for the stabilization of a democratic regime – though not a condition for its establishment – they would argue that the inconsistency is due to the fact that the public 'has still not become completely accustomed' to the functioning of the new institutions. But in this case, there would be at least two other questions which would have to be explained: (a) what are the conditions in which necessity becomes a virtue, i.e. in which the mass public lives the experience of a democracy as something which is a given and which is seen as being valuable in itself? And (b) what is it that explains that in some cases a democratic heritage leads to democratic attitudes, and in others not?

Thirdly, as we have argued, beliefs and attitudes which legitimate democracy are formed within certain margins of autonomy. We posit that they are spread by political factors that stem from the dynamics of tradition or from the contradictory processes of modernization, and that they do not altogether annul the inertial forces represented by the survival of archaic political practices within the new democratic disposition. Indeed, the interaction between the establishment of democratic institutions and the formation of a democratic culture suffers from the contradictory effects of this inertia. New convictions are not held in an homogeneous way; they do not include all areas of political life; and the mere existence of democratic institutions is not sufficient to get citizens used to the demands of democratic practices.

Working within margins of autonomy, the process of democratic legitimation involves persuasion, and as such implies conscious action on the part of political parties and other actors.

To verify the relevance of this hypothesis, the study turns to the specific role played by democratic beliefs, conceptualizing them as part of a continuum rather than as the components of an homogeneous 'package'. This involves taking data on political regimes, attitudes towards democracy and the repression of political rights. Grouped together as a single factor, a scale was then construed according to Guttman's procedures.[49]

The data in Table 9.8 refer to the results of certain correlations conducted from the scale. They confirm the hypothesis that a step was taken towards the consolidation of democratic convictions at the end of the 1980s. In the first place, it is clear that more than two-thirds of those interviewed, who, classified on a democratic-authoritarian continuum said they favoured the less authoritarian level of the scale, corresponded to those who made an explicit option for a democratic regime. Secondly, it becomes evident that, depending on the indicators used, the intensity of this association varies. This shows that, as suggested above, since the formation of democratic convictions is multi-dimensional, it does not imply homogeneity of responses. This suggests, for instance, the advantage of working on the hypothesis of the formation of various political sub-cultures (as Rockon and Mitchell do) using data for occupation and level of education to explain differences in convictions and the diversity of certain responses. However, due to the limits of space available, this cannot be done here.

Two questions remain to be answered: (a) is there any statistical association between levels of sophistication and positions on the democratic-authoritarian continuum? And (b) is the position of individuals on this continuum and on the scale of sophistication correlated to any extent with commitment to political values? In order to test this latter point, we take as an indicator the nominal responses of those interviewed about their preference to political regime, and then split the responses into those who prefer democracy or dictatorship, and those who declare themselves to be indifferent or unable to answer the question. The results are set out in Tables 9.9 and 9.10.

The most sophisticated tend to classify themselves preponderantly on the democratic end of the continuum; the least sophisticated at the

Table 9.8 Consistency of Attitudes and Opinions about Democracy in accordance with Position in the Democratic–Authoritarian Scale. 1989a. Per cent.

Position in Scale	Position regarding political regime			Interest in Politics		Influence of Politics in your life	
	D*	I*	D**	Yes	No	Yes	No
Democratic	69	15	16	74	26	79	21
Intermediate	44	28	28	66	34	63	37
Authoritarian	34	38	28	57	43	55	45
TOTAL	52	25	23	67	33	67	33
Qui Squared =	130.293		27.749		61.027		
DF =	4		2		2		
SIG. =	.000		.000		.000		
GAMMA =	.35		.24		.35		

D*: Democracy; I*: Indifferent; D**: Dictatorship.

Position in Scale	Vote for Illiterates		Would vote even if not obligatory		Discusses Politics	
	Yes	No	Yes	No	Yes	No
Democratic	67	33	73	27	66	34
Intermediate	60	40	59	41	45	55
Authoritarian	46	54	53	47	39	61
TOTAL	59	41	63	37	52	48
Qui Squared =	130.293	40.404		68.316		
DF =	–	2		2		
SIG. =	.000	.000		.000		
GAMMA =	.27	.28		.36		

Source: *Cultura Política*

authoritarian end. But what is most striking is – as the original hypothesis suggests – that the public situated in the intermediate strata are divided almost equally among the three positions on the continuum. Although not a phenomenon of causation, this shows that starting from the supposition that sophistication precedes commitment to values, we can reach the conclusion that the degree of

Table 9.9 Association between Political Sophistication and Position in the Democratic–Authoritarian Scale: 1989a (%)

	Position in the Scale		
	Democratic	Intermediate	Authoritarian
Sophistication			
Low	26	38	37
Medium	41	36	23
High	69	20	10
(Marginals)	(40)	(34)	(26)

Qui Squared = 111.935 DF = 4
Sign.: .0000 Gamma = −.40
Source: Cultura Política

heterogeneity in relation to the levels of sophistication encountered in middle groups is closely associated with their differentiation in terms of commitment to political values. At the same time, commitment to values (measured by the question about political regime preferences) is more positive among those who classify themselves as 'democrats' and as 'authoritarians' than among those who take an 'intermediate' position. For its part, the lack of sophistication is associated more closely with those who are not committed to values than those who are. But, more importantly, the correlation between sophistication and the position on the democratic-authoritarian continuum, when controlled by the variable of commitment to values shows that the intensity of the association between sophistication and the position on the continuum is greater when those interviewed are committed to political values. This is shown by the gamma coefficient.

Conclusions

As the general public opts for democracy, it is tempting simply to conclude that in post-authoritarian Brazil a political culture sufficient to consolidate a democratic regime has already been formed. But one needs to be careful and distinguish at least two aspects of the problem. On the one hand, the data leave no doubt that, in comparison with orientations and attitudes of the mass public over 20 years, there have been effective and important changes towards what could be described generically as a democratic view of politics. There is also a 'secular' sphere of decision-making in public life, recognized as such, with fairly large margins of autonomy, in relation to which

Table 9.10 Correlation between Political Sophistication and Position in the Democratic–Authoritarian Scale, Controlled by Adherence to Political Values. 1989a. Per cent.

Sophistication	Adherence to Values			Non-adherence to Values		
	Democratic	Intermediate	Authoritarian	Democratic	Intermediate	Authoritarian
Low	30	36	34	19	40	41
Medium	46	35	19	26	40	44
High	70	20	8	55	11	34
(Marginals)	46	33	21	24	38	37

Qui Squared = 71.090 DF = 4
Signif = .0000 Gamma = −.41

Qui Squared = 13.500 DF = 4
Signif = .0009 Gamma = −.17

Source: *Cultura Política*

Figure 9.1 Classification of Situation of Political Consensus and Dissent according to the Proportion of those who share Positive or Negative Orientations about a Democratic Regime.

Positive Orientation (%)	Negative Orientation (%)	Types of situation
0–25	75–100	Anti-democratic consensus
25–40	60–75	Anti-democratic dissent
40–60	40–60	Dissent
60–75	25–40	Democratic dissent
75–100	0–25	Democratic consensus

Source: Flisfisch, A. 'Consenso democrático en el Chile Autoritario' in Lechner, N. *Cultura política y democratización*, FLACSO, 1987.

the public believe they have powers of influence; on the other hand, however, it is necessary to ask whether the reality which the data measure for a specific moment, i.e., the levels which fluctuate between half and two thirds of the citizens opting for these democratic values in 1989–90, actually forms what one could consider both necessary and sufficient for the consolidation of democracy in Brazil in the longer run.

On this point, there is no agreement in the literature on democratization. The positions authors adopt vary between, on the one hand, those who tend to stress a consensual view of democracy, i.e., those who believe that for democracy to be consolidated there has to be near unanimity among members of the community about the basic rules of the game;[50] and on the other hand, there are those who adopt a more conflictual definition of democracy, i.e. although the majority may agree on the rules of the game, not everyone has to do so, and there is always a minority which – for a variety of reasons – would like to try out other alternatives or even not to take part at all in the workings of democracy.[51] The virtue of democracy, it is said, lies in the fact that a diversity of conceptions can coexist without threatening its existence. Leaving the first alternative aside since it can be easily answered on account of its non-democratic nature, the second – with its rider about the need for a majority democratic consensus albeit not an unanimous one, is no less problematic. As Flisfisch[52] stresses, the problem then becomes one of arbitrarily choosing a mathematical equation appropriate to it. In other words, it becomes necessary to decide on the degree of majority from which the normative integration of members of the political community can be considered as helping to stabilize a democratic regime. Using Mann's work (1965) on the integration of mass publics in England and the United States, which proposed five levels of democratic consent and dissent as defined by the attitudes of individuals towards a political regime, we can classify countries in processes of democratization.

Accepting Flisfisch's arbitrary suggestion, and in view of the data in Tables 9.3 and/or 9.6, we can see that Brazil is situated in a position of 'dissent' pure and simple; or at best in a situation that is shifting towards 'democratic dissent'. This means that although the degree of recognition of democratic values is not entirely sufficient, on its own, to achieve the stabilization of democracy, the necessary basis for what some authors have termed a 'reservoir' of legitimacy for the new regime is clearly there. At the same time, it is worth stressing the aspect which stems from it. In the actual current of democratization in Brazil, the public situated in the 'intermediate' strata of the scale of sophistication – i.e. nearly 50 per cent of the electorate – is playing a crucial role in the consolidation of a democratic culture. It is composed of sectors which possess the minimal cognitive and informational resources required for public life to function. It therefore forms the core structure upon which any strategy for consolidating democracy in the long term has to be based. However, owing to limitations of space this point cannot be developed any further.

APPENDIX: CONSTRUCTION OF SCALES

The research project 'Cultura Política e Consolidação da Democracia no Brasil' was carried out through an agreement between CEDEC, Data Folha and the Department of Political Science at USP; the author acted as its director. It involved three surveys (national, urban and rural) done by stratified and aleatory sampling. The total electorate of Brazil was considered as the universe, divided according to regions: south, south-east, north-east, centre-north-west. For the purposes of the sample, municipalities were grouped together according to their regional weight, geographical location, socio-economic level, and stratified by population size. Through successive processes of selection, the neighbourhood was identified, the street down to the individual. In September 1989, 2,083 electors were interviewed; in December, 2,506 and in March 1990, 2,480.

The scales were constructed from factor analysis undertaken for the whole gamut of political and attitudinal questions. For the political sophistication scale, the following questions were used, grouped together in a single factor.

1. 'Whom should the political parties represent?'
2. 'In your opinion, do the President of the Republic and his ministers take important decisions on their own, or are they influenced by other political forces in the country?'
3. 'Do you agree or do you disagree that only an alliance of all political parties could solve the country's problems?'
4. 'Are you interested in national politics, state politics, municipal politics, or are you not interested in politics at all?'
5. 'Does politics influence your life?'
6. 'Are you in the habit of reading or watching political news items?'

7. 'What do you understand to be the right-wing in politics?'
8. 'What do you understand to be the left-wing in politics?'
9. 'For you, what is democracy'?

The first three questions were included in order to test whether the interviewee was able to make use of his/her stock of information about the political system. The three following questions were related to the importance of politics for the interviewee. The three last questions sought to test his/her capacity to conceptualize objects in politics. The points were given cumulatively.

For the democratic-authoritarian scale, the following questions were used:

1. 'Would the country be much better if only one political party existed?'
2. 'So as to maintain order, should the laws always be obeyed even when unjust?'
3. 'Is democracy dangerous because it can provoke disorder?'
4. 'Would the country work much better if the military returned to power?'
5. 'Should the government be allowed to ban political parties?'
6. 'Should the government be allowed to close down the Congress?'

Even though these questions were typical of a single addition scale, the way in which they were presented to the interviewees suggested that they were approached as dichotomies. Given the intensity of the stimuli, for the purposes of interpretation, only a total rejection was considered an indication of non-acceptance of an authoritarian standpoint.

ENDNOTES

Chapter 1 (Alkimar Moura)

1. See Fishlow, Albert (1989), 'A tale of two presidents: the political economy of crisis management', in Stepan, A. (ed.) *Democratizing Brazil* (New York/Oxford, Oxford University Press); Bacha, E. L. and Malan, P. S. (1989), 'Brazil Debt: from the miracle to the Fund', in A. Stepan (ed.), *Democratizing Brazil*; Lamounier, B. and Moura, A. R. (1986), 'Economic Policy and Political Opening in Brazil', in Hartlyn, J. and Morley, S. (eds), *Latin American Political Economy: financial crisis and political change* (Boulder/London, Westview Press); Moura, Alkimar R. (1990), 'Rumo à entropia: a política econômica de Geisel a Collor', in Lamounier, B. (ed.) *De Geisel a Collor: o balanço da transição* (São Paulo, Editora Sumaré); Fundação Getúlio Vargas (1981), 'Choques externos e respostas de política econômica no Brasil', *Estudos Especiais IBRE* no.5, Rio de Janeiro; Castro, Antonio B. and Pires de Sousa, Francisco E. (1985), *A economia brasileira em marcha forçada* (Rio de Janeiro, Paz e Terra); Bresser Pereira, L. Carlos (1989), 'The perverse macroeconomics of debt, deficit and inflation in Brazil', in Fukushi, T. and Kagami, M., *Perspectives on the Pacific Basin Economy: a comparison of Asia and Latin America* (Tokyo, Institute of Developing Economies); Cardoso, Eliana and Fishlow, Albert (1990), 'The macroeconomics of the Brazilian external debt', in Sachs, I. (ed.) *Developing Country Debt and Economic Performance* (Chicago, Chicago University Press); Holanda Barbosa, F. and Sanchez de la Cal, M. (1992), 'Crescimento econômico e renegociação da dívida externa', *Revista de Economia Política*, vol.12, no.1, São Paulo.
2. Senna, J. Julio (1989), *Tempos de incerteza: a economia brasileira nos anos oitenta* (Rio de Janeiro, Livros Técnicos e Científicos).
3. Bodin de Moraes, P. (1990), 'A condução da política monetária durante o Plano Cruzado', *Revista de Economia Política*, São Paulo, vol.10, no.2.
4. Salomon Brothers (1992), 'Private capital flows to Latin America: volume triples to US$ 40 billion in 1991', *Sovereign Assessment Group*, Emerging Markets, New York.
5. SEADE-DIEESE survey on income distribution in the Greater São

Paulo metropolitan area, as reported in *Gazeta Mercantil*, 2 February, 1992, São Paulo.

6. Kiguel, Miguel A. and Liviatan, Nissan (1992), 'When do heterodox stabilization programs work?' in *The World Bank Research Observer*, vol.7, no.1 January.
7. Ibid.

Chapter 2 (Gustavo Franco)

* The author wishes to thank CNPq-Conselho Nacional de Pesquisa for financial support.

1. P. Cagan (1956), 'The Monetary Dynamics of Hyperinflation' in M. Friedman (ed.) *Studies in the Quantity Theory of Money* (Chicago: University of Chicago Press), p. 25.
2. P. Cagan (1987), 'Hyperinflation' in J. Eatwell et al. (eds) *The New Palgrave Dictionary of Economics* (London: Macmillan), vol. 2, p. 704.
3. There are, however, three important exceptions to this generalization, namely the cases of the last few months of hyperinflations in Germany in 1923, Hungary in 1946, and Greece in 1944 in which inflation did indeed behave explosively. It is important to observe that inflation explosion is a phenomenon in its own right, having to do with the introduction of indexed monies or explicit threats of repudiation of the national currency. They are by no means typical. More detail in G. H. B. Franco (1991), *High and Hyperinflations: cross country patterns and the design of stabilization*, Center of Latin American Studies, University of Pittsburgh.
4. These aspirations were connected to the very low levels of real wages immediately after the war, nearly a third, on average, of 1914 levels, and also to the extraordinary mushrooming of union membership and activity occurring after the war. See Franco, *High and Hyperinflations: cross country patterns and the design of stabilization*, p. 185.
5. This refers to the adverse effect of inflation on the real value of tax revenues. On the key role of this phenomenon to the stabilization of European hyperinflations in the 1920s, see Franco (1990), 'Fiscal reforms and stabilization: four hyperinflation cases examined', *The Economic Journal* 100(399) March, p. 184.
6. F. Capie (1986), 'Conditions in which Very Rapid Inflation has Appeared', *Carnegie-Rochester Conference Series on Public Policy* 24.
7. The official figures registered a small surplus, but the economic team of the first civilian government claimed there was a 1.5 per cent deficit, according to the operational concept.
8. Considering the average inflation rate for the last six months of all hyperinflations known. Cf. Franco (1990), 'Hiperinflação: teoria e prática' in *Inflação e hiperinflação: interpretações e retórica* (São Paulo: Nobel).
9. An account of these issues may be found in C. A. Longo (1991), 'O processo orçamentário no Brasil', *Revista de Economia Política*, vol.11, no.2, April.

10. A detailed exposition of this point is provided by F. Giambiagi and J. C. G. Soares (1990), 'Negligencia fiscal, inversión reprimida y deuda externa: una revisión crítica del caso brasileño'. Mimeo.
11. Examples of these views may be found in P. N. Batista (1990), 'Deficit e financiamento do setor público brasileiro: 1983–1988', *Revista de Economia Política*, vol.10, no.4, December; and F. Oliveira (1989), 'Política fiscal e política monetária no Brasil: o estrangulamento imposto pela dívida externa' Campinas, Unicamp, *Texto para Discussão* no. 12.
12. See V. Tanzi (1989), 'Fiscal policy and economic restructuring in Latin America'. Mimeo.

Chapter 3 (Carlos A. Longo)

1. See Simonsen, M. H. (1979), *Inflação gradualismo versus tratamento de choque* (Rio de Janeiro, APEC, 1970).
2. See Pelaez, C. M. and Suzigan, W. (1976), *História monetária do Brasil* (Rio de Janeiro, IPEA, série Monográfica nº 23), pp. 336–67.
3. An expanded version of the arguments in this section can be found in Longo, C. A. (1990), *Estado Brasileiro: diagnósticos e alternativas* (São Paulo, Atlas); 'Crise e Revisão das Contas Públicas', in J. P. Reis Velloso (ed.), *Brasil: agenda para sair da crise – inflação e déficit* (Rio de Janeiro, José Olympio); and 'Brazil: monetary and financial system', in *The New Palgrave Dictionary of Money and Finance* (in press).
4. The budgetary obscurity that results from cross-subsidies between the fiscal budget and state enterprises is characteristic of many developing, newly-industrialized countries. For a comparative analysis, grounded in statistical information and accompanied by suggestions for reform, see World Bank (1988), *World Development Report 1988* (Oxford, Oxford University Press), chapter 8. But this problem is not confined to developing nations; it permeates discussions of deregulation and privatization in Western Europe and the socialist countries. See for example the case of the USSR in V. K. Senchagov et al. (1989), 'Restructuring the Financial System and its Influence on Economic Development', in G. Krause-Junk (ed.) *Proceedings of the 45th Congress of the International Institute of Public Finance*, Buenos Aires, International Institute of Public Finance.
5. See A. Premchand (1988), 'El Estado y las Empresas Públicas: relaciones presupuestarias', in Premchand A. and Antonaya A. L. (eds), *Aspectos del presupuesto público* (Washington, IMF).
6. For a less schematic presentation of the Collor Plan and related issues, see Longo, C. A. (1990), 'O Plano Collor em perspectiva', in C. de Faro (ed.), *Plano Collor, avaliações e perspectivas* (Rio de Janeiro, Livros Técnicos e Científicos); Longo, C. A. (1991), 'O Plano Collor aos nove meses', in J. P. Reis Velloso (ed.), *Condições para a retomada do desenvolvimento* (Rio de Janeiro, Nobel); Longo C. A. (1991), 'A questão da governabilidade', in C. de Faro (ed.), *A Economia pós Plano Collor II* (Rio de Janeiro, Livros Técnicos e Científicos).

7. This section draws heavily on M. Figueira de Mello (1991), 'O Projeto de Privatização Brasileira', unpublished Ph.D thesis, Faculdade de Economia e Administração, University of São Paulo; BNDS (1991), 'The Brazilian Privatization Program' (Rio de Janeiro, BNDES); Rogério L. F. Werneck (1991), 'Setting the Stage: The First year of the new Brazilian Privatization Program', Department of Economics PUC-Rio, mimeo.
8. See Faoro, R. (1957), *Os donos do poder* (Porto Alegre, Globo), vol. I, pp. 64–65.
9. Ibid, pp. 66–9.
10. This section relies on S. D. Silber (1991), 'Uma Avaliação da Política Brasileira de Comércio Exterior', *Informações FIPE*, May 1991; C. Primo Braga (1990), 'Liberalização Comercial e Estabilização', *Informações FIPE*, August 1990; and 'US Policies and the Prospects for Latin American Economic Integration', in Baer, W. and Coes, D. (eds) (1990), *US Policies and the Latin American Economies* (New York, Praeger).

Chapter 4 (Camargo and Barros)

1. Most of the ideas in this paper are discussed in the literature on poverty in Brazil. The objective of this work is simply to organize them in a way which provides the authors with an analytical framework for expressing their views on the kind of policies which should be implemented to reduce poverty in Brazil. For this reason, the authors decided not to overburden the reader with a long bibliography of the original sources of the ideas.
2. See IBGE (1991), *Crianças e adolescentes*, vol. 3, Fundação Instituto Brasileiro de Geografia e Estatística.

Chapter 5 (M. H. G. de Castro)

1. On this subject see V. E. Faria and M. H. G. de Castro (1990), 'Social Policy and Democratic Consolidation in Brazil', in Robert Wilson (ed.), *The Political Economy of Brazil: Public Policies in an Era of Transition* (Austin, Univ. of Texas Press).
2. R. Titmus (1963), *Essays on the Welfare State* (London, Allen & Unwin).
3. G. Esping-Andersen (1990), *The Three Worlds of Welfare Capitalism* (New Jersey, Princeton University Press).
4. According to research developed by E. Noronha (1989), 'Acompanhamento das Greves no Brasil – 1978/89' (Campinas, NEPP/UNICAMP, unpublished research report).
5. According to Santos, 60 per cent of the existing technical and professional associations were created after the 1964 revolution; the number of scientific associations practically doubled between 1975 and 1985. Cf. W. G. dos Santos (1986), 'A Pós-Revolução Brasileira', in Hélio Jaguaribe (ed.), *Brasil sociedade democrática* (Rio de Janeiro, J. Olímpio).
6. Various works analysed different movements organized around particular demands (health care, day nurseries, housing, transport) and its growing importance in the government agenda, especially after the direct elections

for state government in 1982. See R. Bochi (1985), 'A Abertura e a Nova Classe Média na Política Brasileira: 1977–1982' (Aguas de São Pedro, ANPOCS, unpublished paper); R. C. Cardoso, Ruth (1983), 'Movimentos Sociais Urbanos: Balanço Crítico', in M. H. Tavares de Almeida and Bernardo Sorj (eds), *Sociedade e política no Brasil Pós–64* (São Paulo, Brasiliense); and P. Jacobi (1989), *Movimentos sociais e políticas públicas* (São Paulo, Cortez).

7. Under the slogan 'Diretas Já' (Direct Elections Now) there occurred intense mass movements, led by opposition parties (PMDB, PT, PDT), claiming direct presidential elections. Although this campaign did not succeed, it expressed the strong expectation of the population about the urgent return to democracy.
8. See W. E. Faria and M. H. G. de Castro (1990), 'Social Policy and Democratic Consolidation in Brazil'.
9. In particular from the medical-sanitary movement, with historical roots in the Brazilian Communist Party, and strongly articulated within the state apparatus where several of its members were working.
10. This topic sums up part of the research report 'The System of Social Welfare in Brazil' by S. Draibe, M. Helena, G. de Castro, and B. Azevedo, developed within the project 'Social Policies for the Urban Poor in Southern Latin America', CEBRAP-Mellow/Kellogg's, under the coordination of Guilherme O'Donnell and Vilmar Faria, September 1991.
11. S. Draibe (1990), As políticas sociais brasileiras: Diagnóstico e Perspectivas', in IPEA (ed.), *Prioridades e perspectivas de políticas públicas para a década de 90* (Brasília, IPEA/IPLAN).
12. The two next items are based on V. Faria and M. H. G. de Castro, (1990) 'Social Policy and Democratic Consolidation in Brazil', pp. 131–7.
13. Instituto de Geografia e Estatística, *Research on Family Budget*, Brasília, 1988.
14. Macedo, Roberto (1987), 'The (Mis) targeting of Social Programs in Brazil' (São Paulo, USP, unpublished manuscript).
15. G. O'Donnell, P. Schmitter, and L. Whitehead (eds) (1986), *Transitions from Authoritarian Rule: Comparative Perspectives*, 4 vols. (Baltimore and London, Johns Hopkins Univ. Press); B. Lamounier (1985), 'Apontamentos sobre a Questão Democrática Brasileira', in A. Rouquié, B. Lamounier and J. Schwarzer (eds), *Como renascem as democracias* (São Paulo, Brasiliense); M. C. C. de Souza (1988), 'The Brazilian "New Republic": under the "Sword of Damocles"', in Alfred Stepan (ed.), *Democratizing Brazil* (Oxford/New York, Oxford University Press).
16. See S. Draibe (1990), 'As políticas sociais brasileiras: Diagnóstico e Perspectivas', in IPEA (ed.), *Prioridades e perspectivas de políticas públicas para a década de 90* (Brasília, IPEA/IPLAN).
17. S. Draibe (1990), 'As políticas sociais brasileiras: Diagnóstico e Perspectivas'.
18. We refer to PT, PMDB, PSDB, PDT, and PSB, parties which presented reformist electoral programmes in the latest elections, stressing the fundamental role of the state in providing to all social areas.

Chapter 6 (M. H. Tavares de Almeida)

* I wish to express my gratitude to Leila Cristina da Silva, an extremely efficient research assistant, who collected data and references and created most of the tables and graphs; to Eduardo Noronha, who prepared the graph about fulfilment of strike demands using NEPP-UNICAMP's data base on strikes; and William Shelton, who translated the text into English.

1. A. Pizzorno (1978), 'Political exchange and collective identity in industrial conflict', in Crouch, Colin and Pizzorno, Alessandro (eds), *The Resurgence of Class Conflict in Western Europe since 1968*, vol.2, (London, Macmillan Press).
2. I use this expression as defined by Valenzuela, that is, in confrontational unionism 'the majority of labour movement leaders are in opposition, as they attempt to resist state policies through union organization and mobilization rather than through party politics'. This form of union action would be typical of authoritarian or semi-competitive contexts or of situations characterized by great political instability and precarious institutionalization of democratic procedures. J. S. Valenzuela (1983), 'Movimientos obreros y sistemas políticos: un análisis conceptual y tipológico', *Desarrollo Económico*, vol. 23 (91), Oct.–Dec., Buenos Aires.
3. Singer distinguishes between the *struggles against inflation* and the *struggles for wage indexation.* The latter occur and tend to be generalized when inflation is chronic. He also argues that, as price increases accelerated, the struggles for indexation became more and more an effort to reduce the periods between wage settlements, attenuating – though not impeding – the transfers of real income from creditors to debtors. P. Singer (1991), 'Reflexões sobre inflação e estabilização', São Paulo, mimeo.
4. C. Maier (1987), 'The politics of inflation in the twentieth century', in Maier (ed.), *In Search of Stability: explorations in historical political economy* (Cambridge, Cambridge University Press).
5. A good analysis of the Figueiredo government's economic policies and dilemmas can be found in A. Fishlow (1988), 'A tale of two presidents: the political economy of crisis management', in A. Stepan (ed.), *Democratizing Brazil* (New York/Oxford, Oxford University Press).
6. Elaborated in 1981, *Esperança e Mudança* described in some detail a development strategy based on planning and state management of economic expansion. Renegotiation of the foreign debt and fiscal and financial reforms were considered essential in securing a new development policy.
7. L. C. Bresser Pereira (1988), *Ideologias econômicas e democracia no Brasil*, Sao Paulo, mimeo.
8. Sallum Jr, Martins and Graeff (1986) made an excellent analysis of the New Republic's first year. A significant part of our discussion is based on their work. B. Sallum Jr, C. E. Martins, and E. Eduardo (1986), 'Nova República, de Tancredo a Sarney', *Análise de Conjuntura*, vol. 8, no. 2, Curitiba, IPARDES.
9. N. Lechner (1987), *Cultura política y democratización* (Santiago, FLACSO/CLACSO/ICI), p. 36.
10. For an analysis of the economic policy in this period see A. Moura

(1990), 'Rumo à entropia: a política econômica de Geisel a Collor', in B. Lamounier (ed.), *De Geisel a Collor: o balanço da transição* (São Paulo, Editora Sumaré).

11. For an excellent analysis of this process, see Cardoso, for whom, problems of governability were due to the fact that the transition did not include 'effective transformation of the ways of organizing the State, society itself, parties or the parties' relationship with the State'. Consequently there had been a reabsorption of the forces opposed to authoritarianism by the 'old regime' establishment, through clientelistic co-optation and patrimonial practices, with a consequent weakening of the impetus for transformation. F. H. Cardoso (1987), 'A negociação da transição', in J. A. Guilhon de Albuquerque and E. Durham (eds), *A transição política – necessidade e límites da negociação* (São Paulo, USP).
12. E. Noronha (1989), 'Relações trabalhistas', *Brasil, 1987 – relatório sobre a situação social do país* (Campinas, NEPP–UNICAMP).
13. Singer argues: 'When inflation is chronic, its original causes contribute nothing to understanding its current dynamic. This dynamic is made up of waves of price increases, which include wages, rent and indirect taxes. As these prices are costs, the elevation of a certain number of prices unbalance a corresponding quantity of the equation prices versus costs, making the former inferior to the latter. A new wave of increases follows, to correct these imbalances and in turn creates new imbalances which set off the third round and so on. Thus, either indexation incites an increase in contractual income, which constitutes costs for business and families – intensifying, and accelerating the dynamic of inflation.' P. Singer, *Reflexões sobre inflação e estabilização.*
14. This calculation includes all the public sector – direct and indirect administration and public enterprises – and strikes held during the last two months of the military government. Between March and December, under José Sarney's mandate, public sector employees were responsible for 35.7 per cent of work stoppages.
15. Roxborough showed the relation between the frequency that social pact was spoken of in the press and the intensification of strike activity. I. Roxborough (1989), 'Organized Labor: a major victim of the debt crisis', in B. Stalling and R. Kaufman, *Debt and Democracy in Latin America* (Boulder, Westview Press).
16. Sola suggested that inflation was, to a certain extent, useful for union organizing and for empowering leaderships reliant on conflict strategies. Evidence of this, during the period, seems to corroborate that hypothesis. L. Sola (1989), 'Límites políticos ao choque heterodoxo no Brasil – técnicos, políticos e democracia', *Revista Brasileira de Ciências Sociais*, vol. 9, São Paulo, Vértice.
17. Ibid.
18. Opinion polls data from DATAFOLHA.
19. E. Diniz (1988), 'Empresariado, sindicatos e política econômica no Brasil da Nova República: 1985/1987', PREALC/OIT, Santiago, mimeo.
20. Diniz records the first statements by business leaders in late March. They increased when it became clear that there was no definite timetable

for ending the freeze, since it was increasingly linked to the government's and the PMDB's political-electoral goals. For information about the debate see E. Diniz (1988), 'Empresariado, sindicatos e política econômica no Brasil da Nova República: 1985/1987'.

21. According to Noronha, the number of working days lost dropped from 37,070,366 to 10,093,159 in 1986, clearly demonstrating a lower level of conflict in the year of the Cruzado Plan. E. Noronha (1989), 'Relações trabalhistas'.
22. Negotiations were easier and results more favourable for workers in non-oligopolist sectors. Consequently, Camargo and Ramos showed that, during the plan, workers in the most competitive sectors obtained higher real wages than those employed in oligopolist sectors. J. M. Camargo and C. A. Ramos (1988), *A revolução indesejada* (Rio de Janeiro, Ed. Campus).
23. For a detailed description of these pressures on the economic system, see Ibid.
24. On 27 July, the government created the National Development Fund, that was to be funded by resources from a compulsory loan on the purchase of automobiles, fuel, international air tickets and the dollar for tourism abroad. The decree also established that price increases generated by the compulsory loan would not be computed in the Consumer Price Index' (IPC) calculation, used to trigger wage escalator.
25. Statements by CUT's president, Jair Meneguelli, are in *Exame*, 6 June 1986, p. 32. Statement by CGT's leader Joaquim dos Santos Andrade was published in *O Estado de São Paulo*, 24 July 1986, p. 30.
26. Diniz also gives an excellent summary of business leaders' opinions on the theme. E. Diniz 'Empresariado, sindicatos e política econômica'.
27. The measures were numerous. Those having the greatest impact are described by J. M. Camargo and C. A. Ramos, *A revoluçao indesejada*.
28. I have done a more detailed analysis of this experience of social pact in M. H. Tavares de Almeida (1987) 'Difícil Caminho: Sindicatos e Política na Construção da Democracia', in F. W. Reis and G. O'Donnell (eds), *A democracia no Brasil – dilemas e perspectivas* (São Paulo, Vértice).
29. From January to June, 1987, monthly rates of inflation were, respectively: 16.82 per cent, 13.94 per cent, 14.40 per cent, 20.96 per cent, 23.21 per cent and 26.06 per cent.
30. Apud IPEA/IPLAN (1987) 'Inflação reduz rendimentos reais dos trabalhadores no primeiro semestre de 1987', *Boletim de Conjuntura da CES*, no.1, July, Brasília, Coordenadoria de Emprego e Salários, mimeo.
31. E. Noronha, 'Relações trabalhistas'.
32. Public sector unionist participation in CUT's leadership rose systematically during the 1980s. Among the fifteen members of the National Executive Committee elected during I CONCLAT, there was only one unionist from the public sector. That proportion rose from 2/15 in CUT's first directorate, elected in 1984, to 3/15 in the Executive Committee chosen in 1986, and to 5/15 in that elected in 1988. A membership list of CUT's National Executive Committees can be found in L. M. Rodrigues (1990), *CUT: os militantes e a ideologia* (Rio de Janeiro, Paz e Terra).

33. The Bresser Plan established: a) increases in some prices and public tariffs whose values were out of line with other prices; b) a three-month freeze on all prices; c) application of automatic wage trigger on May wages, abolition of wage trigger and establishment of free wage bargaining on the period of annual wage settlements; d) payment of the difference between real inflation and wages frozen in six instalments from the date prices were to be unfrozen; e) monthly correction of prices and wages, after the 90 days freeze according to a new index – the Price Reference Unit – calculated by the average monthly inflation of the three preceding months; f) daily mini-devaluations of the exchange rate and, g) nominal interest rates averaging 12 per cent per month. The full governmental decree was published in *Gazeta Mercantil*, 13-16 June 1987.
34. For an interesting discussion and criticism of the Macroeconomic Consistency Plan, see A. Bier, L. Paulani and R. Messemberg (1987), 'O desenvolvimento em xeque', *Novos Estudos CEBRAP* no. 19, São Paulo, CEBRAP, pp.153–71.
35. One month later, these same percentages were, respectively: worse = 60 per cent, equal = 30 per cent, better = 7 per cent. Data from DATAFOLHA, apud. *Folha de São Paulo*, 12 July 1987, p. A-52.
36. E. Diniz, 'Empresariado, sindicatos e política econômica no Brasil da Nova República: 1985/1987'.
37. The most important pieces of discussion were published in the press and republished in 'Artigos na Imprensa sobre o novo Plano de Estabilização econômica', *Revista de Economia Política*, vol. 8, no. 1, Jan–March, 1988, pp. 132-52.
38. The situation was aggravated by military demand for wage improvement. A description of the conflict and its impact on economic policy can be found in L. C. Bresser Pereira (1988), 'Experiências de um governo', *Cadernos de Conjuntura*, vol. 16, Rio de Janeiro, IUPERJ.
39. Problems in renegotiating the foreign debt, within guidelines proposed by the minister, also helped to weaken him. See his own vision about the issue on Bresser Pereira, 'Experiências de um Governo'.
40. Provisional Measure no.32, as well as the president's speech that introduced it, can be found in *Revista de Economia Política*, vol. 9, no. 2, April–June, 1989, pp. 127-39.
41. Maier considers it a coalition typical of hyperinflation. Although I disagree with his definition of hyperinflation, I think the idea of inflationary coalition can be sustained. C. Maier, 'The politics of inflation in the twentieth century'.
42. For a discussion of inflation as a 'prisoner's dilemma' type of game, see S. Maital and Y. Benjamini, 'Inflation as a prisoner's dilemma', *Journal of Post Keynesian Economics*, n/d, pp. 459–81. This article was already finished when I read the preliminary version of I. Roxborough (1991), *Social Pacts and Inertial Inflation in Mexico and Brazil. The politics of anti-inflationary policies in Brazil and Mexico – Viva Corporatism! viva social-democracy!*, Mexico, preliminary draft. The author presents an interesting

discussion about the usefulness and analytical difficulties of employing the 'prisoner's dilemma' game to understand the stabilization policies dilemmas in Mexico and Brazil.

43. G. H. B. Franco (1987), 'Política de estabilização no Brasil: algumas lições do Plano Cruzado', *Texto para discussão*, no.155, Rio de Janeiro, Department of Economy, PUC/RJ, mimeo.
44. Ibid.
45. I am not saying that co-ordination and incentives for transforming the stabilization process into a 'co-operative game' are a panacea for the grave problems of inflation now ravaging a great number of Latin American countries. Discussion of the roots of the inflationary surge, as well as the range of policies most apt for subduing it, has already consumed rivers of ink and continues to be one of the main bones of contention among Latin American economists and those Anglo-American scholars who specialize in southern perversions. I am only attempting to highlight certain non-economic circumstances that can presumably facilitate stabilization efforts. Even so, I do so cautiously. Available empirical evidence about stabilization experiments in poor capitalist countries during the past twenty years is scanty and accounts for few lasting successes. Therefore, it does not allow for definite conclusions.
46. J. C. Torre (1988), 'Transición democrática y emergencia económica', Buenos Aires, mimeo.
47. G. O'Donnell (1989), 'Argentina de novo', *Novos Estudos – CEBRAP* vol. 24, São Paulo, Cebrap, pp. 3–13.
48. For interpretations located somewhere between these two poles, see L. Sola (1989), 'Límites políticos ao choque heterodoxo no Brasil – técnicos, políticos e democracia' and I. Roxborough (1989), 'Organized Labor: a major victim of the debt crisis'.
49. A. Fishlow (1988), 'A Tale of two presidents: the political economy of crisis management'.
50. I am not dealing with these policies' effects on the political dynamic and on democratic institutions being built, as I considered this question in M. H. Tavares de Almeida (1991), 'El Reformismo Democrático en Tiempo de Crisis', in Norbert Lechner (ed.), *Capitalismo, democracia y reformas* (Santiago, FLACSO).

Chapter 7 (B. Lamounier)

* I am grateful to Antonio Octávio Cintra for his critique of the first version of this article. I also wish to thank Marcelo Cavarozzi, Laurence Whitehead, Amaury de Souza, and João Paulo dos Reis Velloso for their comments. I thank the National Endowment for Democracy and Ford Foundation for the support given to the programme of political and institutional studies at the Institute of Economic, Social, and Political Studies, São Paulo.

1. See Arend Lijphart (1982), 'Os Modelos Majoritário e Consociacional da Democracia,' in Bolivar Lamounier (ed.), *A ciência política nos anos 80* (Brasília: Editora da UnB); (1984), *Democracies: Patterns of Majoritarian and Consensus Government in Twenty Countries* (New Haven: Yale

University Press); and (1991), 'Presidencialismo e Democracia Majoritária,' in Bolivar Lamounier (ed.), *A opção parlamentarista* (São Paulo: Editora Sumaré).

2. See Antônio Octávio Cintra and Plínio Dentzien's comments to Arend Lijphart's article in B. Lamounier (ed.) (1982), *A ciência política nos anos 80* (Brasília: Editora da UnB). The institutional complexity underlying Brazilian presidentialism, differentiating it from other Latin American presidential systems, is also underscored by Sérgio Abranches (1988) in 'Presidencialismo de coalizão: o dilema institutional brasileiro', *Revista Dados* 31:1.
3. See W. H. Morris-Jones (1988), 'The politics of the Indian Constitution,' in Vernon Bogdanor (ed.), *Constitutions in Democratic Politics* (Aldershot, England: Gower Publishing Co. Ltd.) p. 130.
4. On the Brazilian electoral system, see the studies collected by Olavo Brasil de Lima Jr. (1985), in *Sistema Eleitoral Brasileiro: teoria e prática* (Rio de Janeiro: IUPERJ/Rio Fundo Editora); on the federative system, see Wanderley Guilherme dos Santos (1987), *Crise e Castigo* (São Paulo: Ed. Vértice).
5. See Encinar et al. (1991), 'El proceso constituyente: enseñanzas a partir de cuatro casos recientes – España, Portugal, Brasil y Chile' (São Paulo: *Textos Idesp* no. 37); see also Amaury de Souza and Bolívar Lamounier, 'A feitura da nova Constituição: um reexame da cultura política brasileira,' in Bolivar Lamounier (ed.) (1990), *De Geisel a Collor: o balanço da transição* (São Paulo: Ed. Sumaré).
6. Amaury de Souza (1978), 'The Nature of Corporatist Representation' (Cambridge, Mass.: MIT, unpublished Ph.D. Dissertation); Youssef Cohen (1988), *The Manipulation of Consent* (Pittsburgh: Pittsburgh University Press).
7. On the political and institutional changes in the thirties, see Walter Costa Porto (1989), *O voto no Brasil* (Brasília: Senado Federal); Victor Nunes Leal (1976), *Coronelismo, enxada e voto* (São Paulo: Ed. Alfa-Omega, first edition, 1948); J. F. Assis Brasil (1931), *Do voto e do modo de votar* (Rio de Janeiro: Imprensa Nacional); Boris Fausto (ed.) (1981), *O Brasil Republicano*, vol. III (São Paulo: Difel).
8. On the stages of plebiscitarian presidentialism in Brazil, see my essay 'Brasil: rumo ao parlamentarismo' in Bolivar Lamounier (ed.) (1991), *A opção parlamentarista* (São Paulo: Ed. Sumaré).
9. Costa Porto, *O voto no Brasil*, p. 269.
10. On the strengthening of parties between 1945 and 1964, see Antonio Lavareda (1991), *A democracia nas urnas* (Rio de Janeiro: IUPERJ/Rio Fundo Editora); on the dual-party experience of 1965–79, see Maria D'Alva G. Kinzo (1988), *Legal Opposition Politics under Authoritarian Rule in Brazil – the Case of the MDB, 1966–79* (London: MacMillan); Bolivar Lamounier and Rachel Meneguello (1986), *Partidos políticos e consolidação democrática* (São Paulo: Ed. Brasiliense).
11. On the legislative elections of 1990 and the fragmentation of Congress, see Bolivar Lamounier (1991), *Depois da transição: eleições e democracia no Governo Collor* (São Paulo: Ed. Loyola), especially Chapter 5.

12. On public opinion between 1988 and 1991, see Bolivar Lamounier (ed.), (1992), *Ouvindo o Brasil: uma análise da opinião pública brasileira hoje* (São Paulo: Ed. Sumaré/Instituto Roberto Simonsen).

Chapter 8 (M. D. G. Kinzo)

* I wish to thank Marcelo Cavarozzi and Laurence Whitehead for their useful comments on this paper when presented at the conference on Brazil: the Challenges of the 1990s, and Fatiha Serrour for help with the English text. I also gratefully acknowledge a post-doctoral grant from CAPES.

1. It is worth clarifying that the problems of governability to which we refer here, are not necessarily associated with the arguments developed in the 1970s debate about the so-called crisis of democracy in post-industrial societies, namely the idea that problems of governability are the result of a marked expansion of participation and an overload of demands on the political system (see specially M. Crozier, S. Huntington and J. Watanuki (1975), *The Crisis of Democracy – Report on the Governability of Democracies to the Trilateral Commission* (New York University Press). To assess Brazil's crisis of governability using this kind of reasoning would be inaccurate for the simple reason that Brazil's newly democratic polity lacks the political traits of the post-industrial democracies (i.e., a politically active citizenry resulting from better education and other social improvements). Governability is used here in relation to the *output of government*, as suggested by Madgwick and Turner. By their definition, governability refers to (1) the maintenance of order and rule which implies 'the recognisable capacity to maintain, or quickly restore, a minimal level of law and order, a minimal conformity with the legislation and the policies of the government, and the more or less prompt execution of the orders of the government'; (2) the capacity for effective delivery, i.e. 'the recognisable capacity to deliver the services expected of the government, including the effective management of the economy, the promotion of evident prosperity and the delivery of recognisable adequate social services'; and (3) the management and control of the polity, i.e., 'the recognisable capacity to control, restrain or reasonably accommodate individuals and groups seeking influence within the polity, and to moderate or manage the external forces acting on the polity'. P. Madgwick and J. Turner (1989), 'Ungovernability Re-visited', *Studies in Public Policy* no. 171 (Glasgow: Centre for the Study of Public Policy, University of Strathclyde), p. 6. On the debate about governability see also R. Rose (1977), 'Governing and "Ungovernability" – a sceptical inquiry', *Studies in Public Policy* no.1 (Glasgow, Centre for the Study of Public Policy, University of Strathclyde).
2. The state of disarticulation in which collective actors in the polity and society have been left is well characterized by Cavarozzi's suggestive remarks: 'The compliance of individuals with organisations, and their allegiance to collective "projects", have substantially diminished, a trend I would characterize as *intra-organisational* decay. Also, the patterns of

interaction among different collective actors have become more disorganised as the formal and informal rules governing those interactions have lost effectiveness.' M. Cavarozzi (1991), 'Beyond transitions to democracy in Latin America', research paper submitted to the XVI Congress of the Latin American Studies Association, 4–5 April, 1991, Washington D.C.

3. Cf. G. Sartori (1976), *Parties and Party Systems – A Framework for Analysis* (Cambridge University Press).
4. K. Lawson (1988), 'When Linkage Fails', in K. Lawson and P. H. Merkl (eds), *When Parties Fail – Emerging Alternative Organizations* (Princeton University Press), p. 16. Lawson characterizes four forms of linkages which parties can provide: (1) *Participatory linkage* which is particularly characteristic of parties that have strong grass-roots organizations and are 'internally democratic procedurally'; (2) *Electoral linkage* which is prominent in parties that are oligarchically controlled and their mobilization efforts are limited to electoral objectives; (3) *Clientelist linkage* which is provided by parties that function as channels for the exchange of votes for favours. Its grass-roots structures, when there are any, are boss-ruled; and (4) *Directive linkage* which is characteristic of parties that are 'used by those in government office to maintain control over the behaviour of citizens'. (pp. 16-17).
5. For a comprehensive account of the past Brazilian experience of party system see B. Lamounier and R. Meneguello (1986), *Partidos políticos e consolidação democrática – o caso brasileiro* (São Paulo, Brasiliense).
6. On the 1945–64 experience see G. A. D. Soares (1973), *Sociedade e política no Brasil* (São Paulo, Difel); M. C. C. Souza (1976), *Estados e partidos políticos no Brasil* (São Paulo, Alfa-Omega); W. G. Santos (1986), *Sessenta e Quatro – anatomia da crise* (São Paulo, Vértice) and A. Lavareda (1991), *A democracia nas urnas – o processo partidário eleitoral brasileiro* (Rio de Janeiro, Rio Fundo Editora).
7. It is worth mentioning here Souza's perceptive remark regarding clientelistic politics in Brazil. Rather than a specific feature of Brazilian political culture, or a characteristic of a backward stage of political development, clientelism should be seen as 'a modality of control over political resources', used by political organizations (i.e. political parties) as the only means of empowering and consolidating themselves within a political system characterized by a very centralized state structure. 'Clientelism becomes less important as a means of control and a use of political resources when the structure of the state allows the consolidation of political parties as promoters of political alternatives and national objectives; conversely, the existence of a centralized state structure *before* the emergence of the party system blocks the institutionalization of the party system and encourages clientelistic politics.' Cf. M. C. C. Souza (1976), *Estados e partidos politicos no Brasil* (São Paulo, Alfa-Omega).
8. On party politics under the military regime see M. D. G. Kinzo (1988), *Legal Opposition Politics under Authoritarian Rule in Brazil – the case of the MDB, 1966-79* (London, Macmillan).

9. In Brazil parties have the right to free radio and television coverage in two forms: (1) during electoral campaigns they are granted free time in proportion to their representation in the Federal Chamber, though a minimum time is guaranteed to all the parties that run for an election; (2) once a year every party can carry out a party broadcast to publicize its doctrine and programme. Moreover, party broadcasts in Brazil are carried out on all radio and television channels simultaneously. It is quite obvious that this is a very important political resource leading to the flourishing of the so-called *partidos de aluguel* , parties that are created for the sole purpose of serving as an additional resource for one of the main contenders.
10. L. Epstein (1981), 'Political Parties: Organization', in David Butler et al. (eds), *Democracy at the Polls – A Comparative Study of Competitive National Elections* (Washington, American Enterprise Institute for Public Policy Research), p. 56.
11. During the first nine months of the Collor administration, not less than 143 *Medidas Provisórias* were issued by the president.
12. As Neumann points out: 'What is common to all parties, beyond partnership in a particular organization and separation from others, is their participation in the decision-making process, or at least the attempt at and a chance for such mobilization for action.' S. Neumann (ed.), (1975), *Modern Political Parties – Approaches to Comparative Politics* (Chicago, The University of Chicago Press, Midway Reprint), p. 195.
13. As I have pointed out in other work, the activity of organizing the party and promoting participation through the party organization has always been neglected. The politicians' contact with the electorate had been, in general, restricted to periods of elections and this kind of contact was not undertaken via the party organization, but predominantly as individuals competing for votes. Kinzo (1988), *Legal Opposition Politics under Authoritarian Rule*, p. 29.
14. See R. Meneguello (1989), *PT: a formação de um partido, 1979-1982* (Rio de Janeiro, Paz e Terra).
15. Ibid., p. 41.
16. As Cardoso remarks, the way in which the organized associations operate presupposes reaching a consensus, in other words, their internal functioning depends on unanimity. 'Oriented towards immediate demands, these groups get together impelled by a rationale which, in order to be consensual, needs to be nonpartisan and universal.' Consequently, close involvement with party politics brings discord, which threatens the group's own survival. R. C. Cardoso (1988), 'Os Movimentos Populares no Contexto da Consolidação Democrática', in F. W. Reis and G. O'Donnell (eds), *A democracia no Brasil – dilemas e perspectivas* (Sao Paulo, Vértice), p. 375.
17. As Sartori so rightly asserted, political parties not only express demands but also 'aggregate, select, and, eventually, deviate and distort'. Sartori, *Parties and Party Systems*, p. 28.
18. These are data collected in interviews with more than seven hundred deputies from all the state assemblies over the country, carried out by the

author in 1989. The data refer to answers to the question: 'During your electoral campaign did you count on the help of trade unions? Professional associations? Community neighbourhood associations?' and so on.

19. Cf. IBGE (1988), 'Perfil dos Eleitores', in *Pesquisa nacional por amostra de domicílios*, Rio de Janeiro, Fundação Instituto Brasileiro de Geografia e Estatística – IBGE.
20. See A. Singer (1990), 'Collor na Periferia: A Volta por Cima do Populismo', in B. Lamounier (ed.), *De Geisel a Collor: o balanço da transição* (São Paulo, Sumaré); and M. D. G. Kinzo (1991), 'La Elección Presidencial de 1989: El Comportamiento Electoral en una Ciudad Brasileña', *Revista de Estudios Políticos*, no.74, Oct–Dec. 1991, pp. 257-75.
21. See particularly Panebianco who argues that 'the success of the professional-electoral party . . . destroys collective identities, deepening the political system's legitimation crisis, and thus exacerbating the establishment/anti-establishment division. This cleavage contributes to the ungovernability of political systems.' A. Panebianco (1988), *Political Parties: Organization and Power* (Cambridge University Press), p. 272.
22. Moreover, state governors, particularly from the more important states, play an important role in national politics influencing enormously the positions of state representatives in the Chamber of Deputies in matters concerning the individual state's interests.
23. A. Kohli (1991), *Democracy and Discontent – India's Growing Crisis of Governability* (Princeton University Press).
24. S. Huntington (1991), *The Third Wave – Democratization in the Late Twentieth Century* (Norman, University of Oklahoma Press).

Chapter 9 (José Alvaro Moisés)

* I would like to express my gratitude to Maria D'Alva Kinzo, Peter McDonough and Victor Manuel Durand Ponte who carefully read an earlier version of this paper and helped me to improve it. Obviously they bear no responsibility for any inadequacies it might contain. I am also very grateful to the IDB/USP's Agreement and the British Council for the support they provided while I was at St Antony's College, Oxford. This article was translated by John Crabtree and Judith Condor Vidal.

1. In August 1991, in reaction to the coup d'etat against Gorbachev and *perestroika*, 500,000 people in Moscow and nearly a million in St Petersburg (formerly Leningrad) protested in the streets. At Easter 1987, when a military rebellion threatened to overturn the constitutional government of Alfonsín in Argentina, one million occupied the centre of Buenos Aires. In February 1981, during an attempted coup against democratization in Spain, 500,000 demonstrated in the streets of Madrid, leading *El País* to overprint its front page 'The Country for the Constitution'.
2. The privatizing urge of the democratic revolutions of Eastern Europe is the case in point here. But the literature on previous cases of political transition, especially in Latin America, has also shown how often the

price of democratization has been to postpone 'until later' all concern for social justice.

3. The phrase is from G. Pasquini: 'L'America latina: la democrazia senza testa', *Mondoperario* (Feb. 1990).
4. A case that comes immediately to mind is that of the *carapintadas* in Argentina, but it is doubtful that it is unique, as sympathetic reactions amongst the military of various Latin American countries following the recent events in Venezuela have shown.
5. I deal with the question of political culture in two previous essays. J. A. Moisés: 'Sociedade civil, cultura política e democracia: descaminhos da transição política' in M. L. M. Covre (1986), *A cidadania que não temos* (São Paulo, Brasiliense), pp. 119-50; and J. A. Moisés (1990), 'Eleições, participação e cultura política: mudanças e continuidades', *Lua Nova*, no. 22.
6. On this, see R. C. Andrade (1988), 'A democracia e a república no Brasil', CEDEC Mimeo.
7. G. Di Palma (1991), *To Craft Democracies* (Berkeley, University of California Press); A. Przeworski (1986), 'Some Problems in the Study of the Transition to Democracy', in G. O'Donnell, P. Schmitter and L. Whitehead (eds), *Transitions from Authoritarian Rule – Prospects for Democracy* (Baltimore, Johns Hopkins University Press) and (1989) 'Como e onde se bloqueiam as transições para a democracia?', in J. A. Moisés and J. A. G. Albuquerque, *Dilemas da consolidação da democracia* (Rio de Janeiro, Paz e Terra); L. Morlino (1987), 'Crisis autoritaria y cambio de régimen en el sur de Europa', in C. Huneeus, *Para vivir la democracia* (Santiago, Editorial Andante).
8. R. Dahl (1971), *Poliarchy: Participation and Opposition* (New Haven, Yale University Press).
9. A. Przeworski (1986), 'Some Problems in the Study of the Transition to Democracy' and (1989), 'Como e onde se bloqueiam as transições para a democracia?'
10. The concept of *passive consent* comes from Gramsci's analysis on hegemony. See A. Gramsci (1971), *Prison Notebooks* (New York, International Publishers); and (1978), *Antología* (Mexico, Siglo Veintiuno).
11. 'The entire problem of legitimacy is in my view incorrectly posed. What matters for the stability of any regime is not the legitimacy of this particular system of domination but the presence or absence of preferable alternatives.' A. Przeworski (1986), 'Some problems in the study of the transition to democracy', p. 52. Przeworski believes that since preferable alternatives analogous to the democratic one exist, they are chosen as a rational decision by relevant actors without the interference of norms, values or political beliefs.
12. To the authors already mentioned, we should add D. Rustow (1970) whose seminal article 'Transition to Democracy: Toward a Dynamic Model', *Comparative Politics*, vol. 2, no. 2, pp. 337-63, has been a permanent source of inspiration for a goodly part of the literature on transition. There are, however, exceptions to the lack of attention for the

importance of political culture to democratic consolidation: L. Diamond, J. J. Linz and S. M. Lipset (1989), *Democracy in Developing Cultures*, 4 vols. (Boulder and London, Lynne Rienner); N. Lechner et al. (1987), *Cultura política y democratización* (Santiago, Flacso/Clacso/ICI); and in the case of Brazil, F. C. Weffort (1984), *Por que democracia?* (São Paulo, Brasiliense) and B. Lamounier et. al. (1990), *De Geisel a Collor: o balanco da transição* (São Paulo, Sumaré). The prestigious study organized by O'Donnell, Schmitter and Whitehead, in my opinion is a case apart. Although the main authors do not deal specifically with the political culture approach, they do not reject the problem out of hand. This can be seen in the chapter written by O'Donnell and Schmitter 'Tentative Conclusions about Uncertain Democracies'.

13. Although Di Palma, for instance, does not think political culture is indispensable for democratic consolidation, he admits that it can be useful and that it develops when the population manages to become 'accustomed' to democratic procedures. But he doesn't explain how or why this could or should happen. G. Di Palma (1991), *To Craft Democracy*.
14. In recent writings, O'Donnell has given fresh importance to this problem which he says derives from the survival of archaic styles of conducting politics.
15. G. O'Donnell (1990), 'Delegative Democracy?', CEBRAP/Notre Dame, mimeo; F. C. Weffort (1991), 'New democracies. Which democracies?', mimeo.
16. Many opinion polls during the last five years show this to be the case.
17. O'Donnell, 'Delegative Democracy?', p. 9.
18. Weffort, Lechner and Paramio correctly stress the important shift in attitudes among, for example, the Latin American left towards democracy. However, in certain sectors of the Brazilian left, it is already possible to detect criticism of the huge 'delay' with which democratic institutional engineering gets round to addressing problems like misery, poverty and socio-economic inequality.
19. Another example arises from the inclusion in the 1988 Brazilian Constitution of so-called semi-direct mechanisms for popular participation in democracy. In spite of the fragile tradition of representative democracy, these new mechanisms presuppose a widespread disposition towards participation among the population in Brazil. But this is rather doubtful, which leads us to suggest that its disuse may demoralize other democratic institutions even more. I dealt with this in J. A. Moisés (1990), *Cidadania e participacão/Ensaio sobre o plebiscito, o referendo e a iniciativa popular na nova constituição* (São Paulo, Marco Zero).
20. What I term the 'minimalist theory' of democracy sees it as being the 'second-best' available choice. See Di Palma, *To Craft Democracies*.
21. Both Rustow and Przeworski deal with this choice as a necessity, but in my view they do not devote sufficient discussion to the extent to which this stems from the processes of delegitimization of authoritarianism, which as I suggest below could be a crucial factor in the crisis of this regime.

22. The book of T. H. Marshall (1979), *Cidadania, clase social e status* (Rio, Zahar) is still the best treatment of this interaction, taking social pressures in the sense of extending citizenship in the case of England.
23. An interesting approach on this is the work of E. Zimmerman (1986), 'Economic and Political Reactions to the World Economic Crisis of the 1930s in Six European Countries', Chicago, Midwest Political Science Association, Mimeo.
24. Almond and Verba (1963), *The Civic Culture* (Boston, Little Brown and Co.).
25. See D. P. Conrad (1963), 'Changing German Political Culture', in Almond and Verba, *The Civic Culture* (Boston, Little Brown and Co.). Also, O. W. Gabriel (1990), *Cambio social y cultura política/el caso de la República Federal de Alemania* (Barcelona, Gedisa Editora).
26. Authors like Maravall and Paramio show how this consensus was progressively created during the transition period, but López Pintor suggests that, even without being the majority view among the Spanish, the level of commitment to democracy that existed under Franco played an important role in creating this consensus. See J. M. Maravall (1980), *La política de transición* (Madrid, Taurus); L. Paramio (1987) 'Del radicalismo reivindicativo al pluralismo radical', in Lechner, *Cultura política y democratización*; R. L. Pintor (1987), 'El impacto del autoritarismo en la cultura política: la experiencia española en una perspectiva comparada', in C. Huneeus et al., *Para vivir la democracia*.
27. See D. Kavanagh (1980), 'Political Culture in Great Britain: the Decline of the Civic Culture'; and A. Lijphart (1980), 'The Structure of Inference', in G. Almond and S. Verba, *The Civic Culture Revisited* (Boston, Little Brown and Company).
28. See Rustow (1970), 'Transition to Democracy: Toward a Dynamic Model'.
29. See in this respect, A. Pizzorno (1983), 'Sulla razionalita della scelta democratica', *Stato e Mercato*, 7, pp. 3-46.
30. It is rather surprising to see the enormous importance now given by an author like Elster to social norms, as set out in his essay J. Elster (1990), 'Racionalidade e normas sociais', *Revista Brasileira de Ciencias Sociais*, vol. 5, no. 12, pp. 55-69. I owe this observation to Hermínio Martins.
31. G. Di Palma (1991), *To Craft Democracies*.
32. Even Downs is now saying so. See in this respect, A. Downs (1991), 'Social Values and Democracy' in K. R. Monroe, *The Economics Approach to Politics* (Harper Collins Publishers).
33. See, for instance, the text of B. Lamounier (1989), 'Inequality against Democracy' in Diamond, Linz and Lipset, *Democracies in Developing Cultures*, pp. 111-58.
34. T. R. Rochon and M. J. Mitchell (1987), 'The Withering away of the Authoritarian State/Social Bases of the Transition to Democracy in Brazil', Western Political Sciences Association, mimeo.
35. In the mid-1980s it fell to Brazil to experience the mobilization of millions of persons in defence of democracy, as I suggested in Note 1 for

other countries. I deal with the significance of this mobilization in my essay J.A. Moisés (1985) 'A transição política ou o longo percurso dentro do tunel', *Ciências Sociais Hoje*, São Paulo, ANPOCS/Cortez.

36. J. A. Moisés (1990), 'Eleições, participação e cultura política: mudanças e continuidade'.
37. J. A. Moisés (1991), 'Democracy threatened: the Latin American Paradox', *Alternative*, vol.16, no.2.
38. G. Germani (1974), *Política y sociedad en una época de transición* (Buenos Aires, Paidos).
39. P. Schmitter (1977), 'The "Portugalization" of Brazil?', mimeo.
40. Y. Cohen (1979) 'Popular Support for Authoritarian Governments: Brazil under Medici', Doctoral thesis, University of Michigan.
41. Ibid.
42. R. W. Neuman (1986), *The Paradox of Mass Politics* (Cambridge, Harvard University Press).
43. L. W. Milbrath (1965), *Political Participation* (Chicago, Rand McNally College Publishing Company).
44. P. Converse (1964), 'The Nature of Belief Systems in Mass Publics', in D. E. Apter, *Ideology and Discontent* (Glencoe, The Free Press).
45. See J. A. Moisés (in collaboration with J. A. G. Albuquerque), '1974, a avalanche de votos de protesto', in J. A. Moisés, *Cenas de política explícita* (São Paulo, Marco Zero, 1986). Also B. Lamounier and F. H. Cardoso, *Os partidos e as eleições no Brasil* (Rio de Janeiro, Paz e Terra, 1975).
46. W. G. Santos (1986), 'A pos-revolução brasileira', in Jaguaribe, H. et al., *Brasil, sociedade democrática* (Rio de Janeiro, José Olympio).
47. The literature on the political significance of social movements in Brazil is vast, similarly on the formation of political parties from the mid-1970s to the end of the 1980s. See J. A. Moises et al., *Cidade, povo e poder* (Rio de Janeiro, CEDEC/Paz e Terra, 1982); P. Jacobi, 'Movimentos sociais urbanos no Brasil', *BIB-Boletim Informativo Bibliográfico*, 9 Rio, 1980; R. C. L. Cardoso, 'Os movimentos populares no contexto da consolidação democrática', in Reis and O'Donnell, *A democracia no Brasil: dilemas e perspectivas* (São Paulo, Vértice, 1988) pp. 368–82; B. Lamounier, *Partidos e Utopias* (São Paulo, Loyola, 1989).
48. The seminal text on this theme is P. Converse, 'The Nature of Belief Systems in Mass Publics' in D. E. Apter, *Ideology and Discontent* (Glencoe, The Free Press, 1964), pp. 206–61. See also, by the same author, 'Of Time and Partisan Stability' *Comparative Political Studies*, vol. 2, no. 2 (July 1969) pp. 129-71.
49. Statistics obtained for the scale on the continuum democratic-authoritarian are as follows: reproductibility = 0.90; minimum marginal reproductibility = 0.76; percentage of improvement = 0.14; scalability = 0.61.
50. J. Chalmers (1966), *Revolutionary Change* (Boston, Little Brown and Company).

51. N. Bobbio (1986), *O Futuro da democracia – uma defesa das regras do jogo* (Rio de Janeiro, Paz e Terra).
52. A. Flisfisch (1987), 'Consenso democrático en el Chile autoritario', in N. Lechner et al., *Cultura política y democratización* (Santiago, FLACSO/CLACSO/ICI).

INDEX